EDUCATIONAL
FOUNDATIONS

To Pam and Nancy, two great teachers who
chart their own courses and ask the tough questions.
And, of course, to our children, Aly, Lauren, and Rachel.

EDUCATIONAL
FOUNDATIONS

An Anthology of Critical Readings

Edited by

ALAN S. CANESTRARI
Roger Williams University

BRUCE A. MARLOWE
Roger Williams University

SAGE Publications
International Educational and Professional Publisher
Thousand Oaks ▪ London ▪ New Delhi

For information:

Sage Publications, Inc.
2455 Teller Road
Thousand Oaks, California 91320
E-mail: order@sagepub.com

Sage Publications Ltd.
6 Bonhill Street
London EC2A 4PU
United Kingdom

Sage Publications India Pvt. Ltd.
B-42, Panchsheel Enclave
Post Box 4109
New Delhi 110 017 India

Printed in the United States of America

Library of Congress Cataloging-in-Publication Data

Educational foundations: an anthology of critical readings /
[edited by] Alan S. Canestrari, Bruce A. Marlowe.
    p. cm.
Includes bibliographical references and index.
ISBN 0–7619–3030–2 (cloth)—ISBN 0–7619–3031–0 (pbk.)
  1. Critical pedagogy. 2. Teaching. 3. Teachers. I. Canestrari, Alan S.
II. Marlowe, Bruce A.
LC196.E393 2004
370.11´5—dc22

                        2003015570

06 07 08 09 10 9 8 7 6 5 4

Acquisitions Editor:	Diane McDaniel
Editorial Assistant:	Margo Beth Crouppen
Production Editor:	Melanie Birdsall
Typesetter:	C&M Digitals (P) Ltd.
Proofreader:	Teresa Herlinger
Cover Designer:	Janet Foulger

Contents

Preface

In the United States and in virtually every Western democracy, there is a national clash as to what students should learn and how they should learn it. Traditionalists hold that the chief business of school is to transmit organized bodies of academic subject area information, cultural values, and rules of proper conduct, and to annually assess student ability to regurgitate this information. Progressives, on the other hand, maintain that simply transmitting information inevitably results in docile, overly obedient, passive, and, as Rousseau suggested, uniformly dull students (and teachers). Which path makes sense for new teachers?

Despite an avalanche of research supporting the need for more active and student-directed learning, new teachers typically find the easier, well-worn path more alluring. While beginning teachers often know that a traditional educational system based on information-dispensing is wholly inadequate, they lack clear direction as to how to move purposefully in another direction, to ask questions, or to challenge assumptions.

But what questions should teachers ask? What answers should teachers accept? We hope new teachers will consider asking whether their instruction promotes the status quo. How deliberate are their efforts to promote equality and to include the experiences of traditionally marginalized groups in the main curriculum? Is their instruction implemented at a transformational social action level? New teachers need models of critical reflection (and even dissent) in order to help them develop their own critical questions and voices.

We assembled this book because we believe that the current textbooks written on the foundations of education are too broad and too politically cautious to engage students or help them develop their own critical voices. Such texts do a good job of providing a survey of practices, but with very limited reference to the social contexts of teachers or of their students, and without taking a strong stance in favor of one practice over another. In these texts' attempt to cover everything in a curriculum, students have little opportunity to delve deeply into any substantive issues and are instead exposed, in only the most superficial ways, to the important issues facing the field. While the scope of the typical course has become broader in the last several years, the tone has become more dispassionate. As textbook content demands expand, students become responsible for knowing less and less about more and more. The texts on the market, like the textbooks in many fields, are so cursory that they leave professors few options other than assuming highly didactic, teacher-directed approaches to instruction. The texts also tend to promote practices that are antithetical to meaningful instruction: lecture, memorization, and multiple-choice assessment. Finally, the texts, because of their size and scope and their neutral stance, foster acceptance of the status quo without opportunity for in-depth examination, reflection, and discussion.

What you have in your hands is a book that we hope you will find as exciting as we do: an anthology of critical readings for students about to enter the teaching profession and for students interested in carefully examining schools and schooling. We feature provocative, engaging authors whose views are politicized but whose writing and opinions matter not simply because they are gadflies, but because their ideas work and because their achievements as teachers, principals, and policy shapers are so notable.

The major purpose of this book is to help teachers develop habits of critical reflection about schools and schooling before entering the classroom. It is for this reason that we have deliberately chosen authors with strong views that reflect particular biases. We hope that these readings will offer a platform for discussion and debate that may be used by instructors to increase student knowledge of pedagogy and to provide authentic opportunities for potential teachers to think critically about teaching and learning. For example, we are very concerned about the current trend toward standardization of curriculum and instruction, a trend that we believe devalues teaching and increases the distrust of teachers. We believe, like Deborah Meier, that this trend has manifested itself in schools organized around testing and that it is imperative for teachers to actively critique such events and recapture some of the control and power over their work.

This text features several previously published essays. However, Robert DiGiulio and Marilyn Page have agreed to write new pieces, and you will also find two new interviews, one with Alfie Kohn and another with Deborah Meier. Our anthology is organized around the following questions: Why teach? Who are today's students? What makes a good teacher? What do good schools look like? How should we assess student learning? How does one develop a critical voice in the face of state mandates, administrative edicts, and the continuous cycle of reform and retrenchment? Our authors' answers are bold and refreshing. They eschew the unquestioning compliance so characteristic of new teachers and, by taking a hard look at traditional educational practice, they serve as models for the kind of reflective practitioners we hope our students will become when they enter the field.

We frame each chapter with a very brief introductory vignette that provides context for the issues that the authors' essays address and also raises probing questions about teaching and learning.

How *Not* to Use This Book

If you're a professor and you've read this far along in the preface, you may be looking for some guidance in using this book. You won't find any direct instruction here. Instead, we hope that you will think critically about the most effective ways to engage your students with these readings and the issues they raise, without simply telling. Let's be clear: Simply walking through the table of contents, chapter by chapter, and expounding on the views of the authors contained in these pages is not what we have in mind.

If you're a student, we challenge you to ensure that your professors practice what they preach about instruction. Are you sitting through long and boring lectures about why teachers should not lecture? Are you actively engaged in discussion? If not, perhaps it is time to ask your professor, "Why not?"

Acknowledgments

There are too many people who have shaped and supported our thinking, teaching, and writing to name them all. It goes without saying that this anthology is composed of the writing of those who have had the most profound influence. For that we are grateful, but we would be remiss if we did not acknowledge some individual contributions as well. Special thanks to Alfie Kohn for engaging us in thought-provoking conversation, and to Deborah Meier for her perseverance, flexibility, and critical perspectives. We also want to thank Robert DiGiulio and Marilyn Page for agreeing to write new pieces for this anthology.

Great teachers and writers, however, are not our only sources of inspiration or support: special thanks to Pam and Nancy for their criticisms of the manuscript at its various stages. We are also grateful to Gary Canestrari for his artistic sense and input regarding the design of the book's cover, and to Janet Foulger for the final product.

We are extremely fortunate to have wonderful administrative support here at Roger Williams University. Mary Gillette, Jeffrey Hill, and Lauren Montanaro were extremely helpful in keeping the manuscript (and us) organized and on task.

We are also grateful to our students for participating in two 90-minute taped conversations that were the basis of the book's epilogue.

At Sage Publications, Faye Zucker and Todd Armstrong were receptive and supportive of the idea for the anthology from its inception. Several others at Sage were instrumental in shepherding the project through all its phases. They include Diane McDaniel, Veronica Novak, Margo Crouppen, and Melanie Birdsall. The reviewers of the manuscript are gratefully acknowledged: Carolyn Wemlinger, Dominican University; Fred Bedelle, Lincoln Memorial University; Dave Donahue, Mills College; Allison Hoewisch, University of Missouri, St. Louis; Christopher Blake, Mt. St. Mary's College; and Russ Dondero, Pacific University.

About the Editors

Alan S. Canestrari is a veteran social studies practitioner and Assistant Professor of Education at Roger Williams University. He earned his EdD from Boston University. He has had a long career in public schools and universities as a history teacher and department chair, as adjunct professor at Rhode Island College, and as mentor in the Brown University Masters of Teaching Program. In 1992, he was recognized as the Rhode Island Social Studies Teacher of the Year.

Bruce A. Marlowe is the author (with Marilyn Page) of *Creating and Sustaining the Constructivist Classroom* (Corwin Press) and of a six-part video series entitled *Creating the Constructivist Classroom* (The Video Journal of Education). He earned his PhD in Educational Psychology from The Catholic University of America in Washington, D.C., where he also completed two years of postdoctoral training in neuropsychological assessment. He has taught at the elementary, secondary, and university levels and is currently Associate Professor of Educational Psychology and Special Education at Roger Williams University.

Alan and Bruce have both taught courses in the foundations of education; neither is satisfied with any of the foundations texts currently available on the market. Both authors can be reached by mail at Roger Williams University, School of Education, One Old Ferry Road, Bristol, Rhode Island 02809, and also by telephone and email: Alan Canestrari at (401) 254–3749; acanestrari@rwu.edu, and Bruce Marlowe at (401) 254–3078; bmarlowe@rwu.edu.

PART I

Why Teach?

S tudents file into a crowded lecture hall at a small liberal arts college in the Northeast. The class, *Foundations of Education,* is a prerequisite for acceptance into the School of Education program and it is enrolled at maximum capacity. It is the first day of class. Students are expecting that the syllabus for the course will be distributed and read aloud, and if no one asks any questions about the requirements of the class, then the students can cut out early and enjoy the warm September sunshine. After all, nobody bought the book yet. The professor arrives and greets the students.

"Good morning. So, you are all interested in becoming teachers? Wonderful. We need bright, energetic, young teachers in the profession today. Teaching can be a very rewarding career, but I must warn you that it is a challenging time for teachers, especially beginning teachers. Teachers are under tremendous scrutiny. There are also increasing concerns about the deplorable condition of our schools, the lack of parental support, the disturbing behavior of the children, and the general disrespect for teachers by the public at large. So, why teach?"

A long silence fills the hall.

"This is not a rhetorical question. Tell us, why do you want to teach?"

More silence . . . long silence.

Finally, Jennifer offers, "My mom is a teacher. So is my aunt. I guess I have grown up around teaching, and ever since I can remember, I've wanted to teach, too."

Then Erin says, "I just love kids. Like, I just want to make a difference in their lives. I want to teach elementary school. The kids are so cute at that age."

1

Robert adds, "I work as a camp counselor in the summers. My cabin always wins the camp contest. I really connect with kids. I mean, I just know what they like. It is not so hard, plus teachers have summers off."

Sound good? Do Jennifer, Erin, and Robert have it right? Are these the reasons to teach?

1

Educating Esmé

Diary of a Teacher's First Year

Esmé Codell

June 21

Ismene died. That's where I start, because it's with Ismene that my real teaching started.

I cried when I found out. I tried to go to her memorial—I mean, I went—but it was all in Greek, and everybody crossing themselves made me nervous. I couldn't really concentrate on remembering Ismene, her sharp eyes, like a sparrow. She was my guide. I would not be a teacher without her.

I'm not quite a teacher yet—that is, I haven't had a class of my own. That's in September, if I last and if the new school opens on time. I'm surprised Mr. Turner hired me, only twenty-four years old, to help him open a brand-new public school. You would think he would want someone more experienced. The interview was very brief. He asked, "How would you describe your classroom discipline style?"

I answered, "Assertive."

He said, "What does that mean?'

"It means I say what I mean and I mean what I say," I replied.

"Well, say you're having a problem with a student, how would you deal with it?"

"I would document the child's behavior and then try interventions such as using successive approximations toward our goal or home involvement, depending on the individual situation," I explained. After a silence, I added, "I wouldn't call the office every five minutes."

He closed the little notebook on his lap and announced, "You're hired."

I had to go through a perfunctory interview with a panel that asked silly questions like, "What would you do if a child were to say 'fuck' in your classroom?"

"Faint dead away!" I put my hand to my forehead.

"What kind of classroom environment will you create?"

"Do you mean the physical, emotional, or educational environment?"

"I guess I don't know."

"Then I guess I don't know how to answer you;" I confessed, "but I offer examples of each. . . ."

I was teary-eyed the whole cab ride home, thinking that I must not really want the job, to answer questions in such a cavalier manner! Why wasn't I more polite? Me and my big mouth! etc. But when I got home, there was a message from Mr. Turner: "They loved you!"

So now here I am, typing, copying, answering phones, "being flexible," as Mr. Turner calls it. I think that means doing things you're not supposed to do for longer than you ever thought you'd have to do them.

Tomorrow Mr. Turner says I should come see the graduation ceremonies at the school where he was vice-principal. They must be planning to make a hot dog out of him—I can't imagine why he'd let me stop typing for a minute, unless it was to bear witness to his glory.

July 7

I was right about the ceremony. There was another assembly, with all of the children who were coming to the new school. I approached Mr. Turner. "If you have an intention of introducing me, would you please call me Ms. Esmé rather than Mrs. Codell?"

I was surprised at how my request surprised him.

He said, "That's against board policy."

Not having been born yesterday, I replied that in all the other classrooms I had worked in, that is what the children called me.

He seemed bemused. "But it's not your legal name." He smiled helplessly.

"Certainly it is."

"Your *last* name?"

"Let's pretend . . . I haven't got a last name. I'll be like . . . Sade."

He laughed heartily at this, and I laughed too, but then he said, "Well, I think we'll call you Mrs. Cordell." The way he mispronounces my last name makes me wince.

"You can call me what you like." I smiled and tried to maintain a pleasant tone. "But we will see what name I answer to!" We made eye contact. He turned away and mumbled something about "women's libbers."

He introduced me as Ms. Esmé. I felt uncomfortable. I didn't mean to be confrontational, but I think I should be able to decide what name I answer to. Mr. Turner is well-intentioned, but it is not enough. He is not clever, he is not intelligent. At least not to me.

I wrote a proposal for a schoolwide Fairy Tale Festival. Mr. Turner approved it, but he said the idea has to first go through administrators, teachers, and community members. I showed my idea to the librarian-to-be. She was skeptical. That's typical. If you give people an idea these days, they just think you are sharing it with them so they can critique it, play devil's advocate, and so on. It doesn't occur to them that they might help or get enthused or at least have the courtesy to get out of your way. Sometimes this frustrates me, but I try deep inside to move beyond it. Sometimes I think, *Why invent projects? What is the point? How will I ever accomplish what I set out to do, what I imagine?* Then I think of the past, even before I was born, the great small feats people accomplished. I think of things like Mary Martin washing her hair onstage in *South Pacific,* or the Kungsholm puppet operas with sixty puppets on stage at once, or the palace built by the postman in France, or the circus I saw in Copenhagen where a woman wore a coat of live minks, or any of the things I enjoy and value, and I think: *Those people had to work to accomplish those things, they thought of details, they followed through.* Even if I come off as naive and zealous, even if I get on everyone's nerves, I have to follow these examples. Even if I fail, I have to try and try and try. It may be exhausting, but that is beside the point. The goal is not necessarily to succeed but to keep trying, to be the kind of person who has ideas and sees them through.

We'll see. I aim too high, probably. But if I don't aim, how will I hit anywhere near the target?

July 8

I hereby attach a copy of what I expect to be a most interesting curiosity, the crowning jewel of my naiveté: my Fairy Tale Festival proposal. Perhaps

I will look back on this and think, as I was most condescendingly informed yesterday at the Friends of the School Library Committee meeting (which I organized, by the way, after it was explained to me that a committee needed to be invented because a committee needs to exist to approve a proposal), that it was not realistic to do, as I would surely have known had I been teaching awhile. I said everything I proposed I was willing to coordinate, that I just needed help on the actual day of the festival to supervise for the children's safety. The vice principal, Ms. Coil, said no, everything should be a group effort. Then, as a group, they decided they didn't want to put forth the effort. So, the end. Some of my favorite sections:

Fairy Tale Fashion Show

Is fur still "in" for the Three Bears? What is Cinderella wearing to the ball this season? Miss Riding Hood still sizzles in red (ask any wolf), and Sleeping Beauty is a cutie in her pj's. The Paper Bag Princess makes a statement without saying a word, while less is more for the Emperor's New Clothes (boxer shorts)! The possibilities are only as limited as local theaters, closet costumers, good sport volunteer models (adults and children), and our collective imaginations!

Carnival Games

Some ideas:

- *Ugly Duckling Match*. Find the numbers that match on the bottoms of bobbing plastic ducks in a "pond" (plastic tub).
- *Three Billy Goats Gruff Toes*. Three beanbags through holes in a thematically painted board wins.

Bookmarks make good inexpensive prizes. What else? Let's brainstorm!

Bake Sale/Book Sale

How about Frog Prince cupcakes (with green food-colored frosting), Thumbelina finger sandwiches, Giant's magic rings (doughnuts), or cookies from Red Riding Rood's basket? Again, volunteerism and imagination are our only limitations.

I only meant that last line to be cheerleading. I was carried away with the idea of infinite possibility. The same sense of infinite possibility from the sour expressions on the faces of my cohorts that would compel someone to go over Niagara Falls in a barrel. All that is really necessary, after all, is a little "volunteerism and imagination!"

Another gross thing at the meeting: Lillia, a teacher from Italy, about fifty-five years old, was chatting along and came to the word "conspicuous," which she pronounced "copiscuous." Big deal!

But no. Ms. Coil made a gesture of a cascading waterfall beneath her chin and enunciated, "Con-SPICK- you-us."

Lillia just looked.

"Con-Spick-you-us," the vice-principal repeated, clearly wanting Lillia to follow. Wow! Isn't that audacious! I could have smacked her across the nose!

"Yes," Lillia nodded and continued what she was saying. When she came to that word again, she said, "Co-PISS-cue-us."

Congratulate me—I didn't laugh out loud.

Esmé Codell is a former teacher and is currently a librarian and children's literature specialist.

2

The Green Monongahela

John Taylor Gatto

I n the beginning I became a teacher without realizing it. At the time, I was growing up on the banks of the green Monongahela River forty miles southwest of Pittsburgh, and on the banks of that deep green and always mysterious river I became a student too, master of the flight patterns of blue dragonflies and cunning adversary of the iridescent ticks that infested the riverbank willows.

"Mind you watch the ticks, Jackie!" Grandmother Mossie would call as I headed for the riverbank, summer and winter, only a two-minute walk from Second Street, where I lived across the trolley tracks of Main Street and the Pennsylvania Railroad tracks that paralleled them. I watched the red and yellow ticks chewing holes in the pale green leaves as I ran to the riverbank. On the river I drank my first Iron City at eight, smoked every cigarette obtainable, and watched dangerous men and women make love there at night on blankets—all before I was twelve. It was my laboratory: I learned to watch closely and draw conclusions there.

How did the river make me a teacher? Listen. It was alive with paddle-wheel steamers in center channel, the turning paddles churning up clouds of white spray, making the green river boil bright orange where its chemical

NOTE: From *Dumbing Us Down: The Hidden Curriculum of Compulsory Schooling* by John Taylor Gatto. Copyright 1992 New Society Publishers (www.newsociety.com). Reprinted with permission.

undercurrent was troubled; from shore you could clearly hear the loud *thump thump thump* on the water. From all over town young boys ran gazing in awe. A dozen times a day. No one ever became indifferent to them because nothing important can ever really be boring. You can see the difference, can't you? Between those serious boats and the truly boring spacecraft of the past few decades, just flying junk without a purpose a boy can believe in; it's hard to feign an interest even now that I teach for a living and would like to pretend for the sake of the New York kids who won't have paddle-wheelers in their lives. The rockets are dull toys children in Manhattan put aside the day after Christmas, never to touch again; the riverboats were serious magic, clearly demarcating the world of boys from the world of men. Levi-Strauss would know how to explain.

In Monongahela by that river everyone was my teacher. Daily, it seemed to a boy, one of the mile-long trains would stop in town to take on water and coal or for some mysterious reason; the brakeman and engineer would step among snot-nosed kids and spin railroad yarns, let us run in and out of boxcars, over and under flatcars, tank cars, coal cars, and numbers of other specialty cars whose function we memorized as easily as we memorized enemy plane silhouettes. Once a year, maybe, we got taken into the caboose that reeked of stale beer to be offered a bologna on white bread sandwich. The anonymous men lectured, advised, and inspired the boys of Monongahela—it was as much their job as driving the trains.

Sometimes a riverboat would stop in mid-channel and discharge a crew, who would row to shore, lying their skiff to one of the willows. That was the excuse for every rickety skiff in the twelve-block-long town to fill up with kids, pulling like Vikings, sometimes with sticks instead of oars, to raid the "Belle of Pittsburgh" or "The Original River Queen." Some kind of natural etiquette was at work in Monongahela. The rules didn't need to be written down: if men had time they showed boys how to grow up. We didn't whine when our time was up—men had work to do—we understood that and scampered away, grateful for the flash of our own futures they had had time to reveal, however small it was.

I was arrested three times growing up in Monongahela, or rather, picked up by the police and taken to jail to await a visit from Pappy to spring me. I wouldn't trade those times for anything. The first time I was nine, caught on my belly under a parked car at night, half an hour after curfew; in 1943 blinds were always drawn in the Monongahela Valley for fear Hitler's planes would somehow find a way to reach across the Atlantic to our steel mills lining both banks of the river. The Nazis were apparently waiting for a worried mother to go searching for her child with a flashlight after curfew, then *whammo!* down would descend the Teutonic air fleet!

Charlie was the cop's name. Down to the lockup we went—no call to mother until Charlie diagrammed the deadly menace of Goering's Luftwaffe. What a geopolitics lesson that was! Another time I speared a goldfish in the town fishpond and was brought from jail to the library, where I was sentenced to read for a month about the lives of animals. Finally, on VJ Day—when the Japanese cried "Uncle!"—I accepted a dare and broke the window of the police cruiser with a slingshot. Confessing, I suffered my first encounter with employment to pay for the glass, becoming sweep-up boy in my grandfather's printing office at fifty cents a week.

After I went away to Cornell, I saw Monongahela and its green river only one more time, when I went there after my freshman year to give blood to my dying grandfather, who lay in the town hospital, as strong in his dying as he had ever been in his living. In another room my grandmother lay dying. Both passed within twenty-four hours, my grandad, Harry Taylor Zimmer, Sr., taking my blood to his grave in the cemetery there. My family moved again and again and again, but in my own heart I never left Monongahela, where I learned to teach from being taught by everyone in town, where I learned to work from being asked to shoulder my share of responsibility, even as a boy, and where I learned to find adventures I made myself from the everyday stuff around me—the river and the people who lived alongside it.

In 1964, I was making a lot of money. That's what I walked away from to become a teacher. I was a copywriter on the fast track in advertising, a young fellow with a knack for writing thirty-second television commercials. My work required about one full day a month to complete, the rest of the time being spent in power breakfasts, after-work martinis at Michael's Pub, keeping up with the shifting fortunes of about twenty agencies in order to gauge the right time to jump ship for more money, and endless parties that always seemed to culminate in colossal headaches.

It bothered me that all the urgencies of the job were generated externally, but it bothered me more that the work I was doing seemed to have very little importance—even to the people who were paying for it. Worst of all, the problems this work posed were cut from such a narrow spectrum that it was clear that past, present, and future were to be of a piece: a twenty-nine-year-old man's work was no different from a thirty-nine-year-old man's work, or a forty-nine-year-old man's work (though there didn't seem to be any forty-nine-year-old copywriters—I had no idea why not).

"I'm leaving," I said one day to the copy chief.

"Are you nuts, Jack? You'll get profit sharing this year. We can match any offer you've got. Leaving for who?"

"For nobody, Dan. I mean I'm going to teach junior high school."

"When you see your mother next, tell her for me she raised a moron. Christ! Are you going to be sorry! In New York City we don't have schools; we have pens for lost souls. Teaching is a scam, a welfare project for losers who can't do anything else!"

Round and round I went with my advertising colleagues for a few days. Their scorn only firmed my resolve; the riverboats and trains of Monongahela were working inside me. I needed something to do that wasn't absurd more than I needed another party or a new abstract number in my bankbook.

And so I became a junior high school substitute teacher, working the beat from what's now Lincoln Center to Columbia, my alma mater, and from Harlem to the South Bronx. After three months the dismal working conditions, the ugly rooms, the torn books, the repeated instances of petty complaints from authorities, the bells, the buzzers, the drab teacher food in the cafeterias, the unpressed clothing, the inexplicable absence of conversation about children among the teachers (to this day, after twenty-six years in the business, I can honestly say I have never once heard an extended conversation about children or about teaching theory in any teachers' rooms I've been in) had just about done me in.

In fact, on the very first day I taught I was attacked by a boy waving a chair above his head. It happened in the infamous junior school Wadleigh, on 113th Street. I was given the eighth grade typing class—seventy-five students and typewriters—with this one injunction: "Under no circumstances are you to allow them to type. You lack the proper license. Is that understood?" A man named Mr. Bash said that to me.

It couldn't have taken more than sixty seconds from the time I closed the door and issued the order not to type for one hundred and fifty hands to snake under the typewriter covers and begin to type. But not all at once—that would have been too easy. First, three machines began to *clack clack* from the right rear. Quick, who were the culprits? I would race to the corner screaming *stop!*—when suddenly, from behind my back, three other machines would begin! Whirling as only a young man can do, I caught one small boy in the act. Then, to a veritable symphony of machines clicking, bells ringing, platens being thrown, I hoisted the boy from his chair and announced at the top of my foolish lungs I would make an example of this miscreant.

"Look out!" a girl shouted, and I turned toward her voice just in time to see a large brother of the little fellow I held heading toward me with a chair raised above his head. Releasing his brother, I seized a chair myself and raised it aloft. A standoff! We regarded each other at a distance of about ten feet for what seemed forever, the class jeering and howling, when the room door opened and Assistant Principal Bash, the very man who'd given the no-typing order, appeared.

"Mr. Gatto, have these children been typing?"

"No, sir," I said, lowering my chair, "but I think they want to. What do you suggest they do instead?"

He looked at me for signs of impudence or insubordination for a second, then, as if thinking better of rebuking this upstart, he said merely, "Fall back on your resources," and left the room.

Most of the kids laughed—they'd seen this drama enacted before.

The situation was defused, but silently I dubbed Wadleigh the "Death School." Stopping by the office on my way home, I told the secretary not to call me again if they needed a sub.

The very next morning my phone rang at 6:30. "Are you available for work today, Mr. Gatto?" said the voice briskly.

"Who is this?" I asked suspiciously. (Ten schools were using me for sub work in those days, and each identified itself at once.)

"The law clearly states, Mr. Gatto, that we do not have to tell you who we are until you tell us whether you are available for work."

"Never mind," I bellowed, "there's only one school who'd pull such crap! The answer is no! I am never available to work in your pigpen school!" And I slammed the receiver back onto its cradle.

But the truth was none of the sub assignments were boat rides; schools had an uncanny habit of exploiting substitutes and providing no support for their survival. It's likely I'd have returned to advertising if a little girl, desperate to free herself from an intolerable situation, hadn't drawn me into her personal school nightmare and shown me how I could find my own significance in teaching, just as those strong men in the riverboats and trains had found their own significance, a currency all of us need for our self-esteem.

It happened this way. Occasionally, I'd get a call from an elementary school. This particular day it was a third grade assignment at a school on 107th Street, which in those days was nearly one hundred percent non-Hispanic in its teaching staff and 99% Hispanic in its student body.

Like many desperate teachers, I killed most of the day listening to the kids read, one after another, and expending most of my energy trying to shut the audience up. This class had a very low ranking, and no one was able to put more than three or four words together without stumbling. All of a sudden, though, a little girl named Milagros sailed through a selection without a mistake. After class I called her over to my desk and asked why she was in this class of bad readers. She replied that "they" (the administration) wouldn't let her out because, as they explained to her mother, she was really a bad reader who had fantasies of being a better reader than she was. "But look, Mr. Gatto, my brother is in the sixth grade, and I can read every word in his English book better than he can!"

I was a little intrigued, but truthfully not much. Surely the authorities knew what they were doing. Still, the little girl seemed so frustrated I invited her to calm down and read to me from the sixth grade book. I explained that if she did well, I would take her case to the principal. I expected nothing.

Milagros, on the other hand, expected justice. Diving into "The Devil and Daniel Webster," she polished off the first two pages without a gulp. My God, I thought, this is a real reader. What is she doing here? Well, maybe it was a simple accident, easily corrected. I sent her home, promising to argue her case. Little did I suspect what a hornet's nest my request to have Milagros moved to a better class would stir up.

"You have some nerve, Mr. Gatto. I can't remember when a substitute ever told me how to run my school before. Have you taken specialized courses in reading?"

"No."

"Well then, suppose you leave these matters to the experts!"

"But the kid can read!"

"What do you suggest?"

"I suggest you test her, and if she isn't a dummy, get her out of the class she's in!"

"I don't like your tone. None of our children are dummies, Mr. Gatto. And you will find that girls like Milagros have many ways to fool amateurs like yourself. This is a matter of a child having memorized one story. You can see if I had to waste my time arguing with people like you I'd have no time left to run a school."

But, strangely, I felt self-appointed as the girl's champion, even though I'd probably never see her again.

I insisted, and the principal finally agreed to test Milagros herself the following Wednesday after school. I made it a point to tell the little girl the next day. By that time I'd come to think that the principal was probably right—she'd memorized one story—but I still warned her she'd need to know the vocabulary from the whole advanced reader and be able to read any story the principal picked, without hesitation. My responsibility was over, I told myself.

The following Wednesday after school I waited in the room for Milagros' ordeal to be over. At 3:30 she shyly opened the door of the room.

"How'd it go?" I asked.

"I don't know," she answered, "but I didn't make any mistakes. Mrs. Hefferman was very angry, I could tell."

I saw Mrs. Hefferman, the principal, early the next morning before school opened. "It seems we've made a mistake with Milagros," she said curtly. "She will be moved, Mr. Gatto. Her mother has been informed."

Several weeks later, when I got back to the school to sub, Milagros dropped by, telling me she was in the fast class now and doing very well. She also gave me a sealed card. When I got home that night, I found it, unopened, in my suitcoat pocket. I opened it and saw a gaudy birthday card with blue flowers on it. Opening the card, I read, "A teacher like you cannot be found. Signed, Your student, Milagros."

That simple sentence made me a teacher for life. It was the first praise I ever heard in my working existence that had any meaning. I never forgot it, though I never saw Milagros again and only heard of her again in 1988, twenty-four years later. Then one day I picked up a newspaper and read:

OCCUPATIONAL TEACHER AWARD

Milagros Maldonado, United Federation of Teachers, has won the Distinguished Occupational Teacher Award of the State Education Department for "demonstrated achievement and exemplary profession-alism." A secretarial studies teacher at Norman Thomas High School, New York City, from which she graduated, Miss Maldonado was selected as a Manhattan Teacher of the Year in 1985 and was nominated the following year for the Woman of Conscience Award given by the National Council of Women.

Ah, Milagros, is it just possible that I was your Monongahela River? No matter, a teacher like you cannot be found.

John Taylor Gatto is an author and former New York City and New York State Teacher of the Year.

3

Death at an Early Age

The Destruction of the Hearts and Minds of Negro Children in the Boston Public Schools

Jonathan Kozol

S tephen is eight years old. A picture of him standing in front of the bulletin board on Arab bedouins shows a little light-brown person staring with unusual concentration at a chosen spot upon the floor. Stephen is tiny, desperate, unwell. Sometimes he talks to himself. He moves his mouth as if he were talking. At other times he laughs out loud in class for no apparent reason. He is also an indescribably mild and unmalicious child. He cannot do any of his school work very well. His math and reading are poor. In Third Grade he was in a class that had substitute teachers much of the year. Most of the year before that, he had a row of substitute teachers too. He is in the Fourth Grade now but his work is barely at the level of the Second. Nobody has complained about the things that have happened to Stephen because he does not have any mother or father. Stephen is a ward of the State of Massachusetts and, as such, he has been placed in the home of

---

some very poor people who do not want him now that he is not a baby any more. The money that they are given to pay his expenses every week does not cover the other kind of expense—the more important kind which is the immense emotional burden that is continually at stake. Stephen often comes into school badly beaten. If I ask him about it, he is apt to deny it because he does not want us to know first-hand what a miserable time he has. Like many children, and many adults too, Stephen is far more concerned with hiding his abased condition from the view of the world than he is with escaping that condition. He lied to me first when I asked him how his eye got so battered. He said it happened from being hit by accident when somebody opened up the door. Later, because it was so bruised and because I questioned him, he admitted that it was his foster mother who had flung him out onto the porch. His eye had struck the banister and it had closed and purpled. The children in the class were frightened to see him. I thought that they also felt some real compassion, but perhaps it was just shock.

Although Stephen did poorly in his school work, there was one thing he could do well: he was a fine artist. He made delightful drawings. The thing about them that was good, however, was also the thing that got him into trouble. For they were not neat and orderly and organized but entirely random and casual, messy, somewhat unpredictable, seldom according to the instructions he had been given, and—in short—real drawings. For these drawings, Stephen received considerable embarrassment at the hands of the Art Teacher. This person was a lady no longer very young who had some rather fixed values and opinions about children and about teaching. Above all, her manner was marked by unusual confidence. She seldom would merely walk into our class but seemed always to sweep into it. Even for myself, her advent, at least in the beginning of the year, used to cause a wave of anxiety For she came into our class generally in a mood of self-assurance and of almost punitive restlessness which never made one confident but which generally made me wonder what I had done wrong. In dealing with Stephen, I thought she could be quite overwhelming.

The Art Teacher's most common technique for art instruction was to pass out mimeographed designs and then to have the pupils fill them in according to a dictated or suggested color plan. An alternate approach was to stick up on the wall or on the blackboard some of the drawings on a particular subject that had been done in the previous years by predominantly white classes. These drawings, neat and ordered and very uniform, would be the models for our children. The art lesson, in effect, would be to copy what had en done before, and the neatest and most accurate reproductions of the inal drawings would be the ones that would win the highest approval the teacher. None of the new drawings, the Art Teacher would tell me frequently, was comparable to the work that had been done in former times, but at least the children in the class could try to copy good examples. The fact that they were being asked to copy something in which they could not believe because it was not of them and did not in any way correspond to their own interests did not occur to the Art Teacher, or if it did occur she did not say it. Like a number of other teachers at my school and in other schools of the same nature, she possessed a remarkable self-defense apparatus, and anything that seriously threatened to disturb her point of view could be effectively denied.

How did a pupil like Stephen react to a teacher of this sort? Alone almost out of the entire class, I think that he absolutely turned off his signals while she was speaking and withdrew to his own private spot. At his desk he would sit silently while the Art Teacher was talking and performing. With a pencil, frequently stubby and end-bitten, he would scribble and fiddle and cock his head and whisper to himself throughout the time that the Art Teacher was going on. At length, when the art lesson officially began, he would perhaps push aside his little drawing and try the paint and paper that he had been given, usually using the watercolors freely and the paintbrush sloppily and a little bit defiantly and he would come up with things that certainly were delightful and personal and private, and full of his own nature.

If Stephen began to fiddle around during a lesson, the Art Teacher generally would not notice him at first. When she did, both he and I and the children around him would prepare for trouble. For she would go at his desk with something truly like a vengeance and would shriek at him in a way that carried terror. "Give me that! Your paints are all muddy! You've made it a mess. Look at what he's done! He's mixed up the colors! I don't know why we waste good paper on this child!" Then: "Garbage! Junk! He gives me garbage and junk and garbage is one thing I will not have." Now I thought that that garbage and junk was very nearly the only real artwork in the class. I do not know very much about painting, but I know enough to know that the Art Teacher did not know much about it either and that, furthermore, she did not know or care anything at all about the way in which you can destroy a human being. Stephen, in many ways already dying, died a second and third and fourth and final death before her anger.

Sometimes when the Art Teacher was not present in our classroom, and when no other supervisory person happened to be there, Stephen would sneak up to me, maybe while I was sitting at my desk and going over records or totaling up the milk money or checking a paper, so that I would not see him until he was beside me. Then, hastily, secretly, with mystery, with fun, with something out of a spy movie, he would hand me one of his small drawings. The ones I liked the most, to be honest, were often not completely his own, but pictures which he had copied out of comic books and then elaborated, amended, fiddled with, and frequently added to by putting under them some kind of mock announcement ("I AM THE GREATEST AND THE STRONGEST") which might have been something he had wished. I think he must have seen something special and valuable about comic books, because another thing that he sometimes did was just cut out part of a comic book story that he liked and bring it in to me as a present. When he did this, as with his paintings and drawings, he usually would belittle his gift by crumpling it up or folding it up very tiny before he handed it to me. It was a way, perhaps, of saying that he didn't value it too much (although it was clear that he did value it a great deal) in case I didn't like it.

If the Art Teacher came upon us while he was slipping me a picture he had drawn, both he and I were apt to get an effective lashing out. Although she could be as affectionate and benevolent as she liked with other children, with Stephen she was almost always scathing in her comments and made no attempt at seeming mild. "He wants to show you his little scribbles because he wants to use you and your affection for him and make you pity him but we don't have time for that. Keep him away. If you don't, I'll do it. I don't want him getting near you during class."

For weeks after that outburst, when we had been caught in the act of friendship, he stopped coming near me. He stopped bringing me his drawings. He kept to his seat and giggled, mumbled, fiddled. Possibly he felt that he was doing this for my sake in order not to get me into further trouble. Then one day for a brief second he got up his nerve and darted forward. He crumpled up some paper in his fist and handed it to me quickly and got back into his chair. The crumpled paper turned out to be more funnies that he had painstakingly cut out. Another time he dropped a ball of crunched-up math paper on my desk. On the paper he had written out his age—eight years old—and his birthday—which I seem to remember came at Christmas. I also remember that once he either whispered to me or wrote to me on a note that he weighed sixty pounds. This information, I thought, came almost a little boastfully, even though it obviously isn't a lot to weigh if you are almost nine, and I wondered about it for a time until it occurred to me that maybe it was just one of very few things that he knew about himself, one of the half dozen measurable facts that had anything to do with him in the world, and so—like all people, using as best they can whatever they've got—he had to make the most of it.

I think that much of his life, inwardly and outwardly, must have involved a steady and, as it turned out, inwardly at least, a losing battle to survive, he battled for his existence and, like many defenseless humans, he had to use whatever odd little weapons came to hand. Acting up at school was part of it. He was granted so little attention that he must have panicked repeatedly about the possibility that, with a few slight mistakes, he might simply stop existing or being seen at all. I imagine this is one reason why he seemed so often to invite or court a tongue-lashing or a whipping. Doing anything at all that would make a teacher mad at him, scream at him, strike at him, would also have been a kind of ratification, even if it was painful, that he actually was there. Other times, outside of school, he might do things like pulling a fire alarm lever and then having the satisfaction of hearing the sirens and seeing the fire engines and knowing that it was all of his own doing and to his own credit, so that at least he would have proof in that way that his hands and his arm muscles and his mischievous imagi- nation actually did count for something measurable in the world. Maybe the only way in which he could ever impinge upon other people's lives was by infuriating them, but that at least was something. It was better than not having any use at all.

I remember that the Art Teacher once caught him out in the back, in the hallway, in front of a big floor-length coat-closet mirror. She grabbed him by the arm and pulled him into the classroom and announced to me and to the children in the classroom that he was "just standing there and making faces at himself and staring." While she talked, he looked away and examined the floor with his eyes, as he did so often, because he was embarrassed by being exposed like that. I thought it was needlessly cruel of her to have hauled him before the children in that manner, and surely a little hesitation on her part might have given her a moment to think why he might *like* to see himself in a mirror, even if it was only to see a scratched reflection. I didn't think it was shameful for him to be doing that, even to be making funny faces. It seemed rather normal and explicable to me that he might want to check up on his existence. Possibly it was a desperate act, and cer- tainly a curious one, but I do not think it was unnatural. What did seem to me to be unnatural was the unusual virulence of the Art Teacher's reaction.

Another time, seeing him all curled up in one of the corners, I went over to him and tried to get him to look up at me and smile and talk. He would not do that. He remained all shriveled up there and he would not cry and would not laugh. I said to him: "Stephen, if you curl up like that and will not even look up at me, it will just seem as if you wanted to make me think you were a little rat." He looked down at himself hurriedly and then he looked up at me and he chuckled grotesquely and he said, with a pitiful little laugh: "I know I couldn't be a rat, Mr. Kozol, because a rat has got to have a little tail!" I never forgot that and I told it later to a child psychiatrist, whose answer to me made it more explicit and more clear: "It is the absence of a tail which convinces him that he has not yet become a rat." Perhaps that is overly absolute and smacks a bit of the psychiatric dogmatism that seems so difficult to accept because it leaves so little room for uncertainty or doubt; yet in this one instance I do not really think that it carries the point too far. For it is the Boston schoolteachers themselves who for years have been speaking of the Negro children in their charge as "animals" and the school building that houses them as "a zoo." And it is well known by now how commonly the injustices and depredations of the Boston school system have compelled its Negro pupils to regard themselves with something less than the dignity and respect of human beings. The toll that this took was probably greater upon Stephen than it might have been upon some other children. But the price that it exacted was paid ultimately by every child, and in the long run I am convinced that the same price has been paid by every teacher too.

Jonathon Kozol is an author, winner of the National Book Award, and a former teacher.

4

Horace's Compromise

Theodore Sizer

Here is an English teacher, Horace Smith. He's fifty-three, a twenty-eight-year veteran of high school classrooms, what one calls an old pro. He's proud, respected, and committed to his practice. He'd do nothing else. Teaching is too much fun, too rewarding, to yield to another line of work.

Horace has been at Franklin High in a suburb of a big city for nineteen years. He served for eight years as English department chairman, but turned the job over to a colleague, because he felt that even the minimal administrative chores of that post interfered with the teaching he loved best.

He arises at 5:45 A.M., careful not to awaken either his wife or grown daughter. He likes to be at school by 7:00, and the drive there from his home takes forty minutes. He wishes he owned a home near the school, but he can't afford it. Only a few of his colleagues live in the school's town, and they are the wives of executives whose salaries can handle the mortgages. His wife's job at the liquor store that she, he, and her brother own doesn't start until 10:00 A.M., and their daughter, a new associate in a law firm in the city, likes to sleep until the last possible minute and skip breakfast. He washes and dresses on tiptoe.

NOTE: "Prologue" from *Horace's Compromise* by Theodore R. Sizer. Copyright 1984 by Theodore R. Sizer. Reprinted by permission of Houghton Mifflin Company. All rights reserved.

Horace prepares the coffee, makes some toast, and leaves the house at 6:20. He's not the first at school. The custodians and other, usually older, teachers are already there, "puttering around," one of the teachers says.

The teachers' room is large, really two rooms. The inner portion, windowless, is arranged in a honeycomb of carrels, one for each older teacher. Younger or newer teachers share carrels. Each has a built-in desk and a chair. Most have file cabinets. The walls on three sides, five feet high, are festooned with posters, photographs, lists, little sayings, notes from colleagues on issues long past. Horace: Call home. Horace: The following students in the chorus are excused from your Period 7 class—Adelson, Cartwright, Donato. . . .

Horace goes to his carrel, puts down his briefcase, picks up his mug, and walks to the coffee pot at the corner of the outer portion of the teachers' room, a space well lit by wide windows and fitted with a clutter of tables, vinyl-covered sofas, and chairs. The space is a familiar, comfortable jumble, fragrant with the smell of cigarettes smoked hours before. Horace lights up a fresh one, almost involuntarily, as a way perhaps to counteract yesterday's dead vapors. After pouring himself some coffee, he chats with some colleagues, mostly other English teachers.

The warning bell rings at 7:20. Horace smothers his cigarette, takes his still partly filled cup back to his carrel and adds it to the shuffle on his desk, collects some books and papers, and, with his briefcase, carries them down the hall to his classroom. Students are already clattering in, friendly, noisy, most of them ignoring him completely—not thoughtlessly, but without thinking. Horace often thinks of the importance of this semantic difference. Many adults are thoughtless about us teachers. Most students, however, just don't know we're here at all, people to think about. Innocents, he concludes.

7:30, and its bell. There are seventeen students here; there should be twenty-two. Bill Adams is ill; Horace has been told that by the office. Joyce Lezcowitz is at her grandmother's funeral; Horace hasn't been officially told that, but he knows it to be true. He marks Joyce "Ex Ab"—excused absence—on his attendance list. Looking up from the list, he sees two more students arrive, hustling to seats. You're late. Sorry . . . Sorry . . . The bus. . . . Horace ignores the apologies and excuses and checks the two off on his list. One name is yet unaccounted for. Where is Jimmy Tibbetts? Silence. Tibbetts gets an "Abs" after his name.

Horace gets the class's attention by making some announcements about next week's test and about the method by which copies of the next play being read will be shared. This inordinately concerns some students and holds no interest for others. Mr. Smith, how can I finish the play when both Rosalie and I have to work after school? Mr. Smith, Sandy and I are on different buses. Can we switch partners? All these sorts of queries are from girls. There is whispering among some students. You got it? Horace asks, abruptly. Silence, signaling affirmation. Horace knows it is an illusion. Some character will come up two days later and guiltlessly assert that he has no play book, doesn't know how to get one, and has never heard of the plans to share the limited copies. Horace makes a mental note to inform Adams, Lezcowitz, and Tibbetts of the text-sharing plan.

This is a class of juniors, mostly seventeen. The department syllabus calls for Shakespeare during this marking period, and *Romeo and Juliet* is the choice this year. The students have been assigned to read Act IV for this week, and Horace and his colleagues all get them to read the play out loud. The previous class had been memorable: Juliet's suicide had provoked much mirth. Romeo. I come! The kids thought it funny, clumsily melodramatic. Several, sniggering, saw a sexual meaning. Horace knew this to be inevitable; he had taught the play many times before.

We'll start at Scene Four. A rustle of books. Two kids looking helplessly around. They had forgotten their books, even though reading had been a daily exercise for three weeks. Mr. Smith, I forgot my book. You've got to remember, Alice . . . remember! All this with a smile as well as honest exasperation. Share with George. Alice gets up and moves her desk next to that of George. They solemnly peer into George's book while two girls across the classroom giggle.

Gloria, you're Lady Capulet. Mary, the Nurse. George, you're old man Capulet. Gloria starts, reading without punctuation: Hold take these keys and fetch more spices Nurse. Horace: Gloria. Those commas. They mean something. Use them. Now, again. Hold. Take these keys. And fetch more spices. Nurse. Horace swallows. Better . . . Go on, Mary. They call for dates and quinces in the pastry. What's a quince? a voice asks. Someone answers, It's a fruit. Fruit! Horace ignores this digression but is reminded how he doesn't like this group of kids. Individually, they're nice, but the chemistry of them together doesn't work. Classes are too much a game for them. Go on . . . George?

Come. Stir! Stir! Stir! The second cock hath crow'd. Horace knows that reference to "cock" will give an opening to some jokester, and he squelches it before it can begin, by being sure he is looking at the class and not at his book as the words are read.

The curfew bell hath rung. 'Tis three o'clock. Look to the bak'd meats, good Angelica. George reads accurately, but with little accentuation.

Mary: Go. You cot-quean. Go. Horace interrupts, and explains "cot-quean," a touch of contempt by the Nurse for the meddling Capulet. Horace does not go into the word's etymology, although he knows it. He feels that such a digression would be lost on this group, if not on his third-period class. He'll tell them. And so he returns: George, you're still Capulet. Reply to that cheeky Nurse.

The reading goes on for about forty minutes, to 8:15. The play's repartee among the musicians and Peter was a struggle, and Horace cut off the reading-out-loud before the end of the fifth scene. He assigns Act V for the next period and explains what will be on the *Romeo and Juliet* test. Mr. Smith, Ms. Viola isn't giving a test to her class. The statement is, of course, an accusing question. Well, we are. Ms. Viola's class will get something else, don't you worry. The bell rings.

The students rush out as the next class tries to push in. The newcomers are freshmen and give way to the eleventh-graders. They get into their seats expectantly, without quite the swagger of the older kids. Even though this is March, some of these students are still overwhelmed by the size of the high school.

There should be thirty students in this class, but twenty-seven are present. He marks three absences on his sheet. The students watch him; there is no chatter, but a good deal of squirming. These kids have the wriggles, Horace has often said. The bell rings: 8:24.

Horace tells the students to open their textbooks to page 104 and read the paragraph at its top. Two students have no textbook. Horace tells them to share with their neighbors. Always bring your textbook to class. We never know when we'll need them. The severity in his voice causes quiet. The students read.

Horace asks: Betty, which of the words in the first sentence is an adverb? Silence. Betty stares at her book. More silence. Betty, what is an adverb? Silence. Bill, help Betty. It's sort of a verb that tells you about things. Horace pauses: Not quite, Bill, but close. Phil, you try. Phil: An adverb modifies a verb. Horace: O.K., Phil, but what does "modify" mean? Silence. A voice: "Darkly." Who said that? Horace asks. The sentence was "Heathcliff was a darkly brooding character." I did, Taffy says. O.K., Horace follows, you're correct, Taffy, but tell us why "darkly" is an adverb. Taffy: It modifies "character." No, Taffy, try again. Heathcliff? No. Brooding? Yes, now why? Is "brooding" a verb? Silence.

Horace goes to the board, writes the sentence with chalk. He underlines darkly. Betty writes a note to her neighbor.

The class proceeds with this slow trudge through a paragraph from the textbook, searching for adverbs. Horace presses ahead patiently, almost dumbly at times. He is so familiar with the mistakes that ninth-graders make that he can sense them coming even before their utterance. Adverbs are always tougher to teach than adjectives. What frustrates him most are the partly correct answers; Horace worries that if he signals that a reply is somewhat accurate, all the students will think it is entirely accurate. At the same time, if he takes some minutes to sort out the truth from the falsity, the entire train of thought will be lost. He can never pursue any one student's errors to completion without losing all the others. Teaching grammar to classes like this is slow business, Horace feels. The bell rings. The students rush out, now more boisterous.

This is an Assembly Day, Horace remembers with pleasure. He leaves his papers on his desk, turns off the lights, shuts the door, and returns to the teachers' room. He can avoid assemblies; only the deans have to go. It's some student concert, in any event.

The teachers' room is full. Horace takes pleasure in it and wonders how his colleagues in schools in the city make do without such a sanctuary. Having a personal carrel is a luxury, he knows. He'd lose his here, he also knows, if enrollments went up again. The teachers' room was one happy consequence of the "baby bust."

The card game is going, set up on a square coffee table surrounded by a sofa and chairs. The kibitzers outnumber the players; all have coffee, some are smoking. The chatter is incessant, joshingly insulting. The staff members like one another.

Horace takes his mug, empties the cold leavings into the drain of the water fountain, and refills it. He puts a quarter in the large Maxwell House can supplied for that purpose, an honor system. He never pays for his early cup; Horace feels that if you come early, you get one on the house. He moves toward a clutch of fellow English and social studies teachers, and they gossip, mostly about a bit of trouble at the previous night's basketball game. No one was injured—that rarely happens at this high school—but indecorous words had been shouted back and forth, and Coke cans rolled on the gym floor. Someone could have been hurt. No teacher is much exercised about the incident. The talk is about things of more immediate importance to people: personal lives, essences even more transitory, Horace knows, than the odors of their collective cigarettes.

Horace looks about for Ms. Viola to find out whether it's true that she's not going to give a test on *Romeo and Juliet*. She isn't in sight, and Horace remembers why: she is a nonsmoker and is offended by smoke. He leaves his group and goes to Viola's carrel, where he finds her. She is put off by his query. Of course she is giving a test. Horace's lame explanation that a student told him differently doesn't help.

9:53. The third-period class of juniors. *Romeo and Juliet* again. Announcements over the public address system fill the first portion of the period, but Horace and a bunch of kids who call themselves "theater jocks" ignore them and talk about how to read Shakespeare well. They have to speak loudly to overpower the PA. The rest of the class chatter among themselves. The readings from the play are lively, and Horace is able to exhibit his etymological talents with a disquisition on "cot-quean." The students are well engaged by the scene involving the musicians and Peter until the class is interrupted by a proctor from the principal's office, collecting absence slips for the first-class periods. Nonetheless, the lesson ends with a widespread sense of good feeling. Horace never gets around to giving out the assignment, talking about the upcoming test, or arranging for play books to be shared.

10:47, the Advanced Placement class. They are reading *Ulysses,* a novel with which Horace himself had trouble. Its circumlocutions more precious than clever, he thinks, but he can't let on. Joyce likely to be on the AP Exam, which will put him on a pedestal. There are eighteen seniors in this class, but only five arrive. Horace remembers: This is United Nations Week at the local college, and a group of the high school's seniors is taking part, representing places like Mauritius and Libya. Many of the students in the UN Club are also those in Advanced Placement classes. Horace welcomes this remnant of five and suggests they use the hour to read. Although he is annoyed at losing several teaching days with this class, he is still quietly grateful for the respite this morning.

11:36, Lunch. Horace buys a salad on the cafeteria line—as a teacher he can jump ahead of students—and he takes it to the dining room. He nods to the assistant principal on duty as he passes by. He takes a place at an empty table and is almost immediately joined by three physical education teachers, all of them coaches of varsity teams, who are noisily wrangling about the previous night's basketball game controversy. Horace listens, entertained. The coaches are having a good time, arguing with heat because they know the issue is really inconsequential and thus their disagreement will not mean much. Lunch is relaxing for Horace.

12:17. A free period. Horace checks with a colleague in the book storeroom about copies of a text soon to be used by the ninth-graders. Can he get more copies? His specific allotment is settled after some minutes' discussion. Horace returns to the teachers' room, to his carrel. He finds a note to call a Mrs. Altschuler, who turns out to be the stepmother of a former student. She asks, on behalf of her stepson, whether Horace will write a character reference for the young man to use in his search for a job. Horace agrees. Horace also finds a note to call the office. Was Tibbetts in your Period One class? No, Horace tells the assistant principal; that's why I marked him absent on the attendance sheet. The assistant principal overlooks this sarcasm.

Well, he says, Tibbetts wasn't marked absent at any other class. Horace replies, That's someone else's problem. He was not in my class. The assistant principal: You're sure? Horace: Of course I'm sure.

The minutes of the free period remaining are spent in organizing a set of papers that is to be returned to Horace's third junior English class. Horace sometimes alternates weeks when he collects homework so as not totally to bury himself. He feels guilty about this. The sixth-period class had its turn this week. Horace had skimmed these exercises—a series of questions on Shakespeare's life—and hastily graded them, but using only a plus, check, or minus. He hadn't had time enough to do more.

1:11. More *Romeo and Juliet*. This section is less rambunctious than the first-period group and less interesting than that of the third period. The students are actually rather dull, perhaps because the class meets at the end of the day. Everyone is ready to leave; there is little energy for Montagues and Capulets. However, as with other sections, the kids are responsive when spoken to individually. It is their blandness when they are in a group that Horace finds trying. At least they aren't hellraisers, the way some last-period-of-the-day sections can be. The final bell rings at 2:00.

Horace has learned to stay in his classroom at the day's end so that students who want to consult with him can always find him there. Several appear today. One wants Horace to speak on his behalf to a prospective employer. Another needs to get an assignment. A couple of other students come by actually just to come by. They have no special errand, but seem to like to check in and chat. These youngsters puzzle Horace. They always seem to need reassurance.

Three students from the Theater Club arrive with questions about scenery for the upcoming play. (Horace is the faculty adviser to the stage crew.) Their shared construction work on sets behind the scenes gives Horace great pleasure. He knows these kids and likes their company.

By the time Horace finishes in his classroom, it is 2:30. He drops his papers and books at his carrel, selecting some—papers given him by his Advanced Placement students two days previously that he has yet to find time to read—to put in his briefcase. He does not check in on the card game, now winding down, in the outer section of the teachers' room but, rather, goes briefly to the auditorium to watch the Theater Club actors starting their rehearsals.

The play is Wilder's *Our Town*. Horace is both grateful and wistful that the production requires virtually no set to be constructed. The challenge for his stage crew, Horace knows, will be in the lighting.

Horace drives directly to his liquor store, arriving shortly after 4:00. He gives his brother-in-law some help in the stockroom and helps at the counter during the usual 4:30–6:30 surge of customers. His wife had earlier left for home and has supper ready for them both and their daughter at 7:45.

After dinner, Horace works for an hour on the papers he has brought home and on the Joyce classes he knows are ahead of him once the UN Mock Assembly is over. He has two telephone calls from students, one who has been ill and wants an assignment and another who wants to talk about the lighting for *Our Town*. The latter, an eager but shy boy, calls Horace often.

Horace turns in at 10:45, can't sleep, and watches the 11:00 news while his wife sleeps. He finally drifts off just before midnight.

Horace has high standards. Almost above all, he believes in the importance of writing, having his students learn to use language well. He believes in having his students write and be criticized, often. Horace has his five classes of fewer than thirty students each, a total of 120. (He is lucky; his colleagues in inner cities like New York, San Diego, Detroit, and St. Louis have a school board-union negotiated "load" base of 175 students.) Horace believes that each student should write something for criticism at least twice a week—but he is realistic. As a rule, his students write once a week.

Most of Horace's students are juniors and seniors, young people who should be beyond sentence and paragraph exercises and who should be working on short essays, written arguments with moderately complex sequencing and, if not grace exactly, at least clarity.

A page or two would be a minimum—but Horace is realistic. He assigns but one or two paragraphs.

Being a veteran teacher, Horace takes only fifteen to twenty minutes to check over each student's daily homework, to read the week's theme, and to write an analysis of it. (The "good" papers take a shorter time, usually, and the work of inept or demoralized students takes much longer.) Horace wonders how his inner-city colleagues, who usually have a far greater percentage of demoralized students, manage. Horace is realistic: even in his accommodating suburban school, fifteen minutes is too much to spend. He compromises, averaging five minutes for each student's work by cutting all but the most essential corners (the reading of the paragraphs in the themes takes but a few seconds; it is the thoughtful criticizing, in red ball point pen in the margins and elsewhere, that takes the minutes).

So, to check homework and to read and criticize one paragraph per week per student with the maximum feasible corner-cutting takes six hundred minutes or ten hours, assuming no coffee breaks or flagging attention (which is some assumption, considering how enervating is most students' forced and misspelled prose).

Horace's fifty-some-minute classes consume about twenty-three hours per week. Administrative chores chew up another hour and a half. Horace cares about his teaching and feels that he should take a half-hour to prepare for each class meeting, particularly for his classes with older students, who are swiftly moving over quite abstract and unfamiliar material, and his class of ninth-graders, which requires teaching that is highly individualized. However, he is realistic. He will compromise by spending no more than ten minutes' preparation time, on average, per class. (In effect, he concentrates his prep time on the Advanced Placement class, and teaches the others from old notes.) Three of his sections are ostensibly of the same course, but because the students are different in each case, he knows that he cannot satisfactorily clone each lesson plan twice and teach to his satisfaction. (Horace is uneasy with this compromise but feels he can live with it.) Horace's class preparation time per week: four hours.

Horace loves the theater, and when the principal begged him to help out with the afternoon drama program, he agreed. He is paid $800 extra per year to help the student stage crews prepare sets. This takes him in all about four hours per week, save for the ten days before the shows, when he and his crew happily work for hours on end.

Of course, Horace would like time to work on the curriculum with his colleagues. He would like to visit their classes and to work with them on the English department program. He would like to meet his students' parents, to read in his field, and, most important for him, to counsel students as they need such counseling one on one. Being a popular teacher, he is asked to write over fifty recommendations for college admissions offices each year, a Christmas vacation task that usually takes three full days. (He knows he is good at it now. When he was less experienced, the reference writing used to take him a full week. He can now quickly crank out the expected felicitous verbiage.) Yet Horace feels uneasy writing the crucial references for students with whom he has rarely exchanged ten consecutive sentences of private conversation. However, one does what one can and hopes that one is not sending the colleges too many lies.

And so before Horace assigns his one or two paragraphs per week, he is committed for over thirty-two hours of teaching, administration, class preparation, and extracurricular drama work. Collecting one short piece of writing per week from students and spending a bare five minutes per week on each student's weekly work adds ten hours, yielding a forty hour work week. Lunch periods, supervisory duties frequently, if irregularly, assigned, coffee breaks, travel to and from school, and time for the courtesies, civilities, and biological necessities of life are all in addition.

For this, Horace, a twenty-eight-year veteran, is paid $27,000, a good salary for a teacher in his district. He works at the liquor store and earns another $8,000 there, given a good year. The district adds 7 percent of his base salary to an invested pension account, and Horace tries to put away something more each month in an IRA. Fortunately, his wife also works at the store, and their one child went to the state university and its law school. She just received her JD. Her starting salary in the law firm is $32,000.

Horace is a gentle man. He reads the frequent criticism of his profession in the press with compassion. Johnny can't read. Teachers have low Graduate Record Examination scores. We must vary our teaching to the learning styles of our pupils. We must relate to the community. We must be scholarly, keeping up with our fields. English teachers should be practicing, published writers. If they aren't all these things, it is obvious that they don't care. Horace is a trooper; he hides his bitterness. Nothing can be gained by showing it. The critics do not really want to hear him or to face facts. He will go with the flow. What alternative is there?

A prestigious college near Franklin High School assigns its full-time freshman expository writing instructors a maximum of two sections, totaling forty students. Horace thinks about his 120. Like these college freshmen, at least they show up, most of them turn in what homework he assigns, and they give him little hassle. The teachers in the city have 175 kids, almost half of whom may be absent on any given day but all of whom remain the teacher's responsibility. And those kids are a resentful, wary, often troublesome lot. Horace is relieved that he is where he is. He wonders whether any of those college teachers ever read any of the recommendations he writes each Christmas vacation.

Most jobs in the real world have a gap between what would be nice and what is possible. One adjusts. The tragedy for many high school teachers is that the gap is a chasm, not crossed by reasonable and judicious adjustments. Even after adroit accommodations and devastating compromises—only five minutes per week of attention on the written work of each student and an average of ten minutes of planning for each fifty-odd-minute class—the task is already crushing, in reality a sixty-hour work week. For this, Horace is paid a wage enjoyed by age-mates in semiskilled and low-pressure blue-collar jobs and by novices, twenty-five years his junior, in some other white-collar professions. Furthermore, none of these sixty-plus hours is spent in replenishing his own academic capital. That has to be done in addition, perhaps during the summer. However, he needs to earn more money then, and there is no pay for upgrading his teacher's skills. He has to take on tutoring work or increase his involvement at the liquor store.

Fortunately (from one point of view), few people seem to care whether he simply does not assign that paragraph per week, or whether he farms its criticism out to other students. ("Exchange papers, class, and take ten minutes to grade your neighbor's essay.") He is a colorful teacher, and he knows that he can do a good job of lecturing, some of which can, in theory at least, replace the coaching that Horace knows is the heart of high school teaching. By using an overhead projector he can publicly analyze the paragraphs of six of his students. But he will have assigned writing to all of them. As long as he does not let on which six papers he will at the last minute "pull" to analyze, he will have given real practice to all. There are tricks like this to use.

His classes are quiet and orderly, and he has the reputation in the community of being a good teacher. Accordingly, he gets his administrators' blessings. If he were to complain about the extent of his overload, he would find no seriously empathetic audience. Reducing teacher load is, when all the negotiating is over, a low agenda item for the unions and school boards. The administration will arrange for in-service days on "teacher burnout" (more time away from grading paragraphs) run by moonlighting education professors who will get more pay for giving a few "professional workshops" than Horace gets for a year's worth of set construction in the theater.

No one blames the system; everyone blames him. Relax, the consultants advise. Here are some exercises to help you get some perspective. Morphine, Horace thinks. It dulls my pain. Come now, he mutters to himself. Don't get cynical. Don't keep insisting that these "experts" should try my job for a week. They assure me that they understand me, only they say, "We hear you, Horace." I wonder who their English teachers were.

Horace's students will get into college, their parents may remember to thank him for the references he wrote for their offspring (unlikely), and the better colleges will teach the kids to write. The students who do not get the coaching in college, or who do not go to college, do not complain. No one seems upset. Just let it all continue, a conspiracy, a toleration of a chasm between the necessary and the provided and acceptance of big rhetoric and little reality. Horace dares not express his bitterness to the visitor conducting a study of high schools, because he fears he will be portrayed as a whining hypocrite.

Theodore Sizer is the founder of The Coalition of Essential Schools, the former dean of the Graduate School of Education at Harvard, and the founding director of the Annenberg Institute for School Reform.

PART II

Who Are Today's Students?

I like to arrive early at our annual Language Arts Teachers Conference so that I can review the day's agenda one more time before making that fateful choice of which breakout sessions to attend. I have been burned so many times in the past, allured by a snappy title or promises of failsafe methods and free materials. If only I can get lucky and pick an engaging session. Hmm . . . this sounds interesting. Clinic 23 in the Winthrop Room: *Teaching Romeo and Juliet*. The program says this clinic features a sharing of innovative ideas for teaching Shakespeare units. Sounds like there will be lots of discussion and hands-on activities. The elevator is jammed with teachers headed to the fourth floor. They can't all be attending the same clinic that I have chosen. I hustle down the hall knowing that clinics close when the room capacity is met. Whew, a few seats left in the second to the last row.

The presenter, a teacher from Hoover High School, begins by telling the audience that we will collectively design and develop an introductory lesson on *Romeo and Juliet*. He divides us into five cooperative groups, each charged with answering the following questions: What standards will your lesson address? What performance objectives will this lesson meet? What materials and resources will you use? What step-by-step instructional procedures will you follow? How will you assess the students? Okay, would everyone please gather with their groups?

Things are moving along rather smoothly when a gentleman in the second to last row exclaims, "Wait!"

The teachers freeze. The room goes silent.

"Yes?" the presenter responds. "What is it?"

"Well," the teacher begins, "how can we plan a series of lessons when we have not asked the most important question: Who are the students?"

Why is this an important question? Do race, ethnicity, income, and gender, for example, affect the teaching and learning cycle?

5

What Should Teachers Do?

Ebonics and Culturally Responsive Instruction

Lisa Delpit

I will submit that one of the reasons [Ebonics] is a problem, if you will—a controversy—is that you cannot divorce language from its speakers. And if you have people who have been disenfranchised, are neglected, are rejected, it is very difficult for the society at large to elevate their language. And, thus, when you start to try to make a case with legitimizing Ebonics—a way of communicating by some, although not all African-Americans speak it—you, in effect, are talking about legitimizing a group of people. You are talking about bringing them to a status comparable to society at large. And that's always a difficult proposition. So, in a certain sense, we cannot talk about Ebonics separate and distinct from the state of African-American people in the United States as a neglected and as an underclass, marginalized, if you will, people.

Orlando Taylor
Professor of Communications
at Howard University
Emerge magazine, April 1997

The "Ebonics Debate" has created much more heat than light for most of the country. For teachers trying to determine what implications there might be for classroom practice, enlightenment has been a completely nonexistent commodity. I have been asked often enough recently, "What do you think about Ebonics? Are you for it or against it?" My answer must be neither. I can be neither for Ebonics or against Ebonics any more than I can be for or against air. It exists. It is the language spoken by many of our African-American children. It is the language they heard as their mothers nursed them and changed their diapers and played peek-a-boo with them. It is the language through which they first encountered love, nurturance, and joy.

On the other hand, most teachers of those African-American children who have been least well-served by educational systems believe that their students' life chances will be further hampered if they do not learn Standard English. In the stratified society in which we live, they are absolutely correct. While having access to the politically mandated language form will not, by any means, guarantee economic success (witness the growing numbers of unemployed African Americans holding doctorates), not having access will almost certainly guarantee failure.

So what must teachers do? Should they spend their time relentlessly "correcting" their Ebonics-speaking children's language so that it might conform to what we have learned to refer to as Standard English? Despite good intentions, constant correction seldom has the desired effect. Such correction increases cognitive monitoring of speech, thereby making talking difficult. To illustrate, I have frequently taught a relatively simple new "dialect" to classes of preservice teachers. In this dialect, the phonetic element "iz" is added after the first consonant or consonant cluster in each syllable of a word. (Maybe becomes miz-ay-biz-ee and apple, iz-ap-piz-le.) After a bit of drill and practice, the students are asked to tell a partner in "iz" language why they decided to become teachers. Most only haltingly attempt a few words before lapsing into either silence or into Standard

English. During a follow-up discussion, all students invariably speak of the impossibility of attempting to apply rules while trying to formulate and express a thought. Forcing speakers to monitor their language typically produces silence.

Correction may also affect students' attitudes toward their teachers. In a recent research project, middle school, inner-city students were interviewed about their attitudes toward their teachers and school. One young woman complained bitterly, "Mrs. _____ always be interrupting to make you 'talk correct' and stuff. She be butting into your conversations when you not even talking to her! She need to mind her own business!" Clearly this student will be unlikely to either follow the teacher's directives or to want to imitate her speech style.

Group Identity

Issues of group identity may also affect students' oral production of a different dialect. Researcher Sharon Nelson-Barber (1982), in a study of phonologic aspects of Pima Indian language, found that, in grades 1–3, the children's English most approximated the standard dialect of their teachers. But surprisingly, by fourth grade, when one might assume growing competence in standard forms, their language moved significantly toward the local dialect. These fourth graders had the competence to express themselves in a more standard form but chose, consciously or unconsciously, to use the language of those in their local environments. The researcher believes that, by ages eight to nine, these children became aware of their group membership and its importance to their well-being, and this realization was reflected in their language. They may also have become increasingly aware of the school's negative attitude toward their community and found it necessary—through choice of linguistic form—to decide with which camp to identify.

What should teachers do about helping students acquire an additional oral form? First, they should recognize that the linguistic form a student brings to school is intimately connected with loved one's community, and personal identity. To suggest that this form is "wrong" or, even worse, ignorant, is to suggest that something is wrong with the student and his or her family. To denigrate your language is, then, in African-American terms, to "talk about your mama." Anyone who knows anything about African-American culture knows the consequences of that speech act!

On the other hand, it is equally important to understand that students who do not have access to the politically popular dialect form in this country are less likely to succeed economically than their peers who do. How can both realities be embraced in classroom instruction?

It is possible and desirable to make the actual study of language diversity a part of the curriculum for all students. For younger children, discussions about the differences in the ways TV characters from different cultural groups speak can provide a starting point. A collection of the many children's books written in the dialects of various cultural groups can also provide a wonderful basis for learning about linguistic diversity, as can audiotaped stories narrated by individuals from different cultures, including taped books read by members of the children's home communities. Mrs. Pat, a teacher chronicled by Stanford University researcher Shirley Brice Heath (1983), had her students become language "detectives," interviewing a variety of individuals and listening to the radio and TV to discover the differences and similarities in the ways people talked. Children can learn that there are many ways of saying the same thing, and that certain contexts suggest particular kinds of linguistic performances.

Some teachers have groups of students create bilingual dictionaries of their own language form and Standard English. Both the students and the teacher become engaged in identifying terms and deciding upon the best translations. This can be done as generational dictionaries, too, given the proliferation of "youth culture" terms growing out of the Ebonics-influenced tendency for the continual regeneration of vocabulary. Contrastive grammatical structures can be studied similarly but, of course, as the Oakland policy suggests, teachers must be aware of the grammatical structure of Ebonics before they can launch into this complex study.

Other teachers have had students become involved with standard forms through various kinds of role-play. For example, memorizing parts for drama productions allow students to practice and "get the feel" of speaking Standard English while not under the threat of correction. A master teacher of African-American children in Oakland, Carrie Secret, uses this technique and extends it so that students videotape their practice performances and self-critique them as to the appropriate use of Standard English. (But I must add that Carrie's use of drama and oration goes much beyond acquiring Standard English. She inspires pride and community connections that are truly wondrous to behold.) The use of self-critique of recorded forms may prove even more useful than I initially realized. California State University—Hayward professor Etta Hollins has reported that just by leaving a tape recorder on during an informal class period and playing it back with no comment, students began to code-switch—moving between Standard English and Ebonics—more effectively. It appears that they may have not realized which language form they were using until they heard themselves speak on tape.

Young students can create puppet shows or role-play cartoon characters—many "superheroes" speak almost hypercorrect standard English. Playing a role eliminates the possibility of implying that the child's language is inadequate and suggests, instead, that different language forms are appropriate in different contexts. Some other teachers in New York City have had their students produce a news show every day for the rest of the school. The students take on the personae of famous newscasters, keeping in character as they develop and read their news reports. Discussions ensue about whether Tom Brokaw would have said it that way, again taking the focus off the child's speech.

Although most educators think of Black Language as primarily differing in grammar and syntax, there are other differences in oral language of which teachers should be aware in a multicultural context, particularly in discourse style and language use. Harvard University researcher Sarah Michaels and other researchers identified differences in children's narratives at "sharing time" (Michaels & Cazden, 1986). They found that there was a tendency among young white children to tell "topic-centered" narratives—stories focused on one event—and a tendency among Black youngsters, especially girls, to tell "episodic" narratives—stories that include shifting scenes and are typically longer. While these differences are interesting in themselves, what is of greater significance is adults' responses to the differences. C. B. Cazden (1988) reports on a subsequent project in which a white adult was taped reading the oral narratives of Black and white first graders, with all syntax dialectal markers removed. Adults were asked to listen to the stories and comment about the children's likelihood of success in school. The researchers were surprised by the differential responses given by Black and white adults.

Varying Reactions

In responding to the retelling of a Black child's story, the white adults were uniformly negative, making such comments as "terrible story, incoherent" and "[n]ot a story at all in the sense of describing something that happened." Asked to judge this child's academic competence, all of the white adults rated her below the children who told "topic-centered" stories. Most of these adults also predicted difficulties for this child's future school career, such as "This child might have trouble reading," that she exhibited "language problems that affect school achievement," and that "family problems" or "emotional problems might hamper her academic progress."

The Black adults had very different reactions. They found this child's story "well formed, easy to understand, and interesting, with lots of detail and description." Even though all five of these adults mentioned the "shifts" and "associations" or "nonlinear" quality of the story, they did not find these features distracting. Three of the Black adults selected the story as the best of the five they had heard, and all but one judged the child as exceptionally bright, highly verbal, and successful in school (Cazden, 1988).

This is not a story about racism, but one about cultural familiarity. However, when differences in narrative style produce differences in interpretation of competence, the pedagogical implications are evident. If children who produce stories based on differing discourse styles are expected to have trouble reading and viewed as having language, family, or emotional problems, as was the case with the informants quoted by Cazden, they are unlikely to be viewed as ready for the same challenging instruction awarded students whose language patterns more closely parallel the teacher's.

Most teachers are particularly concerned about how speaking Ebonics might affect learning to read. There is little evidence that speaking another mutually intelligible language form, per se, negatively affects one's ability to learn to read (Sim, 1982). For commonsensical proof, one need only reflect on nonstandard English-speaking Africans who, though enslaved, not only taught themselves to read English, but did so under threat of severe punishment or death. But children who speak Ebonics do have a more difficult time becoming proficient readers. Why? In part, appropriate instructional methodologies are frequently not adopted. There is ample evidence that children who do not come to school with knowledge about letters, sounds, and symbols need to experience some explicit instruction in these areas in order to become independent readers. Another explanation is that, where teachers' assessments of competence are influenced by the language children speak, teachers may develop low expectations for certain students and subsequently teach them less (Sims, 1982). A third explanation rests in teachers confusing the teaching of reading with the teaching of a new language form.

Reading researcher Patricia Cunningham (1976-1997) found that teachers across the United States were more likely to correct reading miscues that were "dialect"-related ("Here go a table" for "Here is a table") than those that were "nondialect"-related ("Here is a dog" for "There is a dog"). Seventy-eight percent of the former types of miscues were corrected, compared with only 27 percent of the latter. She concludes that the teachers were acting out of ignorance, not realizing that "here go" and "here is" represent the same meaning in some Black children's language.

In my observations of many classrooms, however, I have come to conclude that even when teachers recognize the similarity of meaning, they are likely to correct Ebonics-related miscues. Consider a typical example:

TEXT: Yesterday I washed my brother's clothes.

STUDENT'S   Yesterday I wash my bruvver close.
RENDITION:

The subsequent exchange between student and teacher sounds something like this:

T: Wait, let's go back. What's that word again? [Points at *washed*.]

S: Wash.

T: No. Look at it again. What letters do you see at the end? You see "e-d." Do you remember what we say when we see those letters on the end of the word?

S: "ed."

T: OK, but in this case we say washed. Can you say that?

S: Wash*ed*.

T: Good. Now read it again.

S: Yesterday I wash*ed* my bruvver.

T: Wait a minute, what's that word again? [Points to *brother*.]

S: Bruvver.

T: No. Look at these letters in the middle. [Points to *brother*.] Remember to read what you see. Do you remember how we say that sound? Put your tongue between your teeth and say /th/. . . .

The lesson continues in such a fashion, the teacher proceeding to correct the student's Ebonics-influenced pronunciations and grammar while ignoring that fact that the student had to have comprehended the sentence in order to translate it into her own language. Such instruction occurs daily and blocks reading development in a number of ways. First, because children become better readers by having the opportunity to read, the overcorrection exhibited in this lesson means that this child will be less likely to become a fluent reader than other children that are not interrupted so consistently.

Second, a complete focus on code and pronunciation blocks children's understanding that reading is essentially a meaning-making process. This child, who understands the text, is led to believe that she is doing something wrong. She is encouraged to think of reading not as something you do to get a message, but something you pronounce. Third, constant corrections by the teacher are likely to cause this student and others like her to resist reading and to resent the teacher.

Language researcher Robert Berdan (1980) reports that, after observing the kind of teaching routine described above in a number of settings, he incorporated the teacher behaviors into a reading instruction exercise that he used with students in a college class. He put together sundry rules from a number of American social and regional dialects to create what he called the "language of Atlantis." Students were then called upon to read aloud in this dialect they did not know. When they made errors he interrupted them, using some of the same statements and comments he had heard elementary school teachers routinely make to their students. He concludes:

> The results were rather shocking. By the time these PhD Candidates in English or linguistics had read 10–20 words, I could make them sound totally illiterate. . . . The first thing that goes is sentence intonation: they sound like they are reading a list from the telephone book. Comment on their pronunciation a bit more, and they begin to subvocalize, rehearsing pronunciations for themselves before they dare to say them out loud. They begin to guess at pronunciations.
>
> They switch letters around for no reason. They stumble; they repeat. In short, when I attack them for their failure to conform to my demands for Atlantis English pronunciations, they sound very much like the worst of the second graders in any of the classrooms I have observed.
>
> They also begin to fidget. They wad up their papers, bite their fingernails, whisper, and some finally refuse to continue. They do all the things that children do while they are busily failing to learn to read.

The moral of this story is not to confuse learning a new language form with reading comprehension. To do so will only confuse the child, leading her away from those intuitive understandings about language that will promote reading development and toward a school career of resistance and a lifetime of avoiding reading.

Unlike unplanned oral language or public reading, writing lends itself to editing. While conversational talk is spontaneous and must be responsive to an immediate context, writing is a mediated process that may be written and rewritten any number of times before being introduced to public scrutiny. Consequently, writing is more amenable to rule application—one may first write freely to get one's thoughts down, and then edit to hone the message and apply specific spelling, syntactical, or punctuation rules. My college students who had such difficulty talking in the "iz" dialect found writing it, with the rules displayed before them, a relatively easy task.

To conclude, the teacher's job is to provide access to the national "standard" as well as to understand the language the children speak sufficiently to celebrate its beauty. The verbal adroitness, the cogent and quick wit, the brilliant use of metaphor, the facility in rhythm and rhyme, evident in the language of Jesse Jackson, Whoopi Goldberg, Toni Morrison, Henry Louis Gates, Jr., Tupac Shakur, and Maya Angelou, as well as in that of many inner-city Black students, may all be drawn upon to facilitate school learning. The teacher must know how to effectively teach reading and writing to students whose culture and language differ from that of the school, and must understand how and why students decide to add another language form to their repertoire. All we can do is provide students with access to additional language forms. Inevitably, each speaker will make his or her own decision about what to say in any context.

But I must end with a caveat that we keep in mind a simple truth: Despite our necessary efforts to provide access to Standard English, such access will not make any of our students more intelligent. It will not teach them math or science or geography—or, for that matter, compassion, courage, or responsibility. Let us not become so overly concerned with the language form that we ignore academic and moral content. Access to the standard language may be necessary, but it is definitely not sufficient to produce intelligent, competent caretakers of the future.

Lisa Delpit is the holder of the Benjamin E. Mays Chair of Urban Educational Excellence at Georgia State University, Atlanta.

6

Racism, Discrimination, and Expectations of Students' Achievement

Sonia Nieto

[Racists have power] only if you let them! We'll stick with (the example of striped shirts): If I go where everyone is wearing solids, and I'm wearing a stripe, and someone comes up to me and tells me, "You don't belong here; you're wearing stripes," I'll say, "I belong anywhere to belong." And I'll stand right there! But there are some people who just say, "Oh, okay," and will turn around and leave. Then the racist has the power.

Linda Howard
Interviewee

L inda Howard is a young woman who has been directly harmed by racism in and out of school, and she has a highly evolved understanding

NOTE: From Nieto, S., (2003), *Affirming Diversity: The Sociopolitical Context of Multicultural Education, 3/e.* Published by Allyn and Bacon, Boston, MA. Copyright 2003 by Pearson Education. Reprinted by permission of the publisher.

of it on both an individual and an institutional level. As you will see in her case study, Linda has thought very deeply about racism. Many teachers and other educators, however, have not. In this chapter, we will explore the impact that racism, other biases, and expectations of student abilities may have on achievement. We will focus on racism as an example of bias, but I will also point out other kinds of personal and situational discrimination when appropriate. These include discrimination on the basis of gender (sexism), ethnic group (ethnocentrism), social class (classism), language (linguicism), or other perceived differences. I will also mention anti-Semitism, discrimination against Jews; anti-Arab discrimination, directed against Arabs; ageism, discrimination based on age; heterosexism, discrimination against gay men and lesbians; and ableism, discrimination against people with disabilities.

Definitions of Racism and Discrimination

Discussions of prejudice and discrimination tend to focus on the biases and negative perceptions of individuals toward members of other groups. For example, Gordon Allport, in his groundbreaking work on the nature of prejudice, quotes a United Nations document defining discrimination as "any conduct based on a distinction made on grounds of natural or social categories, which have no relation either to individual capacities or merits, or to the concrete behavior of the individual person." This definition is helpful but incomplete because it fails to describe the harmful effects of such conduct. More broadly speaking, discrimination denotes negative or destructive behaviors that can result in denying some groups' life necessities as well as the privileges, rights, and opportunities enjoyed by other groups. Discrimination is usually based on prejudice, that is, the attitudes and beliefs of individuals about entire groups of people. These attitudes and beliefs are generally, but not always, negative.

Our society, among many others, categorizes people according to both visible and invisible traits, uses such classifications to deduce fixed behavioral and mental traits, and then applies policies and practices that jeopardize some and benefit others. Classifications based on race, ethnicity, gender, social class, and other physical or social differences are all around us. Frequently, they result in gross exaggerations and stereotypes: Girls are not as smart as boys; African Americans have rhythm; Asians are studious; Poles are simple-minded; Jews are smart; and poor people need instant gratification. Although some of these may appear to be "positive" stereotypes, both "negative" and "positive" stereotypes have negative results because they limit our perspective of an entire group of people. There are two major problems with categorizing people in this way: First, people of all groups begin to believe the stereotypes; and second, both material and psychological resources are doled out accordingly.

We see a clear example of the implications of such categorizations in the case study of Rich Miller. Rich was quite severe in his criticism of other African Americans, whom he characterized as "settling for the easiest way out," "lazy," and "tacky." He had internalized the myth of success based completely on individual endeavor rather than as also influenced by structural issues such as institutional racism and lack of opportunity. It is easy to understand how this happens: In our society, the metaphor of "pulling yourself up by your bootstraps" is powerful indeed; it allows little room for alternative explanations based on structural inequality.

Racism and other forms of discrimination are based on the perception that one ethnic group, class, gender, or language is superior to all others. In the United States, the conventional norm used to measure all other groups is European-American, upper-middle class, English-speaking, and male. Discrimination based on perceptions of superiority is part of the structure of schools, the curriculum, the education most teachers receive, and the interactions among teachers, students, and the community. But discrimination is not simply an individual bias; it is above all an institutional practice.

Most definitions of racism and discrimination obscure the institutional nature of oppression. Although the beliefs and behaviors of individuals may be hurtful, far greater damage is done through institutional discrimination, that is, the systematic use of economic and political power in institutions (such as schools) that leads to detrimental policies and practices. These policies and practices have a harmful effect on groups that share a particular identity (be it racial, ethnic, gender, or other). The major difference between individual and institutional discrimination is the wielding of power, because it is primarily through the power of the people who control institutions such as schools that oppressive policies and practices are reinforced and legitimated. Linda Howard, one of our young interviewees, already understood this distinction. In her case study, she distinguished between prejudice and racism in this way: "We all have some type of person that we don't like, whether it's from a different race, or from a different background, or they have different habits." But she went on to explain, as we saw in the quote at the beginning of this chapter, that a racist is someone who has power to carry out his or her prejudices.

Let me give another example: Let's say that I am prejudiced against tall people. Although my bias may hurt individual tall people because I refuse to befriend them or because I make fun of them, I can do very little to limit their options in life. If, however, I belonged to a group of powerful "non-talls" and we limited the access of tall persons to certain neighborhoods, prohibited them from receiving quality health care, discouraged intermarriage with people of short or average height, developed policies against their employment in high-status professions, and placed all children who were the offspring of "talls" (or who showed early signs of becoming above average in height) in the lowest ability tracks in schools, then my bias would have teeth and its institutional power would be clear. In the discussion that follows, we will be concerned primarily with institutional discrimination.

Institutional discrimination generally refers to how people are excluded or deprived of rights or opportunities as a result of the normal operations of the institution. Although the individuals involved in the institution may not be prejudiced or have any racist intentions or even awareness of how others may be harmed, the result may nevertheless be racist. In this sense, intentional and unintentional racism are different. But because they both result in negative outcomes, in the end it does not really matter whether racism and other forms of discrimination are intentional. Rather than trying to figure out whether the intent was to do harm or not, educators would do better to spend their time addressing the effects of racism.

When we understand racism and other forms of discrimination as a systemic problem, not simply as an individual dislike for a particular group of people, we can better understand the negative and destructive effects it can have. Vanessa Mattison provides a good example of a young person struggling to reconcile our country's lofty ideals of equality and fair play with the reality of the injustice she saw around her. Vanessa was committed to social justice, but she saw it primarily as working to change the attitudes and behaviors of individuals. She had not yet made the connection between racism and institutional oppression, and she did not grasp that institutional racism was far more harmful than individual biases or acts of meanness. But she was beginning to see that certain norms existed that were unfair to Blacks, women, and gays and lesbians. In her words: "There's all these underlying rules that if you're not this, you can't do that."

This is meant neither to minimize the powerful effects of individual prejudice and discrimination, which can be personally painful, nor to suggest that discrimination occurs only in one direction, for example, from Whites toward Blacks. There is no monopoly on prejudice and individual discrimination; they happen in all directions, and even within groups. However, interethnic and intraethnic biases and personal prejudices, while negative and hurtful, simply do not have the long-range and life-limiting effects of institutional racism and other kinds of institutional discrimination.

As an illustration of institutional racism, let us look at how testing practices are sometimes used in schools: Students from dominated groups may be stigmatized and labeled because of their performance on standardized tests. What places these students at a disadvantage is not that particular teachers have prejudiced attitudes about them; teachers may, in fact, like the students very much. What places the students at jeopardy is the fact that they may be labeled, grouped, and tracked, sometimes for the length of their schooling, because of their score on an ethnocentric and biased test. In this case, it is institutions—schools and the testing industry—that have the major negative impact on students from culturally dominated groups.

Prejudice and discrimination, then, are not just personality traits or psychological phenomena; they are also a manifestation of economic, political, and social power. The institutional definition of racism is not always easy to accept because it goes against deeply held notions of equality and justice in our nation. According to Beverly Tatum, "An understanding of racism as a system of advantage presents a serious challenge to the notion of the United States as a just society where rewards are based solely on one's merits." Racism as an institutional system implies that some people and groups benefit and others lose. Whites, whether they want to or not, benefit in a racist society; males benefit in a sexist society. Discrimination always helps somebody—those with the most power—which explains why racism, sexism and other forms of discrimination continue.

According to Meyer Weinberg, racism is a system of privilege and penalty. That is, one is rewarded or punished in housing, education, employment, health, and so on, by the simple fact of belonging to a particular group, regardless of one's individual merits or faults. He goes on to explain, "Racism consists centrally of two facets: First, a belief in the inherent superiority of some people and the inherent inferiority of others; and second, the acceptance of distributing goods and services—let alone respect—in accordance with such judgments of unequal worth." In addressing the institutional nature of racism, he adds, " . . . racism is always collective. Prejudiced individuals may join the large movement, but they do not cause it." According to this conception, the "silence of institutional racism" and the "ruckus of individual racism" are mutually supportive. It is sometimes difficult to separate one level of racism from the others, as they feed on and inform one another. What is crucial, according to Weinberg, is understanding that the doctrine of White supremacy is at the root of racism.

The History and Persistence of Racism in U.S. Schools

As institutions, schools respond to and reflect the larger society. It therefore is not surprising that racism finds its way into schools in much the same way that it finds its way into other institutions such as housing, employment, and the criminal justice system. Overt expressions of racism may be less frequent in schools today than in the past, but racism does not just exist when schools are legally segregated or racial epithets are used against Black students. Racism is also manifested in rigid ability tracking, low expectations of students based on their identity, and inequitably funded schools.

Racism and other forms of discrimination—particularly sexism, classism, ethnocentrism, and linguicism—have a long history in our schools and their effects are widespread and long lasting. The most blatant form of discrimination is the actual withholding of education, as was the case with African Americans and sometimes with American Indians during the nineteenth century. To teach enslaved Africans to read was a crime punishable under the law and it became a subversive activity that was practiced by Blacks in ingenious ways. Other overt forms of discrimination include segregating students, by law, according to their race, ethnicity, or gender, as was done at one time or another with African American, Mexican American, Japanese, and Chinese students, as well as with females; or forcing them into boarding schools, as was done with American Indian students. In such groups, children have been encouraged to adopt the ways of the dominant culture in sundry ways, from subtle persuasion to physical punishment for speaking their native language. This, too, is a bitter reminder of the inequities of U.S. educational history.

Unfortunately, the discrimination that children face in schools is not a thing of the past. School practices and policies continue to discriminate against some children in very concrete ways. Recent studies have found that most students of color are still in schools that are segregated by race and social class, and the situation is worsening rather than improving. At the impetus of the civil rights movement, many school systems throughout the United States were indeed desegregated. But less than rigorous implementation of desegregation plans, "White flight," and housing patterns have succeeded in resegregating many schools. Segregation invariably results in school systems that are "separate and unequal" because segregated schools are differently funded, with fewer resources provided to schools in poor communities and vastly superior resources provided to schools in wealthier communities.

Segregation often results in students receiving differential schooling on the basis of their social class, race, and ethnicity. In addition, schools that serve students of color tend to provide curricula that are watered down and at a lower level than schools that serve primarily White students. Also, teachers in poor urban schools tend to have less experience and less education than colleagues who teach in schools that serve primarily European American and middle-class students. Even when they are desegregated, many schools resegregate students through practices such as rigid ability tracking. Consequently, desegregating schools in and of itself does not guarantee educational equity.

Manifestations of Racism and Discrimination in Schools

Racism and discrimination are manifested in numerous school practices and policies. Policies most likely to jeopardize students at risk of educational failure are most common precisely in the institutions in which those students are found. For example, many studies have found that rigid tracking is most evident in poor communities with large numbers of African American, Latino, and American Indian students.

It is sometimes difficult to separate what is racist or discriminatory from what appear to be neutral school policies and practices or behaviors of individual teachers. An early study cited by Ray McDermott can help illustrate this point. Through filmed classroom observations, he found that a White teacher tended to have much more frequent eye contact with her White students than with her Black students. Was this behavior the result of racism? Was it because of cultural and communication differences? Or was poor teacher preparation responsible for her behavior?

David and Myra Sadker cite many anecdotes in their powerful report on sexism in schools that bring up similar questions. They found that well-intentioned and otherwise excellent teachers often treat their female students far differently from their male students, interacting with them less frequently, asking them fewer questions, and giving them less feedback than they give male students. Because boys are expected to be more verbal and active and are both praised and reproached more often by their teachers, girls become invisible in the classroom. Girls are singled out neither for praise nor for disciplinary action. They are simply expected, as a group, to be quiet, attentive, and passive. Is this because of inherent sexism? Are teachers simply unaware of how such practices may jeopardize girls and, in a different way, boys as well?

In another example of how difficult it is to separate racism from individual teachers' behaviors or seemingly neutral policies, Patricia Gandara found, in a study of 50 low-income and high-achieving Mexican Americans, that most were either light-skinned or European-looking. Few of the sample, according to Gandara, looked "classically Mexican in both skin color and features." Does this mean that teachers intentionally favored them because of their light skin? Did teachers assume that their light-skinned students were smarter?

These questions are impossible to answer in any conclusive way; it is probable that institutional racism and teachers' biases both play a role in negative outcomes such as those described in the studies. The results, however, are very clear: In the study by McDermott, the Black children had to strain three times as hard to catch the teacher's eye, looking for approval, affection, and encouragement. In the Sadker and Sadker report, the researchers concluded that girls are frequently denied an equal education simply because of their gender, rather than because of any personal talents or deficits. In Gandara's study, the light-skinned students were able to derive more benefits from their schooling than their darker-skinned peers.

Thus students' educational success or failure cannot be explained solely by family circumstance, social class, race, gender, or language ability. Racism and other forms of institutional discrimination also play a part. African American, Latino, American Indian, and poor children in general continue to achieve below grade level, drop out in much greater numbers, and go to college in much lower proportion than their middle-class and European American peers. Two concrete examples illustrate this point: Black students are chronically underrepresented in programs for the gifted and talented, being only half as likely to be placed in a class for the gifted as are White students, even though they may be equally gifted. Latino students drop out of school at a rate higher than any other major ethnic group; and in some places, the rate has been as high as 80 percent. If educational failure were caused only by students' background and other social characteristics, it would be difficult to explain why similar students are successful in some classrooms and schools and not in others. For instance, students at Central Park East High School in East Harlem, one of the most economically impoverished communities in New York City, have reached unparalleled levels of success compared to their peers in other neighborhood schools who are similar to them in every way.

School structures have also proved to be sexist in organization, orientation, and goals. Most schools are organized to meet best the needs of White males; that is, the policy and instruction in schools generally reflect what is most effective for the needs of their male students, not the needs of either females or students of color. This organization includes everything from the curriculum, which follows the developmental level of males more closely than that of females, to instructional techniques, which favor competition as a preferred learning style, although it is not necessarily the best learning environment for either females or most students of color. The effect of such discrimination on female students is to reinforce the persistent message that they are inferior. In fact, high-achieving female students tend to receive the least attention of all from their teachers.

Discrimination based on social class is also prevalent in our public schools. In a study of affluent and low-income youth in a secondary school, Ellen Brantlinger found that students' social class was highly correlated with their academic placement, with most low-income students in special education or low tracks and all the high-income students in college preparatory classes. This was the case in spite of the fact that two of the high-income students were classified as "learning disabled." Using data from 1993, the National Center for Education Statistics also found a significant correlation between social class and dropping out of school. While only 6 percent of high-income students dropped out, over 40 percent of low-income students did so.

The hidden curriculum, that is, subtle and not-so-subtle messages that are not part of the intended curriculum, may also have an impact on students. These messages may be positive (e.g., the expectation that all students are capable of high quality work) or negative (e.g., that children of working-class backgrounds are not capable of aspiring to professional jobs), although the term is generally used to refer to negative messages. These frequently unintentional messages may contradict schools' stated policies and objectives. For instance, Carolyn Persell found that, in spite of schools' and teachers' stated commitment to equal education, social class is repeatedly related to how well students do in school. In fact, she found that students are more different from one another when they leave school than when they enter it, thus putting to rest the myth of school as the "great equalizer." Persell found that differences in academic achievement experienced by students of different economic and cultural backgrounds are due primarily to a number of specific factors: the kinds of schools the students attend, the length of time they stay in school, the curriculum and pedagogy to which they are exposed, and societal beliefs concerning intelligence and ability.

Rather than eradicate social class differences, then, it appears that schooling reflects and even duplicates them. This finding was confirmed by Samuel Bowl and Herbert Gintis in their ground-breaking class analysis of schooling. They compared the number of years of schooling of students with the socioeconomic status of their parents and found that students whose parents were in the highest socioeconomic group tended to complete the most years of schooling. They concluded that schooling in and of itself does not necessarily move poor children out of their parents' low economic class. More often, schooling maintains and solidifies class divisions.

Intentional or not, racism, classism, and other forms of discrimination are apparent in the quality of education that students receive. A graphic example of discrimination based on both race and class is found in the differential resources given to schools. As is evident in Jonathan Kozol's searing indictment of the funding of public education, the actual money spent on schools is very often directly correlated with the social class and race of the student body. Furthermore, a review of relevant literature by Carol Ascher and Gary Burnett reported that disparities in funding between rich and poor states, and between rich and poor districts in the same state, has actually grown in the recent past.

In the case of African American youth, Angela Taylor found that to the extent that teachers harbor negative stereotypes about them, African American children's race alone is probably sufficient to place them at risk for negative school outcomes. Of course, many teachers and other educators prefer to think that students' lack of academic achievement is due solely to conditions inside their homes or inherent in their cultures. But the occurrence of racism in schools has been widely documented. In a report about immigrant students in California, more than half of the students interviewed indicated that they had been the victims of teachers' biases, citing instances where they were punished, publicly embarrassed, or ridiculed because of improper use of English. They also reported that teachers had made derogatory comments about immigrant groups in front of the class. Most of the middle and high school students interviewed in a study by Mary Poplin and Joseph Weeres also had witnessed incidents of racism in school. And in a study in an urban high school in the Northeast, Karen Donaldson found that an astounding 80 percent of students surveyed said they had experienced or witnessed racism or other forms of discrimination in school.

Studies focusing specifically on Latino youth have reported similar results. Marietta Saravia-Shore and Herminio Martinez interviewed Puerto Rican youths who had dropped out of school and were currently participating in an alternative high school program. These youths keenly felt the discrimination of their former teachers, who they said were "against Puerto Ricans and Blacks." One young woman said that a former teacher had commented, "Do you want to be like the other Puerto Rican women who never got an education? Do you want to be like the rest of your family and never go to school?" In Virginia Zanger's study of high-achieving Latino and Latina high school students in Boston, one young man described his shock when his teacher called him "spic" right in class. Although the teacher was later suspended, the incident had clearly affected how this young man perceived school and his teachers. If we keep in mind that these are successful students, who are apt to hear far fewer of such damaging comments than other students, we can begin to grasp the enormity of the problem confronted by young people who are not as successful in school.

The effect of discrimination on students is most painfully apparent when students themselves have the opportunity to speak. Their thoughts concerning their education are revealing. In her study, Karen Donaldson found that students were affected by racism in three major ways: White students experienced guilt and embarrassment when they became aware of the racism to which their peers were subjected; students of color sometimes felt they needed to compensate and overachieve to prove they were equal to their White classmates; and at other times, students of color said that their self-esteem was badly damaged. However, self-esteem is a complicated issue that includes many variables. It does not come fully formed out of the blue, but is created in particular contexts and responds to conditions that vary from situation to situation. Teachers' and schools' complicity in creating negative self-esteem cannot be discounted. This point was illustrated by Lillian, a young woman in a study of an urban high school by Nitza Hidalgo. Lillian commented, "That's another problem I have, teachers, they are always talking about how we have no type of self-esteem or anything like that. . . . But they're the people that's putting us down. That's why our self-esteem is so low."

Racism, Discrimination, and Silence

Many times, unintentional discrimination is practiced by well-meaning teachers who fear that talking about race will only exacerbate the problem. As a consequence, most schools are characterized by a curious absence of talk about differences, particularly about race. The process begins with the preparation of teachers. In one study, Alice Mcintyre interviewed a group of White female student teachers working in urban schools in order to understand how they made meaning of their Whiteness in relation to teaching. She found that these pre-service teachers were reluctant to discuss racism or to consider their individual or collective role in perpetuating it. Because they saw their students primarily as victims of poverty and parental neglect, these student teachers preferred to place themselves in relationship to their students as protective "White Knights." This patronizing stance facilitated their denial of racism.

Silence and denial about racism are still quite prevalent when student teachers become teachers. In a follow-up study to her initial research concerning students' experiences with racism, Karen Donaldson had a hard time recruiting White teachers to take part in an antiracist education teacher study because most White teachers were not aware (or claimed not to be aware) of racial biases in schools and of how these biases could influence students' achievement. In another study, Julie Wollman-Bonilla found that a sizable proportion of the teachers in her children's literature courses explicitly rejected children's books about race and racism or use with their students. Whether it was to shield their students from unpleasant realities, or to uphold particular societal myths, Wollman-Bonilla concluded that many teachers lack the courage to present views that differ from the mainstream perspective. As a result, their role becomes one of maintaining the status quo rather than helping children question social inequality and injustice. That this attitude can be taken to an extreme is evident in research by Ellen Bigler: When she asked a middle school librarian in a town with a sizable Puerto Rican community if there were any books on the Hispanic experience, the librarian answered that carrying such books was inadvisable because it would interfere with the children's identification of themselves as "American"!

Silence pervades even schools committed to equity and diversity. This was a major finding in a study by Kathe Jervis of the first year of a New York City middle school consciously designed to be based on these principles. Although she had not originally intended to focus her study on race, Jervis found that there was an odd silence on the part of most teachers to address it. Their reluctance to discuss race resulted in their overlooking or denying issues of power that are imbedded in race. Jervis concluded that "even in the 'best' schools, where faculty try hard to pay attention to individuals, Whites' blindness to race clouds their ability to notice what children are really saying about themselves and their identities."

Failure to discuss racism, unfortunately, will not make it go away. As you will see in her case study, Linda Howard's close relationship with Mr. Benson, her English teacher, was no doubt partly due to the fact that they were able to talk openly about racism and other biases. Racism, classism, and other forms of discrimination play a key role in setting up and maintaining inappropriate learning environments for many students. A related phenomenon concerns the possible impact of teachers' expectations on student achievement.

Expectations of Students' Achievement

Much research has focused on teachers' interactions with their students, specifically teacher expectations. The term *self-fulfilling prophecy,* coined by Robert Merton in 1948, means that students perform in ways that teachers expect. Student performance is based on both overt and covert messages from teachers about students' worth, intelligence, and capability. The term did not come into wide use until 1968, when a classic study by Robert Rosenthal and Lenore Jacobson provided the impetus for subsequent extensive research on the subject. In this study, several classes of children in grades one through six were given a nonverbal intelligence test (the researchers called it the "Harvard Test of Influenced Acquisition"), which researchers claimed would measure the students' potential for intellectual growth. Twenty percent of the students were randomly selected by the researchers as "intellectual bloomers," and their names were given to the teachers. Although the students' test scores actually had nothing at all to do with their potential, the teachers were told to be on the alert for signs of intellectual growth among these particular children. Overall these children, particularly in the lower grades, showed considerably greater gains in IQ during the school year than did the other students. They were also rated by their teachers as being more interesting, curious, and happy, and thought to be more likely to succeed later in life.

Rosenthal and Jacobson's research on teacher expectations caused a sensation in the education community, and controversy surrounding it continues to be present. From the beginning, the reception to this line of research has been mixed, with both supporters and detractors. But one outcome was that the effect of teachers' expectations on the academic achievement of their students was taken seriously for the first time. Before this research, students' failure in school was usually ascribed wholly to individual or family circumstances. Now, the possible influence of teachers' attitudes and behaviors and the school's complicity in the process had to be considered as well. The most compelling implications were for the education of those students most seriously disadvantaged by schooling, that is, for students of color and the poor.

Early research by Ray Rist on teachers' expectations is also worth mentioning here. In a groundbreaking study, he found that a kindergarten teacher had grouped her class by the eighth day of class. In reviewing how she had done so, Rist noted that the teacher had already roughly constructed an "ideal type" of student, most of whose characteristics were related to social class. By the end of the school year, the teacher's differential treatment of children based on who were "fast" and "slow" learners became evident.

The "fast" learners received more teaching time, more reward-directed behavior, and more attention. The interactional patterns between the teacher and her students then took on a "castelike" appearance. The result after three years of similar behavior by other teachers was that teachers' behavior toward the different groups influenced the children's achievement. In other words, the teachers themselves contributed to the creation of the "slow" learners in their classrooms.

In the research by Rist, all the children and teachers were African American but represented different social classes. But similar results have been found with poor and working-class children of any race. Persell, in a review of relevant research, found that expectations for poor children were lower than for middle-class children even when their IQ and achievement scores were similar. Teachers' beliefs that their students are "dumb" can become a rationale for providing low-level work in the form of elementary facts, simple drills, and rote memorization. Students are not immune to these messages. On the other hand, a study by Diane Pollard found that the academic performance of African American students is enhanced when they perceive their teachers and other school staff to be supportive and helpful.

Some of the research on teacher expectations is quite old. Although it is reasonable to expect that, with the increasing diversity in our schools, it no longer holds true, there are still numerous examples of teachers' low expectations of students. A recent study by Francisco Rios underscores the problem. Rios studied teachers in an urban city in the Midwest to determine what principles of practice they used for teaching in culturally diverse classrooms. Among the 16 teachers he studied, he found that most of the comments they made about their students were negative; further, none of the teaching principles that they identified focused on academic achievement and only one teacher said that her students wanted to learn.

These findings are particularly problematic when we consider the impact that such beliefs can have on students. Given the increasing diversity in our public schools, the problem is even more acute because many teachers know little or nothing about the background of their students. Consequently, teachers may consider their students' identity to be at fault. This was the result found by Bram Hamovitch in an ethnographic study of an urban after-school program for adolescents at risk of dropping out of school. In his study, Hamovitch concluded that the program failed to meet its objective of motivating students to continue their education because "it allegorically asks them to dislike themselves and their own culture."

Teachers' attitudes about the diversity of their students develop long before they become teachers, however. In a review of recent literature,

Kenneth Zeichner found that teacher education students, who are mostly White and monolingual, by and large view diversity of student backgrounds as a problem. He also found that the most common characteristics of effective teachers in urban schools are a belief that their students are capable learners, and an ability to communicate this belief to the students. Martin Haberman reached a similar conclusion, identifying a number of functions of successful teachers of the urban poor. Most significant, he found that successful teachers did not blame students for failure and they had consistently high expectations of their students. Rich Miller offers compelling evidence of this reality. According to Rich, standards would be higher in his high school if there were more White students. But the reason was not because White students are smarter, but because White teachers don't push the Black students as much as they push White students. On the other hand, Black teachers, Rich said, have "expectations that are higher than White teachers . . . because they know how it was for them."

What happens when teachers develop high expectations of their students? In a wonderful example of how changing the expectations of students can influence achievement in a positive direction, Rosa Hernandez Sheets recounted her own experience with five Spanish-speaking students who had failed her Spanish class. Just one semester after placing them in what she labeled her "advanced" class, the very same students who had previously failed, passed the AP Spanish language exam, earning college credits while just sophomores and juniors. A year later, they passed the AP Spanish Literature exam. As a result of the change in her pedagogy, over a three-year period, Latino and Latina students who had been labeled "at risk" were performing at a level commonly expected of honors students.

The issue of labeling is key in this situation. In a similar case, Ruben Rumbaut found that the self-esteem of immigrant students is linked to how they are labeled by their schools. Specifically, he found that students' self-esteem is diminished when they are labeled "Limited English Proficient." If this is the case with a seemingly neutral term, more loaded labels no doubt have a much greater impact. But explicit labeling may not even be needed. According to Claude Steele, the basic problem that causes low student achievement is what he terms "stigma vulnerability" based on the constant devaluation faced by Blacks and other people of color in society and schools. In schools, this devaluation occurs primarily through the harmful attitudes and beliefs that teachers communicate, knowingly or not, to their students. Steele maintains, "Deep in the psyche of American educators is a presumption that black students need academic remediation, or extra time with elemental curricula to overcome background deficits."

Although disadvantage may contribute to the problem, Steele contends that Blacks underachieve even when they have sufficient material resources, adequate academic preparation, and a strong value orientation toward education. To prove his point, he reviewed a number of programs that have had substantial success in improving the academic achievement of Black students without specifically addressing either their culturally specific learning orientations or socioeconomic disadvantage. What made the difference? In these programs, student achievement was improved simply by treating students as if they were talented and capable. Steele concludes, "That erasing stigma improves black achievement is perhaps the strongest evidence that stigma is what depresses it in the first place."

Research on teachers' expectations is not without controversy. First, it has been criticized as unnecessarily reductionist because, in the long run, what teachers expect matters less than what teachers do. Second, the term itself and the research on which it is based imply that teachers have the sole responsibility for students' achievement or lack of it. This is both an unrealistic and an incomplete explanation for student success or failure. The study by Rosenthal and Jacobson, for example, is a glaring indication of the disrespect with which teachers have frequently been treated and raises serious ethical issues in research. Blaming teachers, or "teacher bashing," provides a convenient outlet for complex problems, but it fails to take into account the fact that teachers function within contexts in which they usually have little power.

There are, of course, teachers who have low expectations of students from particular backgrounds and who are, in the worst cases, insensitive and racist. But placing teachers at the center of expectations of student achievement shifts the blame to some of those who care most deeply about students and who struggle every day to help them learn. The use of the term *teachers' expectations* distances the school and society from their responsibility and complicity in student failure. That is, teachers, schools, communities, and society interact to produce failure.

Low expectations mirror the expectations of society. It is not simply teachers who expect little from poor, working-class, and culturally dominated groups. Garfield High School in East Los Angeles, a school made famous by the extraordinary efforts of Jaime Escalante and other teachers in propelling an unprecedented number of students to college in spite of poverty and discrimination, was visited by George Bush when he was running for U.S. president. Rather than build on the message that college was both possible and desirable for its students, Bush focused instead on the idea that a college education is not needed for success. He told the largely Mexican American student body that "we need people to build our buildings . . . people who do the hard physical work of our society." It is doubtful that he would even have considered uttering these same words at Beverly Hills High School, a short distance away. The message of low expectations to students who should have heard precisely the opposite is thus replicated even by those at the highest levels of a government claiming to be equitable to all students.

The Complex Connections Between Diversity and Discrimination

Because societal inequities are frequently reflected in schools, institutional racism and other biases are apparent in inequitable school policies and practices in complex ways. Let us take the example of language. The fact that some children do not enter school speaking English cannot be separated from how their native language is viewed by the larger society or from the kinds of programs available for them in schools. Each of these programs—whether ESL, immersion, or two-way bilingual education—has an underlying philosophy with broad implications for students' achievement or failure. As a consequence, each approach may have a profound influence on the quality of education that language minority children receive. But linguistic and other differences do not exist independently of how they are perceived in the general society or by teachers; there is a complex relationship between students' race, culture, native language, and other differences with institutional discrimination, school practices, and teachers' expectations.

Social class provides another example of the complex links between difference and discrimination. In spite of the firm belief in our society that social class mobility is available to all, classism is a grim reality because economic inequality is now greater in the United States than in any other industrial or postindustrial country in the world; in fact, social class inequality has actually increased in the past 20 years. Related to this reality is the widely accepted classist view among many educators that poverty causes academic failure. Yet although poverty may have an adverse effect on student achievement, the belief that poverty and failure go hand-in-hand is questionable. Research by Denny Taylor and Catherine Dorsey-Gaines provides evidence that by itself poverty is not an adequate explanation for the failure to learn. In their work with Black families living in urban poverty, they found inspiring cases of academically successful students. They discovered children who consistently did their homework, made the honor roll, and had positive attitudes about school. The parents of these children motivated them to learn and study, had high hopes for their education, were optimistic about the future, and considered literacy an integral part of their lives—this in spite of such devastating conditions as family deaths; no food, heat, or hot water; and a host of other hostile situations.

Similarly, an in-depth study by David Hartle-Schutte of four Navajo students, who might be identified as "at risk" by their teachers because of poverty and culture, found that these students came from homes where literacy was valued. But their school failed to recognize and build on the many literacy experiences they had in their homes to help them become successful readers. These cases point out that home background can no longer be accepted as the sole or primary excuse for the school failure of large numbers of students.

Examples such as these demonstrate that although poverty is certainly a disadvantage, it is not an insurmountable obstacle to learning. The economic condition of African American and other poor students has often been used as an explanation for academic failure, but as Kofi Lomotey, in a review of the education of African American youths, states: " . . . there are clear examples of environments that have, over long periods of time, been successful in educating large numbers of African-American students. These models can be replicated; the situation is not hopeless." In fact, one major explanation for students' lack of academic achievement lies in the lack of equitable resources given to students of different social classes and cultural backgrounds. For instance, one of the most disturbing patterns found in the 1997 National Condition of Education report was that, compared with middle-class White children, children of color and low-income students were much more likely to be taught by teachers who had little academic preparation for their teaching field. Furthermore, the skills differentials that result from this inequity will lead to earnings differentials as adults to a much greater extent than was the case even 20 years ago.

In the ideal sense, education in the United States is based on the lofty values of democracy, freedom, and equal access. Historically, our educational system proposed to tear down the rigid systems of class and caste on which education in most of the world was (and still is) based and to provide all students with an equal education. Education was to be, as Horace Mann claimed, "the great equalizer." On the other hand, some educational historians have demonstrated that the common school's primal purposes were to replicate inequality and to control the unruly masses. Thus, the original goals of public school education were often at cross purposes.

Mass public education began in earnest in the nineteenth century through the legislation of compulsory education and its most eloquent democratic expression is found in the early-twentieth-century philosophy of John Dewey. The commitment that Dewey articulated for educational equity continues today through policies such as desegregation and nonsexist education and through legislation and policies aimed at eradicating many existing inequalities. But the legacy of inequality also continues through policies and practices that favor some students over others, including unequal funding, rigid tracking, and unfair tests. As a result, schools have often been sites of bitter conflict.

Race is another pivotal way in which privilege has been granted on an unequal basis. Based on his research, the historian David Tyack asserts that the struggle to achieve equality in education is nothing new, and that race has often been at the center of this struggle. He adds: "Attempts to preserve white supremacy and to achieve racial justice have fueled the politics of education for more than a century." But resistance on the part of parents, students, and teachers has been crucial in challenging the schools to live up to their promise of equality. That is, schools were not racially desegregated simply because the courts ordered it, and gender-fair education was not legislated only because Congress thought it was a good idea. In both cases, as in many others, educational opportunity was expanded because many people and communities engaged in struggle, legal or otherwise, to bring about change.

Although in theory education is no longer meant to replicate societal inequities but rather to reflect the ideals of democracy, we know that such is not always the reality. Our schools have consistently failed to provide an equitable education for all students. The complex interplay of student differences, institutional racism and discrimination, teachers' biases that lead to low expectations, and unfair school policies and practices all play a role in keeping it this way.

Conclusion

Focusing on the persistence of racism and discrimination and low expectations is meant in no way to deny the difficult family and economic situation of many poor children and children of color, or its impact on their school experiences and achievement. Drug abuse, violence, and other social ills, as well as poor medical care, deficient nutrition, and a struggle for the bare necessities for survival harm children's lives, including their school experiences. The fact that poor children and their parents do not have at their disposal the resources and experiences that economic privilege would give them is also detrimental.

But blaming poor people and people from dominated racial or cultural groups for their educational problems is not the answer to solving societal inequities. Teachers can do nothing to change the conditions in which their students may live, but they can work to change their own biases as well as the institutional structures that act as obstacles to student learning. As we have seen, racism and other forms of discrimination play a central role in educational failure, as does the related phenomenon of low expectations.

Sonia Nieto is a professor of Teacher Education at the University of Massachusetts.

7

Full Inclusion as
Disclosing Tablet

Revealing the Flaws in
Our Present System

Mara Sapon-Shevin

I f we include a student like Travis, we'll have to change our curriculum. . . .

If we include students like Larissa, we'll have to change our teaching methods, too—lecture just doesn't work with those kids. . . .

If we include a student like Justin, the other kids will destroy him. The kids in my class have no tolerance for kids who are different in any way. . . .

And if we have to plan for a student like Marianna, our teachers will need time to meet and plan together. . . .

The above statements are representative of the hue and cry that has been raised by the prospect of full inclusion in many school districts. Full inclusion, the movement to include students with disabilities as full-time members of general education classrooms, has come under sharp criticism of late,

NOTE: From Sapon-Shevin, M. (1996). Full inclusion as disclosing tablet: Revealing the flaws in our present system. *Theory into Practice, 35*(1), 35–41. Copyright by the College of Education, The Ohio State University. All rights reserved.

and has been blamed for a host of problems—overworked teachers, falling academic standards, lack of discipline, and poor teacher morale (Willis, 1994). Although some of these criticisms are consistent with the often inadequate and half-hearted ways in which inclusion has been implemented, negative responses to planning and implementing full inclusion tell us as much (or more) about the quality and responsiveness of the schools as it does about the challenges presented by the students themselves.

When children are being taught proper dental hygiene, the dentist sometimes gives them a little red pill to chew after they have brushed. The red dye sticks to any areas that have been inadequately brushed, thus making it obvious where problems remain. These pills are called "disclosing tablets" because they disclose the areas that require further attention.

It is possible to look at full inclusion as a disclosing tablet. Attempting to integrate students with significant educational and behavioral challenges tells us a lot about the ways in which our schools are unimaginative, under-resourced, unresponsive, and simply inadequate. Full inclusion did not create these problems, but it shows us where the problems are. Children who stretch the limits of the system make it painfully clear how constricting and narrow those limits are. Full inclusion reveals the manner in which our educational system must grow and improve in order to meet the needs of all children.

Consider again the original set of complaints cited at the beginning of the article. What do these statements tell us about our schools?

We'll have to change the curriculum . . .

Yes, we will need to change the curriculum if we want to include students with disabilities. But don't we believe that the curriculum already needs changing, is changing, and will be improved for all children by being reconceptualized more broadly and divergently?

We'll have to change the way we teach . . .

Yes, we will need to look at teaching structures and practices. Teachers whose teaching repertoires are limited to frontal, lecture style instruction will need to explore more interactive, engaging ways of teaching. Isn't that what the research tells us needs to happen anyway?

We'll have to pay close attention to the social dynamics . . .

Yes, including a child with a significant difference will mean that we need to pay closer attention to the social climate of the school. But, clearly, if children who are "different" in any way are routinely mocked, scorned, or excluded, this is not a productive learning environment. Why do we assume that a classroom in which a child with Down's Syndrome would be teased is a comfortable classroom for children who are African-American, overweight, from single parent families, or non-English speaking? Wouldn't improvements in classroom climate have a salutary effect on all students?

We'll have to support teachers in their efforts at change . . .

It is true that including a student with a disability will require that teachers have time for collaborative planning and preparation. The kinds of creative, multilevel instruction and assessment necessitated by full inclusion make it imperative that teachers be given adequate time to think and plan together. But doesn't all good teaching require planning and preparation? And don't all teachers rise to higher expectations when they are treated as professionals who need thinking and planning time?

There is bad news and good news about full inclusion—and it is the same news. The "news" is that to do inclusion well will require changes in curriculum, pedagogy, staff development, school climate, and structures. This can be characterized as "bad news" because it means that mere tinkering on the edges of existing structures will not work; simply dumping children with disabilities into classrooms without adequate preparation, commitment, and support will certainly not work. But this same news—the need for wide-ranging change—is good news because there is considerable evidence that the kinds of changes necessitated by inclusion are consistent with and often can be a catalyst for broader, far-reaching school restructuring and reform efforts (Stainback & Stainback, 1992; Villa, Thousand, Stainback, & Stainback, 1992).

Like all reform efforts, the range of policies and practices implemented in the name of full inclusion has varied tremendously in quality and depth. Some school systems have simply eliminated costly special education services and teachers in the name of inclusion, dumping those students into inadequately prepared and supported classrooms. But in other schools, full inclusion has served as a spark, an organizing principle for wide-ranging change. In these schools, the inclusion of students with disabilities has been part of school reform and school restructuring that reaches far beyond the handful of labeled students identified as the purview of "special education" (Villa et al., 1992). Like all reform movements that are clouded by misinformation debated by experts, and shrouded by emotion, it can be difficult to discern what full inclusion really means.

This article explores the vision and possibilities of full inclusion by addressing and responding to myths about full inclusion that block thoughtful and comprehensive implementation. Responding to these myths can help us to better understand the promise and the practice of full inclusion.

Myth: Inclusion is being imposed on schools by outside ideologues and unrealistic parents who do not accept their child's disability

Inclusion did not spring, fully-formed, from any particular group. The evolution of the movement can be traced through changes in language and terminology. Twenty years ago, our efforts were directed toward "mainstreaming"—putting selected students with disabilities into general classrooms when a good "match" could be made. When those efforts proved inadequate to the task of changing classrooms so that students would fit in, we focused our efforts on "integration"—trying to mesh the systems of general and special education. Those efforts taught us about the need for unified services and collaboration and the importance of good communication and problem solving.

We have now articulated our task as inclusion—changing existing classrooms and structures so that all students can be served well within a unified system. Rather than merging two systems, we are trying to create a new, improved, more inclusive system for all students.

While parents have certainly played an important role in the inclusion movement, they have not acted alone. Teachers and administrators have shown great leadership in designing creative solutions to the problems inherent within pullout programs and remedial education. In the best case scenarios, parents and teachers have worked together to create programs that are effective and realistic. Inclusion is a product of many people's rethinking of the nature and quality of special education, as well as a by-product of new ways of thinking about teaching and curriculum.

Myth: Inclusionists only care about students with significant disabilities

This is a complaint often raised by those whose primary concern is for students with mild disabilities, particularly learning disabilities. They fear that the educational needs of their students will get lost in the shuffle of full inclusion, while students with extensive challenges (of which there are fewer) will become the organizing focus of inclusion. These are valid concerns, and no inclusion advocate I know is callous to the very real learning needs of students with mild disabilities who are often abandoned without support in general education classrooms under the name of inclusion.

But, by definition, inclusion involves changing the nature and quality of the general education classroom. And there is no reason that the instructional strategies and modifications provided for students with learning disabilities in segregated settings cannot be provided in more typical classrooms if we are willing to reconceptualize those classrooms.

Justin Maloney (1994/1995) of the Learning Disabilities Association of America argues against full inclusion and for a continuum of services; yet, she herself acknowledges that

> . . . students with learning disabilities would have a better chance of success in the general education setting if more of the strategies developed by special education, such as collaborative learning, cooperative teaching, peer tutoring and some of the innovative scheduling and planning developed in education reform models, became commonplace, rather than showpieces. (p. 25)

Myth: Inclusionists are driven only by values and philosophy—there is no research and no data

The research in the field of inclusion is relatively recent, because it is difficult to collect data on programs and options until they exist. Advocates of full inclusion provide data indicating that students with disabilities educated in general education classrooms do better academically and socially than comparable students in noninclusive settings (Baker, Wang, & Walberg, 1994/1995). Those who do not support inclusion cite studies indicating that special education programs are superior to general education classrooms for some types of children (Fuchs & Fuchs, 1994/1995).

The controversy about the research and what it tells us is indicative of more fundamental disagreements about (a) what counts as research and (b) what research is of value and what it is of value for. Should inclusion programs have to prove they are better than segregated programs, or should the burden of proof be on those who would maintain students in more restrictive environments? What data are collected? Are reading scores the best indications of student success? Is growth in social and communicative skills considered of primary or secondary importance? And what about benefits to "typical" students? How should these be measured and valued? The lack of agreement on the quality and value of the research data gathered to this point is indicative of more basic conflicts about the value and purposes of inclusion.

Myth: Segregation is not inherently a problem—it is only *bad* segregation that is a problem

Many anti-inclusionists have been angry about parallels drawn between racial segregation (Brown v. Board of Education's "segregation is inherently unequal") and the segregation of students with disabilities. Kauffman (quoted in O'Neil, 1994/1995) asserts:

> Certainly racial segregation is a great evil and segregation that is forced and universal and unrelated to legitimate educational purposes certainly is wrong. But when separate programs are freely chosen and placement decisions are made on a case-by-case basis—not forced, not universal—I think it's inappropriate to call that segregation. (p. 9)

But most of the segregation that has been part of special education has been forced, has not been freely chosen, and has not been made on a case-by-case basis. Often parents have been forced to accept segregated special education services or nothing and have not been presented with a range of options. More importantly, it is not clear that segregating students with disabilities is directly related to a legitimate educational purpose! When all school districts offer parents and their children the choice of a well-developed, fully inclusive classroom, then we may be able to talk differently about the advisability and appropriateness of more segregated settings; until then, we cannot call segregation a legitimate choice.

Myth: The system isn't broken—why are we messing with it?

The eagerness with which educators embrace school reform in general and inclusion in particular is definitely related to the extent to which they believe that the existing system needs changing. Inclusion advocates do not believe the system (two systems, actually) is working. The disproportionate number of students of color in special education, the lack of mobility out of special education settings, the limited community connections for students with disabilities, and the human and financial costs of supporting two separate systems of teacher education, classroom programs, and curricular materials and resources have led many educators to welcome changes in the ways in which special education services are conceptualized and delivered.

Even those who recognize the need for change, however, do not necessarily agree on the nature or extent of that change. Some supporters of maintaining a continuum of services believe that we only need to do special education "better" to make it work. Inclusion advocates tend to look for more systemic, structural change; they do not see the problems as being linked to the quality or commitment of those who provide services but as more basic, requiring changes in more than just personnel.

Myth: Inclusionists think we need change because special educators are bad or incompetent

This myth is closely related to the previous one. Those who promote inclusion in no way impugn the hard work, motives, or competence of special educators. Rather, they seek to find new ways to use those talents and skills so that all students can benefit from highly specialized teaching strategies and adaptations.

Myth: Inclusion advocates believe special educators are extinct (or should become that way)

Again, closely linked to the above two, inclusion will require that special educators reconceptualize their roles, acting more often as coteachers or resources than as primary sources of instruction or services. Conceiving of special education as a set of services rather than as a place allows us to conceive of special educators as educators with special skills, rather than as educators who work with "special" children.

Myth: It takes a special person to work with "those kids"

Idealizing the special educator as someone with unique personality characteristics (often patience) and a set of instructional tricks foreign to general education classroom teachers has served to deskill general education teachers, removing the motivation and the need to develop a wider repertoire of skills. "Those kids" need good teaching, as do all students. Our goal should be to have skilled (special education) teachers share what they know with others, rather than to isolate them in ways that minimize their breadth and long-term effectiveness.

Myth: Inclusion is beyond the reach of the already overburdened general education teacher

There is no question that many general education teachers are overburdened and undersupported. Adding students with disabilities without committing the necessary resources and support is unethical as well as ineffective. We must make huge improvements in the kinds and quality of support we provide for teachers. Although many general education classroom teachers initially say, "If I take that kid, I'll need a full-time aide," more experienced inclusion teachers identify many kinds of support as important (sometimes eliminating the need for a full-time aide), including: planning and collaboration time with other teachers, modified curriculum and resources, administrative support, and ongoing emotional support.

Myth: We're talking about the same "regular classrooms" you and I grew up with

This myth is a difficult one. It is true that many special education programs were developed because the "regular" classroom was inadequate for the learning needs of children with disabilities. So talk of "returning" such students seems illogical—if those classrooms were not good before, why should they be appropriate now? The answer is that inclusive classrooms are not and cannot be the same rigidly structured, everyone-on-the-same-page, frontal teaching, individually staffed classrooms we all remember. Successful inclusion involves radical changes in the nature of the general education classroom.

Myth: The curriculum of the general education classroom will get watered down and distorted

There is a fear that inclusion will force teachers to "dumb down" the curriculum, thus limiting the options for "typical students" and especially for "gifted and talented" students. The reality is that the curriculum in inclusive classrooms must be structured as multi-level, participatory and flexible.

For example, all the students might be working on the Civil War, but the range of books and projects undertaken and the ways in which learning is pursued can vary tremendously. Some students might be working on computer simulations, while others might write and perform skits or role plays. A wide range of books on the Civil War could allow students who read at a range of levels to find and share information. Inclusion invites, not a watered-down curriculum, but an enhanced one, full of options and creative possibilities (Thousand, Villa, & Nevin, 1994).

Myth: Special services must take place in special places

Those who are fearful or antagonistic about full inclusion believe that we must maintain a continuum of placements in order to serve all children well. Inclusion advocates support the need for a continuum of services (e.g., occupational therapy, speech therapy, physical therapy) but propose that those services be provided in the most integrated way possible, sometimes in the general education classroom and sometimes with other nonhandicapped students participating.

Inclusion does not mean abandoning the special help and support that students with disabilities truly need. Rather, it means providing those services within more normalized settings and without the isolation and stigma often associated with special education services.

Myth: Without special education classes, children with disabilities will not learn functional life skills—the things they really need to know

In many special education classes, students are still learning money skills by working with pretend coins and bills, doing workbook problems. In more inclusive settings, a student with a disability may be working at the school store, making change, and interacting with real customers using real money. Creative teachers (with adequate support) can find numerous ways to incorporate functional life skills into more typically "academic" settings, often benefiting all the students in the class.

Myth: The only way to keep "special children" safe is to keep them away from other children. If you include them you are setting them up to be victims; you are setting them up for failure. They can only feel good about themselves if they're with their "own kind"

No parent wants their child to be a victim of cruelty or violence, friend-less and alone, abandoned and outcast in school. But when we think of the bigger picture—the future beyond school—it becomes evident that we cannot keep students with disabilities safe by sheltering them. They must learn repertoires of accommodation and adaptation (how to deal with teasing and rejection) and, more importantly, we must take active steps to shape the understanding, commitment, and active friendship of students without disabilities who will be the lifelong peers of people with disabilities.

When students grow up together, sharing school experiences and activities, they learn to see beyond superficial differences and disabilities and to connect as human beings. This applies to differences in race, religion, economic status, and skill and ability, as well as physical, emotional, and learning differences. It is vital that all students feel safe and welcome in the world, and inclusion provides us with an excellent way to model and insist on a set of beliefs about how people treat one another with respect and dignity.

Myth: Inclusion values "social goals" above "educational goals"

The accusation that inclusion advocates only care about "social" integration and that valuing social growth means that academic progress is not considered relevant or important has persisted for many years. In fact, all learning is social and all learning occurs in a social environment. Learning to talk, make friends, ask questions and respond, and work with others are all educational goals, important ones, and foundational ones for other learning.

There is little doubt that certain specific, concrete drill and practice skills can be better taught within intensified, one-on-one instructional settings; what is less clear is that those are the skills that matter or whether such learning will generalize to more "normal" environments. There is also little evidence that most special education settings are particularly effective at teaching academic skills. Some of the original motivation for mainstreaming, then integration, and then inclusion, was the recognition of the low expectations and distorted goals that were set for students with disabilities within more segregated settings.

Myth: Inclusion is a favor we are doing for children with disabilities at the cost of other children's education

There is no evidence that the education of other students suffers in any way from the inclusion process. Al Shanker, president of the American Federation of Teachers (AFT) and a leading anti-inclusion force, commented on the students pictured in the Academy Award-winning film, *Educating Peter* (Wurzberg & Goodwin, 1992), which detailed the classroom experience of Peter, a boy with Down's syndrome, during his third grade year:

> I wonder whether the youngsters in that class had spent a whole year in adjusting to how to live with Peter and whether they did any reading, whether they did any writing, whether they did any mathematics, whether they did any history, whether they did any geography.
>
> And it seems to me that it's a terrible shame that we don't ask that question. Is the only function of the schools to get kids to learn to live with each other? Would we be satisfied if that's what we did and if all the youngsters came out not knowing any of the things they're supposed to learn academically?
>
> Will any of them, disabled or non-disabled, be able to function as adults? (Shanker, 1994, p. 1)

The answer, Mr. Shanker, is that their teacher, Martha Stallings (1993, 1994) reports that the students in her class all had a wonderful year, learned their math and their history and their geography, did a great deal of writing and reading, and learned to be decent caring human beings as well. That seems like an incredibly successful year to me!

Will any of them be able to function as adults? Yes, they will function as adults who, in addition to knowing long division and the states and their capitals, also know how to actively support a classmate who is struggling and know not to jump to early conclusions about whether or not someone can be a friend.

Myth: It takes years of planning and preparation before you can start to do inclusion

Planning and preparation certainly help inclusion to work well. And there is no denying that adequate lead time and thoughtful groundwork improve the quality of what can happen when students with disabilities are included. But it is also true that no teacher, school, and district ever feel truly ready to begin inclusion, and what is most necessary is ongoing support and commitment. Even schools that are well known for their inclusion programs acknowledge that there are always new issues and concerns. Although some aspects of the inclusion process become easier, they still require time and planning because every child and every situation is different.

The AFT has requested an inclusion moratorium, citing the many problems that schools experience when they attempt to implement inclusion. Shanker (1994/1995) cites lack of adequate preparation for teachers and lack of ongoing support as the two major barriers to successful inclusion. I would agree with his analysis completely. His conclusion, however, is quite different from mine. His solution to the lack of preparation and support is to call for a moratorium on inclusion. My solution is to commit the resources we know are required to do inclusion well.

Myth: If we just ignore inclusion long enough and hard enough, it will go away

I cannot imagine that parents who fought so hard for the right to have their children included in general education classrooms will be willing to go back to segregated programming. And teachers who have experienced successful inclusive teaching are not likely to want to return to a segregated system. But is society willing to commit the funds and the human resources necessary to do inclusion well? That is a larger question that brings us to the very heart of our values and our priorities about children and their educational futures.

Conclusion

Examining these myths and the responses to them allows us to see how much is affected by our decision to include students with disabilities and how much change will be required for it to be successful. At stake is not just our special education programs, or even our educational system. What is at stake is our commitment as a democracy to educate all children to the best of their abilities and to teach them all to be responsible, caring citizens, cognizant of their interrelationships and their mutual needs. A stirring song by Bernice Reagan, performed by the group "Sweet Honey in the Rock," says, "We who believe in freedom cannot rest until it comes." An appropriate paraphrase for *this* struggle might be: We who believe in inclusion cannot rest until it's done (well)!

References

Baker, E., Wang, M., & Walberg, H. (1994/1995). The effects of inclusion on learning. *Educational Leadership, 52*(4), 33–35.

Fuchs, O., & Fuchs, L. (1994/1995). Sometimes separate is better. *Educational Leadership, 52*(4), 22–26.

Maloney, J. (1994/1995). A call for placement options. *Educational Leadership, 52*(4), 25.

O'Neil, J. (1994). Can inclusion work? A conversation with Jim Kauffman and Mara Sapon-Shevin. *Educational Leadership, 52*(4), 7–11.

Shanker, A. (1994, Fall). A full circle? Inclusion: A 1994 view in the circle. Atlanta, GA: Governor's Council on Developmental Disabilities.

Shanker, A. (1994/1995). Full inclusion is neither free nor appropriate. *Educational Leadership, 52*(4), 18–21.

Stainback, S., & Stainback, V. (1992). *Curriculum considerations in inclusive classrooms: Facilitating learning for all students.* Baltimore: Paul Brookes.

Stallings, M. (1993, May). When Peter came to Mrs. Stallings' class. *NEA Today,* p. 22.

Stallings, M. (1994, December). *Educating Peter.* Presentation at the Association for Persons With Severe Handicaps Conference, Alliance for Action, Atlanta.

Thousand, J., Villa, L., & Nevin, A. (1994). *Creativity and collaborative learning: A practical guide for empowering students and teachers.* Baltimore: Paul Brookes.

Villa, R., Thousand, I., Stainback, W., & Stainback, S. (1992). *Restructuring for caring and effective education.* Baltimore: Paul Brookes.

Willis, S. (1994, October). Making schools more inclusive. MCD curriculum update, pp. 1–8.

Wurzberg, G., & Goodwin, C. (1992). *Educating Peter.* Home Box Office Video.

Mara Sapon-Shevin is a professor at Syracuse University.

8

Making the Most of
the Classroom Mosaic

Bruce Marlowe and Marilyn Page

R ecently, we visited a student teacher in a small elementary school in the northwestern corner of rural Vermont. Imagine our surprise to find a sign on the front door for parents, written in Vietnamese! Schools are changing, and they are changing fast. The arrival of new immigrant groups, the mainstreaming of children with disabilities, and the precipitous rise in poverty among children have all contributed to making our classrooms more diverse—and in more ways—than at any other time in our nation's history. In fact, children are the most diverse segment of American society. Although student diversity makes teaching more challenging, this is problematic only if the focus is on how the teacher will deliver instruction rather than on how the students will learn. Classroom settings with students from different cultures, abilities, needs, and interests provide rich learning opportunities, in part because they so clearly reflect one of the central tenets of constructivism: There is virtually an infinite variety of ways to know the world. The magnitude of student diversity underscores this point in ways impossible to ignore by even the most traditional of teachers.

How Are Our Schools Changing?

Consider the following.

- Close to 60% of the nation's entire immigrant population entered the United States in the 1980s. A century ago, the nations that sent the largest numbers of immigrants had a common European culture (England, Ireland, Germany, and Italy). The nations that send the most immigrants now—and that are projected to do so through at least the year 2000—come from every corner of the globe. In rank order, they are Mexico, the Philippines, Korea, China, Taiwan, India, Cuba, the Dominican Republic, Jamaica, Canada, Vietnam, the United Kingdom, and Iran (Hodgkinson, 1993).
- As a group, children are America's poorest citizens. During the 1980s, the poverty rate for children reached an unprecedented 11%; by 1993, the level had increased to 23% (or more than 1 in 5 school-aged children; Hodgkinson, 1993).
- The two largest minority groups are African Americans (30 million) and Hispanic Americans (20 million). Together, they compose about one third of the total school enrollment; currently, non-European American students are the majority in the 25 largest school districts in the country (Hodgkinson, 1992).
- More than 15% of students in the schools of New York, Chicago, Los Angeles, Washington, D.C., and San Francisco are of limited English proficiency (Hodgkinson, 1992).
- The United States Bureau of the Census estimates that there are 329 languages other than English spoken in the United States (Sileo, Sileo, & Prater, 1996).

Do These Differences Affect Learning?

Simply put, "Yes." There is overwhelming evidence that such factors as a student's country of origin, cultural heritage, linguistic background, and religious beliefs, as well as the socioeconomic status of the student's parents, all, in their own way, influence learning. Teachers who fail to recognize how the values of traditional schooling may clash with particular cultural values (Kugelmass, 1995) often face classrooms of disengaged, unmotivated, and/or disruptive learners who may find school irrelevant, or even hostile, to their values.

The Problem

As suggested above, today's teachers are required to be sensitive to a wider range of multicultural differences than ever before. Most teachers in the

United States are white. By century's end, more than one third of the school-aged population will be nonwhite; "minority" students already are the majority culture in many large urban school districts. Although eager to learn, teachers as a group believe they are unprepared to teach students from diverse cultures (Barry & Lechner, 1995). Can teachers package content into a single format that all children can understand? Or should they continuously repackage the content for each of the cultural, religious, and ethnic groups represented in their classrooms?

Liberating Ourselves

Framing the issues in this way reveals the potency of teacher commitment to thinking about teaching as information dispensing. As Barry and Lechner (1995) report, teachers are concerned primarily with how they will relate content in multiple ways to meet the needs of a very diverse student body. It should come as no surprise that teachers feel that this is a daunting task for which they are ill-prepared. In fact, this is not a daunting task at all; it is an impossible one. Although some find this enormously distressing, we believe it is very liberating; as teachers, we cannot simultaneously be all things to all children. Nor can we present one approach based on a kind of average of student difference. Rather, we must reframe our questions about teaching and learning. We must do so to allow for student exploration and inquiry in a way that allows them to connect content knowledge to what they already know. How is this possible for students with limited English proficiency? How can teachers meet the needs of Mexican American children, children of Asian Pacific descent, and African American children, all of whom are in the same classroom?

Focusing on Students Experiences

Ethnic differences are real, but continually seeking to alter our teaching style to conform to our beliefs about each student (based solely on his or her ethnic identity) perpetuates an overgeneralization about ethnic groups and puts the focus of the teaching/learning experience in the wrong place. Knowing that Asian children as a group are quieter and more submissive to authority will not enhance the learning of students of Asian descent if, as a teacher armed with this knowledge, you continue to focus on what you will do to cover the curriculum as opposed to focusing on the ways you can help your students connect content to the most important factors in student learning—the students' experiences and prior knowledge (Ausubel, 1968).

The value of constructivism is that it respects and allows each student to use his or her unique knowledge and experience in the learning process. This is so whether the student is from a 10,000-acre ranch in Billings, Montana, or a one-room flat in Springfield, Massachusetts.

Classroom Culture and Ethnic Culture: A Dynamic Relationship

Looking at Two Ethnic Groups: Vietnamese and Navajo

Many books that address the teaching of different ethnic groups describe Vietnamese (and in general Asian) children as being quiet, submissive, and reluctant to speak publicly, and Navajo children as being nonverbal, nonanalytical, and even disengaged. Review Table 1, but be advised: It is detrimental to the learning health of your students.

In Traditional Classrooms

The traits described in Table 1 appear primarily when the diverse classroom is one where the teacher dispenses knowledge. In these classrooms, teachers of minority students spend more time talking than do teachers of white children; thus, minority children "spend considerably more time listening than being heard" (Moran in McCarty, Lynch, Wallace, & Benally, 1991, p. 54), when communication is controlled by the teacher, when students are singled out to answer direct questions about subjects "for which they have little background knowledge" (Collier, Laatsch, & Ferrero, 1972, p. 70).

This very classroom culture reinforces submissiveness and makes certain minority groups appear, as groups, to be nonverbal, nonanalytical, or disengaged.

In Constructivist Classrooms

The situation is different in constructivist classrooms. Where

... teachers and students share talk, where the expression of students' ideas is sought and clearly valued, where curricular content meaningfully incorporates the students' social environment and where students use their cultural and linguistic resources to solve new problems, Native American students respond eagerly and quite verbally to questioning, even in their second language. (McCarty et al., 1991, p. 53)

Table 1   Questioning Stereotypes

Ethnicity	Learning Style	Implications for Teaching
Asian	Quiet, submissive, obedient, prefer not to call attention to themselves, prefer to work independently, reluctant to engage in "free discussion," prefer not to partake in brainstorming exercises.	Didactic methods important; teachers should transmit information, strategies, etc. through lecture. Teachers should understand that if student does not ask questions, it is because the student is reluctant to challenge assumptions/methods of teacher, or otherwise appears unengaged.
Navajo	Nonanalytical, nonverbal, visual learners, "doers" rather than "talkers' (McCarty, Lynch, Wallace, & Benally, 1991), may consider it rude to disagree in public, or not worth the risk of hurting someone's feelings by stating an opinion in class, often slow to respond verbally.	Teacher should employ "right hemisphere" approaches, emphasizing dance, art, and music. Teachers should employ a lot of wait time after questions. Try to avoid asking direct questions that put students on the spot.

According to Steinberg (1996), Asian students outperform all other groups (including whites) on measures of school performance. They earn higher grades, do more homework, cut class less often, and report less mind-wandering. One of Steinberg's most striking findings, however, is that compared to all other ethnic groups, Asians so frequently "turn to each other for academic assistance and consultation" (p. 47). They collaborate, they work in groups, they pose questions, and they work on them together. This is hardly what one would expect based on Table 1, which characterizes Asians as independent, passive, and reluctant to ask questions.

In a study by McCarty and colleagues (1991), the use of a pilot curriculum that emphasized open-ended questioning, collaborative group work, and student-directed learning (not exactly the approach suggested in Table 1) was shown to enhance student engagement, content mastery, and analytic reasoning in Navajo youth. As suggested in Table 1, this approach was widely considered to be antithetical to the Navajo learning style. As Au pointed out (in McCarty et al., 1991), "Native American children may in no way be characterized as nonverbal . . . though . . . there are settings in which they may appear so" (p. 53). Unfortunately, these settings all too often are our classrooms.

Disabilities and Academic Failure

Individuals With Disabilities Education Act

Since the passage of the Education of All Handicapped Children Act (PL 94–142) in 1975, all children, regardless of disability, have been entitled to a free and appropriate public education. This federal law (amended in 1990 and now referred to as the Individuals With Disabilities Education Act (or IDEA) is both a civil rights landmark and a landmark in the history of American education. IDEA prohibits the exclusion of disabled students from public schools (which was routine in some states prior to 1975) and requires that children with disabilities be educated with their nondisabled peers to the maximum extent appropriate (i.e., in the least restrictive environment). IDEA also requires school personnel to:

- construct individualized education plans (for students with disabilities);
- closely monitor student progress; and
- evaluate the academic achievement and cognitive ability of identified students on a regular basis.

Despite the progressive nature of special education legislation, individuals with identified disabilities, as a group, continue to fare poorly both in our schools and in their transition to adulthood. Who are the students with disabilities in our schools? Table 2 provides some of the answers.

Educational Outcomes for Students With Disabilities

Here is some of what we know:

- Although about 1 in 10 students receives special education services, many more school-aged children are presumed to have disabilities. Nationally, about 65% of students with disabilities receive at least some of their instruction in the context of the regular classroom. In some states (e.g., Colorado and Vermont), more than 80% of students with disabilities spend most, if not all, of their day in a regular classroom (Turnbull, Turnbull, Shank, & Leal, 1995).

Table 2   Disability Type and Incidence

Disability	Percentage of All Students With Disabilities
Specific learning disabilities: Students of average intellectual ability or higher with significant difficulty in one or more academic domains (e.g., reading)	49.9
Speech or language impairment: Students with significant difficulty in producing language (e.g., following directions)	22.2
Mental retardation: Students with significantly below-average measured intellectual ability and age-appropriate social skills (e.g., communication, independent living, etc.)	12.3
Serious emotional disturbance: Students with chronic emotional, behavioral, or interpersonal difficulties extreme enough to interfere with learning	8.9
Multiple disabilities: Students with more than one disability	2.2
Orthopedic impairments: Students who have limited functional use of legs, feet, arms, hands, or other body parts	1.1
Other health impairments: Students with chronic conditions that limit strength, vitality, or alertness (e.g., epilepsy, arthritis, asthma)	1.3
Hearing impairments: Students with significant hearing loss in one or both ears	1.3
Visual impairments: Students with low vision, even when corrected	0.5
Deaf-blindness: Students with both significant hearing loss and low vision	<0.1
Autism: Students with significant difficulty in both social interaction and communication	<0.1
Traumatic brain injury: Students who have had brain injury as the result of external force (e.g., car accident) or internal occurrence (e.g., stroke)	<0.1

SOURCE: Yeseldyke and Algozzine, 1995

- In 1992, about 3 million children were receiving child protective services for abuse and/or neglect (Turnbull et al., 1995).
- One in 5 school-aged children is estimated to have reading disabilities (Lyon, 1995; Shaywitz & Shaywitz, 1995). Eighty percent of students with weak reading skills who fail to make significant reading progress by the age of 9 will continue to be unskilled readers in the 10th grade (Shaywitz & Shaywitz, 1995).
- Since 1977, the identification of emotional-behavioral disorders has risen by 32%; in some states, this number has increased by more than 75% (Carnine, 1994). Nationally, the identification of learning disabilities has more than doubled between 1977 and 1994. There are currently well more than 2 million school-aged children identified with learning disabilities (Turnbull et al., 1995).
- Close to 3 million school-aged children take Ritalin every day.
- Nationally, the dropout rate is 25%; only about 50% of students with disabilities graduate from high school.
- Between 1980 and 1990, the prison population in the United States increased by 139% (Hodgkinson, 1992); recent rate increases are estimated at 300% (Carnine, 1994). Of America's prisoners, 82% are high school dropouts; 75% to 80% of the prison population is estimated to have specific learning disabilities and/or serious emotional disturbance.
- Juel (1988) found that about 40% of unskilled readers in the 4th grade would prefer cleaning their rooms to reading.

Connections to Traditional Classrooms?

Why is the "dropout" rate so high for students with disabilities? Why is academic underachievement so prevalent? Why have behavioral problems increased so dramatically? Why do students prefer cleaning their rooms to reading? The answers to these questions are complex and multifaceted, and they are clearly beyond the scope of this book. We must ask, though, to what extent teaching approaches that focus on the transmission of information contribute to student failure, disengagement, and disenfranchisement. Is it plausible in all (or even most) cases of student failure that students and/or their families are to blame for weak academic skills and/or behavioral problems? Goodlad (1984) found that students spend a little more than 10% of their time in school asking questions, reading, writing, or engaged in some other form of active learning. Is there something wrong with our children, or are schools and teachers contributing to this state of affairs? Could 5,000 reports be right in finding that no student difficulty was related to shortcomings in school practice? Or would Carnine's (1994) question about this finding ring more true: "If 5,000 medical files of patients who failed to respond to [medical] treatment were analyzed, would there be an absence of professional shortcomings in all 5,000 cases?" (Carnine, 1994, p. 341).

Could it be the teaching approach that makes difference in the classroom so deadly? Can some school difficulties be attributed to shortcomings related to school practice?

The Challenge

Disabilities make learning and classrooms more challenging. Some disabilities may even make the learning of some things impossible. As teachers, we must create opportunities for learning that are more exciting, more enriching, and more rewarding—in short, more appealing—than the desire to clean one's room, leave school, get involved in criminal activity, or become a ward of the state. During the 1980s, in Massachusetts, some urban school systems reported 20% or more of the entire student population in special education programs. Where did all these special education students come from? "Were they sitting undetected in regular classrooms, or have special education mandates provided a fast track out of regular education for problem learners?" (Henley, Ramsey, & Algozzine, 1993, p. 183). Others have noted that a focus on the ways in which students do not fit into traditional classrooms (in addition to putting system and teacher needs ahead of student needs) also often reflects cultural biases. For example:

> Only when formal education came to the Indian Nations were labels supplied to the differences between children. Public Law 94–142 . . . caused multitudes of children to be labeled mentally retarded or learning disabled who up until that time were not considered handicapped in their cultures. (Locust, in Tumbull et al., 1995, p. 15)

The Regular Education Initiative and the Full Inclusion Movement

Full Inclusion Is Changing Classrooms

For the last 20 years, most special education students received a large part of their education in public schools—but on a "pull-out" basis. Most still do. That is, students leave their regular classrooms for part or all of the day to work with a special education teacher or aide in a resource room on individual academic skills or behavioral goals. Most students with disabilities still receive the bulk of their education in resource rooms; however, including students with disabilities in regular classrooms for most or all of their day (regardless of the severity of their disability) has become increasingly popular around the nation. This change in thinking has been variously described as the "full inclusion" or "mainstreaming" movement. Several persuasive arguments have driven this change.

Problems With Pull-Out Programs

First, research on the ineffectiveness of tracking by ability groups demonstrates that, in general students perform better academically in heterogeneous, rather than homogeneous, groupings (Lewis, 1990). Madeline Will, once the Assistant Secretary for Special Education and Rehabilitative Services, noted, in a frequently cited address (1985) that special education students were dropping out of school at very high rates each year, despite intensive efforts. She argued that special and regular education be merged, because in her view the negative side effects of special education—its high cost, the stigmatization of students, the fragmentation of instruction into self-contained special and regular education units, the student dropout rate—outweighed any benefit it might confer on students with disabilities.

Although research shows (Henley et al., 1993) that special needs students appear to do better in regular classrooms than in special education settings, recent surveys indicate that most teachers are uncomfortable with special education students in their classrooms because they feel that they do not have the proper training to work with students with disabilities. Are these fears justified? Perhaps, but in some sense, this appears irrelevant, as virtually every public school classroom (K–12) has at least one student with a disability; teachers must learn to adjust to mainstreaming, regardless of their politics. Still, legitimate questions remain. Do students with disabilities require something regular education teachers cannot provide? What is it that special education teachers provide that is so critical to the needs of students with disabilities? What additional training do regular education teachers need to ensure that students with disabilities receive an appropriate education in their classrooms?

What's So Special About Special Education?

As it turns out, very little. There is some good news about what works (and what does not) for students with disabilities. What we can say with certainty about what students with disabilities need is contrary to what many regular (and special) educators believe.

False Assumptions

For example, many classroom teachers operate under the assumption that only specialized training in fields like learning disabilities, mental retardation, and speech and language disorders will allow them to work effectively with disabled students in their classrooms. Similarly, many special educators believe that they are somehow uniquely qualified (by virtue of their training) to work with children with disabilities. Many assume that the magic bullet for working with students with disabilities is finding the right placements and particular academic or behavioral curricula that match the disability in question. We now know, from a variety of research, that all these assumptions are false. In fact, Ysseldyke and Algozzine (1995) have summarized these findings by noting that research in special education has been unable to demonstrate that

- specific instructional practices/techniques match or work better with specific learner characteristics; research has not supported the view that children with mental retardation need X, whereas children with learning disabilities need Y;
- certain placements result in improved academic achievement; or
- special educators are more effective in working with students with disabilities than are regular educators.

How Can I Teach Special Education Kids in My Classroom?

As you probably could have guessed by now, this is the wrong question.

Asking the Right Question

How do students learn? How can I spark their curiosity, facilitate their learning, and get out of their way? These questions are ultimately more important, particularly for students with disabilities, who are at increased risk of school failure. The high school dropout rate for students with disabilities continues to be very high. Without a compelling reason to stay, and with little academic success and much frustration, this should come as no surprise. For many students with disabilities, school is deadly boring; it is irrelevant to their lives, needs, and interests; and for many others, it is extremely punishing as well.

What Do Students With Disabilities Need?

The value of special education can be summed up as follows: What's good for the goose is necessary for the gander. That is, although all students benefit from good teachers, students with a history of academic and/or behavioral challenges (for whatever reason) need good teachers and the kind of classroom experiences supported by and driven by constructivist propositions, including the proposition that student talent and ability can be key to developing knowledge. If a teacher is simply delivering information, he cannot ever deal with the infinite variety of perspectives (in the case of ethnic questions) or with the different ways of knowing and learning that students with disabilities present. To remain interested and engaged in learning, students need opportunities to discover, create, and problem solve. What if problem solving skill is precisely what they lack?

Building Bridges: Putting Students in Control of Their Learning

Two Approaches

Many teachers treat students with disabilities as if they have a defect that needs correcting. To fix the disability, some professionals believe that students need high levels of teacher-directed information transmission. This approach often relies on prepackaged remedial programs such as the Orton-Gillingham Reading Method and standardized ways to assess learning. At the other extreme, some advocate fostering student strengths (wherever they may be), following the students' lead in learning, and letting students choose whether or not to attempt to improve the academic skill areas in which they may struggle. The first approach often results in the temporary memorization of increased content knowledge. Resource room teachers, for example, often report a threshold effect: When students leave the resource room and cross the door's threshold, everything they learned seems to have vanished. The second approach also is inappropriate for many students with disabilities because most disabilities, including specific learning disabilities and attention disorders (the majority of the disability pie), are frequently characterized by weak ability to approach tasks in a planned, strategic manner and to carefully monitor ongoing performance (Marlowe, 1990). Thus, the majority of students with disabilities do not spontaneously initiate problem-solving behaviors, and they demonstrate difficulty sustaining attention, inhibiting impulsive responding, and remaining cognitively flexible. Students with this profile need a bridge from traditional special education to constructivist learning experiences. We may summarize these differing views as in Table 3.

The Bridge Model

Many students with disabilities do not benefit from either the medical model or the constructivist one until they have the tools necessary to learn. The learning strategies model is a middle ground on this continuum and was designed, ideally, so that students could initiate their own learning; sustain attention for complex, multistep tasks; form hypotheses; and evaluate their own performance. Although there are many kinds of learning strategy models, perhaps the easiest and most practical of these approaches is Bonnie Camp's *Think Aloud* Program. The *Think Aloud* Program is designed to increase student self-control by the explicit teaching of self-talk strategies for solving a range of problems. Because many children with disabilities lack verbal mediation skills, this is a natural step to move them toward constructivist activity. You can easily incorporate this into whole-class instruction. You would simply introduce four questions students can ask themselves as they set about to learn. They involve

- identifying problems ("What am I to do?" "How can I find out?");
- choosing a plan or strategy ("How can I do it? "What are some plans?");
- self-monitoring ("Am I using my plan?"); and
- self-evaluation ("Is my plan working? How did I do? Do I need a new plan?").

When students use these questions in the context of the curriculum (and not separate from it), together with a menu of problem-solving strategies (such as brainstorming, means-end analysis, mnemonic memory strategies, etc.), they quickly acquire a wide repertoire of powerful learning tools.

Powerful Ideas for Inclusive Classrooms

Buddy Systems or the Value of Teaching Others

Revisiting Jan's Classroom

Ironically, perhaps one of the most powerful learning approaches for students with disabilities is to prepare them to teach others. We observed this

Table 3   A Comparison of Approaches in Special Education

Criteria for Classifying Instruction	Medical Model: Special Education	The Bridge: Learning Strategy Model	Constructivist: Special Education
Pace of learning	Carefully controlled by teacher	Initially controlled by teacher. As student masters use of self-questioning, control turned over to student	Controlled by student
Sequence of learning	Prescribed by commercially available system	Controlled by teacher	Based on consultation between student and teacher
Selection of materials	Controlled by teacher or prescribed by curriculum	Controlled by teacher	Selected and/or created by student
Way student spends time	Student is active but frequently on drill and learning-restricted content in particular academic domains, usually in response to teacher directions and/or requests	Teacher presents problems. Student practices self-questioning and problem-solving strategies	Student produces material, teaches others, or frames questions. Often in nontraditional activities (music, art, construction)
Way of confirming and acknowledging learning	Teacher, or results of standardized testing, determines when, and how much, learning has occurred	Initially, controlled by teacher. As student masters self-questioning through (guided) practice and the use of appropriate problem-solving strategies, student gains control	Production of artifacts and their collection (e.g., in portfolios), demonstrations, performances, and community activity

(and it was dramatic) very recently in Jan Carpenter's classroom. Steve, a student with severe attentional and organizational difficulties, typically arrived unprepared for school—he rarely arrived with his books or writing utensils, had difficulty settling down for class work, and often appeared confused shortly after directions had been given. Many special educators and proponents of collaborative groups emphasize the importance of pairing students like Steve with academically advanced students who can model appropriate classroom and social behaviors. Jan chose a seemingly counterintuitive approach and paired Steve with a student whose organizational skills were weaker than his own. After a variety of interventions that often resulted in Steve becoming upset and Jan becoming frustrated, she asked Steve if he could help a student with mild autism named Maria to get organized in the morning, to keep her materials tidy, and to remember to bring her books home for homework assignments. On the first day of Steve's teaching, Steve approached Maria at the end of the school day and asked the following questions: "Maria, what do you need to do to make sure you have everything you need? How can you remember to bring these materials home? What will you do tomorrow morning to remember to bring your homework to school?"

Jan's strategy worked brilliantly. Steve began to rehearse verbally the very strategies and questions he needed to ask himself to become more focused, responsible, and engaged with school assignments. For the first time, Steve began to feel empowered, as if learning was something within his control. For the first time, Steve saw at first hand the value of self-questioning, of teaching, and of collaborating with another. Finally, Steve became a model for Maria, and slowly she began to learn. Who might she teach next?

Accommodations

For most students who are eligible for special education service, disabilities are life span issues. The ways in which they approach material, the challenges they face, and the compensatory strategies they use—all these things are unlikely to change over time. If students are struggling in your class, this means it is imperative (because students are unlikely to change) that you think about the ways in which challenged students can fit into the environment without affecting your other students. How is this possible? Many years ago, one of us was involved in a consultation with a 10th grade chemistry teacher who complained that a hyperactive student in her class continually tapped his pencil on the lab table, disrupting her and other students. The teacher shared with us that most days ended with arguments (because the student would continue tapping moments after he was asked to stop) and an occasional angry exchange. From the teacher's point of view, it was unclear whether the tapping was a willful attempt to continually disrupt the classroom or a manifestation of a behavior out of the boy's control. Either way, the behavior had to stop. Thinking about this behavior as something that must be changed (i.e., thinking that the student must be changed) is a mindset that guarantees teacher frustration and anger, student resentment, and very often feelings of inferiority and impotence in both. One way to frame this dilemma is the following: The student needs to tap, and the teacher needs a distraction-free environment. Accepting for a moment that both are in fact true needs (and that the student is not simply trying to be difficult), are these needs mutually exclusive? Of course not. Readers who already have begun to think about how we can change the environment and not the student already know this. For the rest of you, the solution to this dilemma can be found at the end of the chapter.

What About Fairness?

Unfortunately, many teachers believe that accommodating an individual student need is somehow unfair to other students. As Richard Lavoie has elegantly pointed out on his well-known video about the F.A.T. city workshop (1989), it is not about the *other* students! Lavoie points out that a teacher who fails to make accommodations to a student with a disability because she feels she may be unfair to the others is using the same logic as a teacher skilled in CPR who refuses to administer resuscitation to a student who collapses in the middle of her room because she doesn't have time to administer CPR to *all* the students in her room. Obviously, all the students do not need CPR. Fairness is about need.

Ignore Bloom's Taxonomy

If you're a preservice teacher, it's probably too late to try to forget Bloom after the amount of time you've spent hearing about his hierarchy of learning. For many students with disabilities, however, Bloom simply needs to be ignored if you are to facilitate learning. When we think about constructivist classrooms, whether or not they include students like those discussed in this section (and almost every classroom does), we need to focus on how individual students learn—not on a predetermined sequence or hierarchy that is perhaps true for some students. "Some students" are not *your* students. Your students will differ in many ways, and you must follow their lead, their needs, and their strengths. Many students may, for example, be able to make informed judgments (Bloom: "evaluate") about Plato's ideas—even though they may not be able to read or remember (Bloom: "knowledge") specific factual information about how to spell his name, when he lived, or where he was from. Similarly, many students are ready for sophisticated mathematical concepts despite being unable to perform simple calculations.

Tough Questions

1. Should all students, regardless of the severity of disability, be educated in regular classrooms? Why? Why not?

2. At what age, if ever, should a decision be made that a student should pursue vocational preparation instead of a more academically based education? Who should be involved in such a decision?

3. Is there a value to labeling students? Why? Why not?

4. Given the projected increases in the number of Spanish-speaking students, should learning Spanish be required of all new teachers? Why or why not?

5. Should students learn about cultural diversity issues even if they live in regions of the country that are fairly homogeneous? If so, given the lack of diversity in the area, what would be the context for learning?

6. Should the makeup of your classroom, school, or district have some bearing on curriculum requirements? That is, should schools emphasize more of an international perspective when establishing standards for the study of literature, art, history and other subjects, or should we continue to focus on the contributions of Europeans and North Americans?

The Pen-Tapping Dilemma Solution

A rubber pad was placed on the lab table, allowing the student to tap to his heart's content without disturbing his classmates or the teacher.

References

Ausubel, D. P. (1968). *Educational psychology: A cognitive view*. New York: Holt, Rinehart & Winston.

Barry, N. H., & Lechner, J. V. (1995). Preservice teachers' attitudes about and awareness of multicultural teaching and learning. *Teaching and Teacher Education, 11*(2), 149–161.

Carnine, D. (1994). Introduction to the mini series: Diverse learners and prevailing, emerging, and research-based educational approaches and their tools. *School Psychology Review, 23*(3), 341–350.

Collier, J. J., Laatsch, M., & Ferrero, P. (1972). *Film analysis of the Rough Rock Community school—phase one*. (Manuscript on file at Rough Rock, Chinle, AZ).

Goodlad, J. I. (1984). *A place called school: Prospects for the future*. New York: McGraw-Hill.

Henley, M., Ramsey, R. S., & Algozzine, R. (1993). *Characteristics of and strategies for teaching students with mild disabilities*. Boston: Allyn & Bacon.

Hodgkinson, H. L. (1992). *A demographic look at tomorrow*. Washington, DC: Institute for Educational Leadership Center for Demographic Policy.

Hodgkinson, H. L. (1993). American education: The good, the bad, and the task. *Phi Delta Kappan, 84*(8), 619–623.

Juel, C. (1988). Learning to read and write: A longitudinal study of fifty-four children from first through fourth grade. *Journal of Educational Psychology, 80*(4), 437–447.

Kugelmass, J. W. (1995). Educating children with learning disabilities in Foxfire classrooms. *Journal of Learning Disabilities, 28*(9), 545–553.

Lavoie, R. (1989). *Understanding learning disabilities: Frustration, anxiety, tension, the F.A.T. city workshop* (produced by Peter Rosen for Eagle Hill School Outreach). Alexandria, VA: PBS Video.

Lewis, A. C. (1990). Tracking the national goals. *Phi Delta Kappan, 72*(7), 496–506.

Lipsitz, J. (1984). *Successful school for young adolescents*. New Brunswick, NJ: Transaction.

Lyon, G. R. (1995, August). *Dyslexia*. Paper presented at Disabilities Unifying Services Across the Lifespan, Johnson, VT.

MacInnis, C., & Hemming, H. (1995). Linking the needs of students with learning disabilities to a whole language curriculum. *Journal of Learning Disabilities, 28*(9), 535–544.

Marlowe, B. A. (1990). *Identifying learning disabilities in the deaf population*. Unpublished doctoral dissertation, Catholic University of America, Washington, DC.

McCarty, T. L., Lynch, R. H., Wallace, S., & Benally, A. (1991). Classroom inquiry and Navajo learning styles: A call for reassessment. *Anthropology and Education Quarterly, 22*(1), 42–59.

Shaywitz, S. (1995, July). *Implications of the Connecticut longitudinal study.* Paper presented at Disabilities Unifying Services Across the Lifespan, Johnson, VT.

Sileo, T. W., Sileo, S. P., & Prater, M. A. (1996, January). Parent and professional partnerships in special education: Multicultural considerations. *Intervention in School and Clinic,* pp. 145–153.

Steinberg, L. (1996). *Beyond the classroom: Why school reform has failed and what parents need to do.* New York: Simon & Schuster.

Turnbull, A. P., Turnbull, H. R., Shank, M., & Leal, D. (1995). *Exceptional lives: Special education in today's schools.* Englewood Cliffs, NJ: Prentice Hall.

Ysseldyke, J. E., & Algozzine, R. (1995). *Special education: A practical approach for teachers* (3rd ed.). Boston: Houghton Mifflin.

Bruce Marlowe is an associate professor at Roger Williams University.

Marilyn Page is an assistant professor at Pennsylvania State University.

PART III

What Makes a Good Teacher?

Vignette 1

Cathy Johnson is charged with teaching her tenth grade biology class about the digestive system of sheep, their eating habits, and their grazing preferences. Here is her plan: From Monday to Wednesday, she will present a forty minute lecture, fielding questions as they arise; Thursday is scheduled for review; and on Friday she'll give a multiple choice test based on the information that she covered during the week.

Let's take a glimpse at a typical exchange between Cathy and her students.

On Tuesday, after twenty-five minutes of lecture, Billy raises his hand and, after being acknowledged by Ms. Johnson, says, "I still don't understand. How come sheep can digest grass but people can't?"

"We covered this yesterday. Can someone help Billy out? Who knows why sheep can digest grass. Come on, people. Anyone? Anyone?"

Jessica dutifully raises her hand. When called on, she says, "Sheep are ruminants. They have three extra specialized stomach sections and humans have one stomach section."

"Thank you, Jessica. At least I know one person is listening."

On Friday, Cathy administers her multiple-choice test. A few students fail, but most earn passing grades. Even though she will not return to the subject of sheep for the remainder of the year, Cathy feels confident that the generally strong test scores indicate that she has adequately covered the content and that her students have learned the material.

Vignette 2

Monday through Thursday, Frankie Stevens, an elder Navajo sheep herder, spends forty minutes each afternoon with tribal children, listening to their questions about sheep's eating habits and grazing preferences. When a child asks a question, the elder often replies, "What do *you* think?" and continues to encourage further observation and inquiry. On Friday, Mr. Stevens asks the students to herd the sheep without him, to rely on one another, and to return prepared to demonstrate what they have learned.

Is Cathy Johnson a good teacher? Is Frankie Stevens teaching? How might Mr. Stevens answer Billy's question to Ms. Johnson in the first vignette?

9

The Banking
Concept of Education

Paulo Freire

A careful analysis of the teacher-student relationship at any level, inside or outside the school, reveals its fundamentally narrative character. This relationship involves a narrating Subject (the teacher) and patient listening objects (the students). The contents, whether values or empirical dimensions of reality, tend in the process of being narrated to become lifeless and petrified. Education is suffering from narration sickness.

The teacher talks about reality as if it were motionless, static, compartmentalized, and predictable. Or else he expounds on a topic completely alien to the existential experience of the students. His task is to "fill" the students with the contents of his narration—contents which are detached from reality, disconnected from the totality that engendered them and could give them significance. Words are emptied of their concreteness and become a hollow, alienated, and alienating verbosity.

The outstanding characteristic of this narrative education, then, is the sonority of words, not their transforming power. "Four times four is sixteen; the capital of Para is Belem." The student records, memorizes, and repeats these phrases without perceiving what four times four really means,

NOTE: From *Pedagogy of the Oppressed* by Paulo Freire. Copyright 1970, 1993 by the author. Reprinted by permission of The Continuum International Publishing Group.

or realizing the true significance of "capital" in the affirmation "the capital of Para is Belem," that is, what Belem means for Para and what Para means for Brazil.

Narration (with the teacher as narrator) leads the students to memorize mechanically the narrated account. Worse yet, it turns them into "containers," into "receptacles" to be "filled" by the teachers. The more completely she fills the receptacles, the better a teacher she is. The more meekly the receptacles permit themselves to be filled, the better students they are.

Education thus becomes an act of depositing, in which the students are the depositories and the teacher is the depositor. Instead of communicating, the teacher issues communiques and makes deposits which the students patiently receive, memorize, and repeat. This is the "banking" concept of education, in which the scope of action allowed to the students extends only as far as receiving, filing, and storing the deposits. They do, it is true, have the opportunity to become collectors or cataloguers of the things they store. But in the last analysis, it is the people themselves who are filed away through the lack of creativity, transformation, and knowledge in this (at best) misguided system. For apart from inquiry, apart from the praxis, individuals cannot be truly human. Knowledge emerges only through invention and re-invention, through the restless, impatient continuing, hopeful inquiry human beings pursue in the world, with the world, and with each other.

In the banking concept of education, knowledge is a gift bestowed by those who consider themselves knowledgeable upon those whom they consider to know nothing. Projecting an absolute ignorance onto others, a characteristic of the ideology of oppression, negates education and knowledge as processes of inquiry. The teacher presents himself to his students as their necessary opposite; by considering their ignorance absolute, he justifies his own existence. The students, alienated like the slave in the Hegelian dialectic, accept their ignorance as justifying the teacher's existence—but unlike the slave, they never discover that they educate the teacher.

The raison d'etre of libertarian education, on the other hand, lies in its drive towards reconciliation. Education must begin with the solution of the teacher-student contradiction, by reconciling the poles of the contradiction so that both are simultaneously teachers and students.

This solution is not (nor can it be) found in the banking concept. On the contrary, banking education maintains and even stimulates the contradiction through the following attitudes and practices, which mirror oppressive society as a whole:

a. the teacher teaches and the students are taught;

b. the teacher knows everything and the students know nothing;

c. the teacher thinks and the students are thought about;

d. the teacher talks and the students listen—meekly;

e. the teacher disciplines and the students are disciplined;

f. the teacher chooses and enforces his choice, and the students comply;

g. the teacher acts and the students have the illusion of acting through the action of the teacher;

h. the teacher chooses the program content, and the students (who were not consulted) adapt to it;

i. the teacher confuses the authority of knowledge with his or her own professional authority, which she and he sets in opposition to the freedom of the students;

j. the teacher is the Subject of the learning process, while the pupils are mere objects.

It is not surprising that the banking concept of education regards men as adaptable, manageable beings. The more students work at storing the deposits entrusted to them, the less they develop the critical consciousness which would result from their intervention in the world as transformers of that world. The more completely they accept the passive role imposed on them, the more they tend simply to adapt to the world as it is and to the fragmented view of reality deposited in them.

The capability of banking education to minimize or annul the student's creative power and to stimulate their credulity serves the interests of the oppressors, who care neither to have the world revealed nor to see it transformed. The oppressors use their "humanitarianism" to preserve a profitable situation. Thus they react almost instinctively against any experiment in education which stimulates the critical faculties and is not content with a partial view of reality but always seeks out the ties which link one point to another and one problem to another.

Indeed, the interests of the oppressors lie in "changing the consciousness of the oppressed, not the situation which oppresses them,"[1] for the more the oppressed can be led to adapt to that situation, the more easily they can be dominated. To achieve this, the oppressors use the banking concept of education in conjunction with a paternalistic social action apparatus, within which the oppressed receive the euphemistic title of "welfare recipients."

They are treated as individual cases, as marginal persons who deviate from the general configuration of a "good, organized and just" society. The oppressed are regarded as the pathology of the healthy society which must therefore adjust these "incompetent and lazy" folk to its own patterns by changing their mentality. These marginals need to be "integrated," "incorporated" into the healthy society that they have "forsaken."

The truth is, however, that the oppressed are not "marginals," are not living "outside" society. They have always been "inside" the structure which made them "beings for others." The solution is not to "integrate" them into the structure of oppression, but to transform that structure so that they can become "beings for themselves." Such transformation, of course, would undermine the oppressors' purposes; hence their utilization of the banking concept of education to avoid the threat of student conscientizacao.

The banking approach to adult education, for example, will never propose to students that they critically consider reality. It will deal instead with such vital questions as whether Roger gave green grass to the goat, and insist upon the importance of learning that, on the contrary, Roger gave green grass to the rabbit. The "humanism" of the banking approach masks the effort to turn women and men into automatons—the very negation of their ontological vocation to be more fully human.

Those who use the banking approach, knowingly or unknowingly (for there are innumerable well-intentioned bank-clerk teachers who do not realize that they are serving only to dehumanize), fail to perceive that the deposits themselves contain contradictions about reality. But sooner or later, these contradictions may lead formerly passive students to turn against their domestication and the attempt to domesticate reality. They may discover through existential experience that their present way of life is irreconcilable with their vocation to become fully human. They may perceive through their relations with reality that reality is really a process, undergoing constant transformation. If men and women are searchers and their ontological vocation is humanization, sooner or later they may perceive the contradiction in which banking education seeks to maintain them, and then engage themselves in the struggle for their liberation.

But the humanist revolutionary educator cannot wait for this possibility to materialize. From the outset, her efforts must coincide with those of the students to engage in critical thinking and the quest for mutual humanization. His efforts must be imbued with a profound trust in people and their creative power. To achieve this, they must be partners of the students in their relations with them.

The banking concept does not admit to such partnership—and necessarily so. To resolve the teacher-student contradiction, to exchange the role of depositor, prescriber, domesticator, for the role of student among students would be to undermine the power of oppression and serve the cause of liberation.

Implicit in the banking concept is the assumption of a dichotomy between human beings and the world: a person is merely in the world, not with the world or with others; the individual is spectator, not re-creator. In this view, the person is not a conscious being (*corpo consciente*); he or she is rather the possessor of a consciousness: an empty "mind" passively open to the reception of deposits of reality from the world outside. For example, my desk, my books, my coffee cup, all the objects before me—as bits of the world which surround me—would be "inside" me, exactly as I am inside my study right now. This view makes no distinction between being accessible to consciousness and entering consciousness. The distinction, however, is essential: the objects which surround me are simply accessible to my consciousness, not located within it. I am aware of them, but they are not inside me.

It follows logically from the banking notion of consciousness that the educator's role is to regulate the way the world "enters into" the students. The teacher's task is to organize a process which already occurs spontaneously, to "fill" the students by making deposits of information which he or she considers to constitute true knowledge.[2] And since people "receive" the world as passive entities, education should make them more passive still, and adapt them to the world. The educated individual is the adapted person, because she or he is better "fit" for the world. Translated into practice, this concept is well suited for the purposes of the oppressors, whose tranquility rests on how well people fit the world the oppressors have created and how little they question it.

The more completely the majority adapt to the purposes which the dominant majority prescribe for them (thereby depriving them of the right to their own purposes), the more easily the minority can continue to prescribe. The theory and practice of banking education serve this end quite efficiently. Verbalistic lessons, reading requirements,[3] the methods for evaluating "knowledge," the distance between the teacher and the taught, the criteria for promotion: everything in this ready-to-wear approach serves to obviate thinking.

The bank-clerk educator does not realize that there is no true security in his hypertrophied role, that one must seek to live with others in solidarity. One cannot impose oneself, nor even merely co-exist with one's students. Solidarity requires true communication, and the concept by which such an educator is guided fears and proscribes communication.

Yet only through communication can human life hold meaning. The teacher's thinking is authenticated only by the authenticity of the students' thinking. The teacher cannot think for her students, nor can she impose her thought on them. Authentic thinking, thinking that is concerned about reality, does not take place in ivory tower isolation, but only in communication. If it is true that thought has meaning only when generated by action upon the world, the subordination of students to teachers becomes impossible.

Because banking education begins with a false understanding of men and women as objects, it cannot promote the development of what Fromm calls "biophily," but instead produces its opposite: "necrophily."

> While life is characterized by growth in a structured functional manner, the necrophilous person loves all that does not grow, all that is mechanical. The necrophilous person is driven by the desire to transform the organic into the inorganic, to approach life mechanically, as if all living persons were things. . . . Memory, rather than experience; having, rather than being, is what counts. The necrophilous person can relate to an object—a flower or a person— only if he possesses it; hence a threat to his possession is a threat to himself, if he loses possession he loses contact with the world . . . He loves control, and in the act of controlling he kills life.[4]

Oppression—overwhelming control—is necrophilic; it is nourished by love of death, not life. The banking concept of education, which serves the interests of oppression, is also necrophilic. Based on a mechanistic, static, naturalistic, spatialized view of consciousness, it transforms students into receiving objects. It attempts to control thinking and action, leads women and men to adjust to the world, and inhibits their creative power.

When their efforts to act responsibly are frustrated, when they find themselves unable to use their faculties, people suffer. "This suffering due to impotence is rooted in the very fact that the human has been disturbed."[5] But the inability to act which causes men's anguish also causes them to reject their impotence, by attempting

> . . . to restore [their] capacity to act. But can [they], and how? One way is to submit to and identify with a person or group having power. By this symbolic participation in another person's life, [men have] the illusion of acting, when in reality [they] only submit to and become a part of those who act.[6]

Populist manifestations perhaps best exemplify this type of behavior by the oppressed, who, by identifying with charismatic leaders, come to feel that they themselves are active and effective. The rebellion they express as they emerge in the historical process is motivated by that desire to act effectively. The dominant elites consider the remedy to be more domination and repression, carried out in the name of freedom, order, and social peace (that is, the peace of the elites). Thus they can condemn—logically, from their point of view—"the violence of a strike by workers and [can] call upon the state in the same breath to use violence in putting down the strike."[7]

Education as the exercise of domination stimulates the credulity of students, with the ideological intent (often not perceived by educators) of indoctrinating them to adapt to the world of oppression. This accusation is not made in the naive hope that the dominant elites will thereby simply abandon the practice. Its objective is to call the attention of true humanists to the fact that they cannot use banking educational methods in the pursuit of liberation, for they would only negate that very pursuit. Nor may a revolutionary society inherit these methods from an oppressor society. The revolutionary society which practices banking education is either misguided or mistrusting of people. In either event, it is threatened by the specter of reaction.

Unfortunately, those who espouse the cause of liberation are themselves surrounded and influenced by the climate which generates the banking concept, and often do not perceive its true significance or its dehumanizing power. Paradoxically, then, they utilize this same instrument of alienation in what they consider an effort to liberate. Indeed, some "revolutionaries" brand as "innocents," "dreamers," or even "reactionaries" those who would challenge this educational practice. But one does not liberate people by alienating them. Authentic liberation—the process of humanization—is not another deposit to be made in men. Liberation is a praxis: the action and reflection of men and women upon their world in order to transform it.

Those truly committed to liberation must reject the banking concept in its entirety, adopting instead a concept of women and men as conscious beings, and consciousness as consciousness intent upon the world. They must abandon the educational goal of deposit-making and replace it with the posing of the problems of human beings in their relations with the world. "Problem-posing" education, responding to the essence of consciousness—intentionality—rejects communiques and embodies communication. It epitomizes the special characteristic of consciousness: being conscious of, not only as intent on objects but as turned in upon itself in a "Jasperian split"—consciousness as consciousness of consciousness.

Liberating education consists in acts of cognition, not transferals of information. It is a learning situation in which the cognizable object (far from being the end of the cognitive act) intermediates the cognitive actors—teacher on the one hand and students on the other. Accordingly, the practice of problem-posing education entails at the outset that the teacher-student contradiction to be resolved. Dialogical relations—indispensable to the capacity of cognitive actors to cooperate in perceiving the same cognizable object—are otherwise impossible.

Indeed, problem-posing education, which breaks with the vertical characteristic of banking education, can fulfill its function of freedom only if it can overcome the above contradiction. Through dialogue, the teacher-of-the-students and the students-of-the-teacher cease to exist and a new term emerges: teacher-student with students-teachers. The teacher is no longer merely the-one-who-teaches, but one who is himself taught in dialogue with the students, who in turn while being taught also teach. They become jointly responsible for a process in which all grow. In this process, arguments based on "authority" are no longer valid; in order to function authority must be on the side of freedom, not against it. Here, no one teaches another, nor is anyone self-taught. People teach each other, mediated by the world, by the cognizable objects which in banking education are "owned" by the teacher.

The banking concept (with its tendency to dichotomize everything) distinguishes two stages in the action of the educator. During the first he cognizes a cognizable object while he prepares his lessons in his study or his laboratory; during the second, he expounds to his students about that object. The students are not called upon to know, but to memorize the contents narrated by the teacher. Nor do the students practice any act of cognition, since the object towards which that act should be directed is the property of the teacher rather than a medium evoking the critical reflection of both teacher and students. Hence in the name of the "preservation of culture and knowledge" we have a system which achieves neither true knowledge nor true culture.

The problem-posing method does not dichotomize the activity of teacher-student: she is not "cognitive" at one point and "narrative" at another. He is always "cognitive," whether preparing a projector or engaging in dialogue with the students. He does not regard objects as his private property, but as the object of reflection by himself and his students. In this way, the problem-posing educator constantly re-forms his reflections in the reflection of the students. The students—no longer docile listeners— are now critical co-investigators in dialogue with the teacher. The teacher presents the material to the students for their consideration, and re-considers her earlier considerations as the students express their own. The role of the problem-posing educator is to create, together with the students, the conditions under which knowledge at the level of the doxa is superseded by true knowledge at the level of the logos. Whereas banking education anesthetizes and inhibits creative power, problem-posing education involves a constant unveiling of reality. The former attempts to maintain the submersion of consciousness; the latter strives for the emergence of consciousness and critical intervention in reality.

Students, as they are increasingly posed with problems relating to themselves in the world and with the world, will feel increasingly challenged and obliged to respond to that challenge. Because they apprehend the challenge as interrelated to other problems within a total context not as a theoretical question, the resulting comprehension tends to be increasingly critical and thus constantly less alienated. Their response to the challenge evokes new challenges, followed by new understandings; and gradually the students come to regard themselves as committed.

Education as the practice of freedom—as opposed to education as the practice of domination—denies that man is abstract, isolated, independent and unattached to the world; it also denies that the world exists as a reality apart from people. Authentic reflection considers neither abstract man nor the world without people, but people in their relations with the world. In these relations consciousness and world are simultaneous: consciousness neither precedes the world nor follows it.

La conscience et le monde sont dormes d'un meme coup: exterieur par essence a la conscience, le monde est, par essence relatif a elle.[8]

In one of our culture circles in Chile, the group was discussing (based on a codification) the anthropological concept of culture. In the midst of the discussion, a peasant who by banking standards was completely ignorant said: "Now I see that without man there is no world." When the educator responded: "Let's say, for the sake of argument, that all the men on earth were to die, but that the earth remained, together with trees, birds, animals, rivers, seas, the stars . . . wouldn't all this be a world?" "Oh no," the peasant replied. "There would be no one to say: 'This is a world.'"

The peasant wished to express the idea that there would be lacking the consciousness of the world which necessarily implies the world of consciousness. I cannot exist without a non-I. In turn, the non-I depends on that existence. The world which brings consciousness into existence becomes the world of that consciousness. Hence, the previously cited affirmation of Sartre: "La conscience et le monde sont dormes dun meme coup."

As men, simultaneously reflecting on themselves and on the world, increase the scope of their perception, they begin to direct their observations towards previously inconspicuous phenomena:

In perception properly so-called, as an explicit awareness [Gewahren], I am turned towards the object, to the paper, for instance. I apprehend it as being this here and now. The apprehension is a singling out, every object having a background inexperience. Around and about the paper lie books, pencils, inkwell and so forth, and these in a certain sense are also "perceived" perceptually there, in the "field of intuition"; but whilst I was turned towards the paper there was no turning in their direction, nor any apprehending of them, not even in a secondary sense. They appeared and yet were not singled out, were posited on their own account. Every perception of a thing has such a zone of background intuitions or background awareness, if "intuiting" already includes the state of being turned towards, and this also is a "conscious experience," or more briefly a "consciousness of" all indeed that in point of fact lies in the co-perceived objective background.[9]

That which had existed objectively but had not been perceived in its deeper implications (if indeed it was perceived at all) begins to "stand out," assuming the character of a problem and therefore of challenge. Thus, men and women begin to single out elements from their "background awareness" and to reflect upon them. These elements are now objects of their consideration, and, as such, objects of their action and cognition.

In problem-posing education, people develop their power to perceive critically the way they exist in the world with which and in which they find themselves; they come to see the world not as a static reality, but as a reality in process, in transformation. Although the dialectical relations of women and men with the world exist independently of how these relations are perceived (or whether or not they are perceived at all), it is also true that the form of action they adopt is to a large extent a function of how they perceive themselves in the world. Hence, the teacher-student and the students-teachers reflect simultaneously on themselves and the world without dichotomizing this reflection from action, and thus establish an authentic form of thought and action.

Once again, the two educational concepts and practices under analysis come into conflict. Banking education (for obvious reasons) attempts, by mythicizing reality, to conceal certain facts which explain the way human beings exist in the world; problem-posing education sets itself the task of demythologizing. Banking education resists dialogue; problem-posing education regards dialogue as indispensable to the act of cognition which unveils reality. Banking education treats students as objects of assistance; problem-posing education makes them critical thinkers. Banking education inhibits creativity and domesticates (although it cannot completely destroy) the intentionality of consciousness by isolating consciousness from the world, thereby denying people their ontological and historical vocation of becoming more fully human. Problem-posing education bases itself on creativity and stimulates true reflection and action upon reality, thereby responding to the vocation of persons as beings only when engaged in inquiry and creative transformation. In sum: banking theory and practice, as immobilizing and fixating forces, fail to acknowledge men and women as historical beings; problem-posing theory and practice take the people's historicity as their starting point.

Problem-posing education affirms men as beings the process of *becoming*— as unfinished, uncompleted beings in and with a likewise unfinished reality. Indeed, in contrast to other animals who are unfinished, but not historical, people know themselves to be unfinished; they are aware of their incompletion. In this incompletion and this awareness lie the very roots of education as an human manifestation. The unfinished character of human beings and the transformational character of reality necessitate that education be an ongoing activity.

Education is thus constantly remade in the praxis. In order to be, it must become. Its "duration" (in the Bergsonian meaning of the word) is found in the interplay of the opposites permanence and change. The banking method emphasizes permanence and becomes problem-posing education—which accepts neither a "well-behaved" present nor a predetermined future— roots itself in the dynamic present and becomes revolutionary.

Problem-posing education is revolutionary futurity. Hence it is prophetic (and as such, hopeful). Hence, it corresponds to the historical nature of humankind. Hence, it affirms men as beings who transcend themselves, who move forward and look ahead, for whom immobility represents a fatal threat for whom looking at the past must only be a means of understanding more clearly what and who they are so that they can more wisely build the future. Hence, it identifies with the movement which engages people as beings aware of their incompletion—an historical movement which has its point of departure, its Subjects and its objective.

The point of departure of the movement lies in the men themselves. But since men do not exist apart from the world, apart from reality, the movement must begin with the men-world relationship. Accordingly, the point of departure must always be with men and women in the "here and now," which constitutes the situation within which they are submerged, from which they emerge, and in which they intervene. Only by starting from this situation—which determines their perception of it—can they begin to move. To do this authentically they must perceive their state not as fated and unalterable, but merely as limiting—and therefore challenging.

Whereas the banking method directly or indirectly reinforces men's fatalistic perception of their situation, the problem-posing method presents this very situation to them as a problem. As the situation becomes the object of their cognition, the naive or magical perception which produced their fatalism gives way to perception which is able to perceive itself even as it perceives reality, and can thus be critically objective about that reality.

A deepened consciousness of their situation leads people to apprehend that situation as an historical reality susceptible of transformation. Resignation gives way to the drive for transformation and inquiry, over which men feel themselves to be in control. If people, as historical beings necessarily engaged with other people in a movement of inquiry, did not control that movement, it would be (and is) a violation of their humanity. Any situation in which some individuals prevent others from engaging in the process of inquiry is one of violence. The means used are not important; to alienate human beings from their own decision-making is to change them into objects.

This movement of inquiry must be directed towards humanization—the people's historical vocation. The pursuit of full humanity, however, cannot be carried out in isolation or individualism, but only in fellowship and solidarity; therefore it cannot unfold in the antagonistic relations between oppressors and oppressed. No one can be authentically human while he prevents others from being so. Attempting to be more human, individualistically, leads to having more, egotistically, a form of dehumanization. Not that it is not fundamental to have in order to be human. Precisely because it is necessary, some men's having must not be allowed to constitute an obstacle to others' having, must not consolidate the power of the former to crush the latter.

Problem-posing education, as a humanist and liberating praxis, posits as fundamental that the people subjected to domination must fight for their emancipation. To that end, it enables teachers and students to become Subjects of the educational process by overcoming authoritarianism and an alienating intellectualism; it also enables people to overcome their false perception of reality. The world—no longer something to be described with deceptive words—becomes the object of that transforming action by men and women which results in their humanization.

Problem-posing education does not and cannot serve the interests of the oppressor. No oppressive order could permit the oppressed to begin to question: Why? While only a revolutionary society can carry out this education in systematic terms, the revolutionary leaders need not take full power before they can employ the method. In the revolutionary process, the leaders cannot utilize the banking method as an interim measure, justified on grounds of expediency, with intention of later behaving in a genuinely revolutionary fashion. They must be revolutionary—that is to say, dialogical—from the outset.

Notes

1. Simon de Beauvoir. La Pensee de Droite, Aujord'hui (Paris); ST, El Pensamiento politico de la Derecha (Buenos Aires, 1963), p. 34.

2. This concept corresponds to what Sartre calls the "digestive" or "nutritive" in which knowledge is "fed" by the teacher to the students to "fill them out." See Jean-Paul Sartre, "Une idee fundamentals de la phenomenologie de Husserl: L'intentionalite," Situations I (Paris, 1947).

3. For example, some professors specify in their reading lists that a book should be read from pages 10 to 15—and do this to "help" their students!

4. Fromm, op. cit. p. 41.

5. Ibid. p. 31.

6. Ibid. p. 7.

7. Reinhold Niebuhr, *Moral Man and Immoral Society* (New York, 1960), p. 130.

8. Sartre, op. cit., p. 32.

9. Edmund Husserl, *Ideas: General Introduction to Pure Phenomenology* (London, 1969), pp. 105–106.

Paulo Freire (deceased) was an author and social activist.

10

On Stir-and-Serve Recipes for Teaching

Susan Ohanian

The notion that just about any Joe Blow can walk in off the street and take over a classroom is gaining ground. It makes me nervous. No, more than that: it infuriates me. We should squash once and for all the idea that schools can be adequately staffed by 32 bookkeepers and a plumber. The right teacher-proof curriculum is not sufficient; children need real teachers, and real teachers must be trained.

Nor am I charmed by the idea of signing up out-of-work computer programmers and retired professors to teach math and science. The mass media like to scoff that current certification requirements would keep Albert Einstein from teaching in the public schools. That news is not all bad. Is there any evidence that Einstein worked particularly well with young children? A Nobel Prize does not guarantee excellence in the classroom.

Having sat through more stupid education courses than I wish to recall, I am not altogether comfortable defending schools of education. But I suspect that the blame for worthless courses lies as much with the teachers who take them as with the professors who teach them. As a group, we teachers are intransigently anti-intellectual. We demand from our professors carry-out

NOTE: Reprinted with kind permission from the author.

formulae, materials with the immediate applicability of scratch-and-sniff stickers. We are indignant when they try instead to offer ideas to grow on, seeds that we have to nurture in our own gardens.

We teachers frequently complain that education courses do not prepare us for the rigorous, confusing work ahead—that they do not show us how to run our classrooms. We refuse to admit that no course or manual can give us all the help we crave. We should not expect professors to set up our classroom systems, as though each of us were heading out to operate a fast-food franchise. There is no instant, stir-and-serve recipe for running a classroom.

Too often, teachers judge the success of education courses by the weight of the materials they cart away—cute cutouts or "story starters," all ready for immediate use. One popular journal for teachers promises 100 new ideas in every issue. "You can use them on Monday" is the promise. No one gets rich admitting that genuinely good ideas are hard to come by.

I understand only too well this yearning for the tangible, the usable. We are, after all, members of a profession ruled by pragmatism. People who sit in judgment on us don't ask about our students, "Are they happy? Are they creative? Are they helpful, sensitive, loving? Will they want to read a book next year?" Instead, these people demand, "What are their test scores?" as if those numbers, though they passeth understanding, will somehow prove that we're doing a good job.

During my first 12 years of teaching I was desperate for new ideas, constantly foraging for schemes with which to engage the children. My frenetic activity was due, in part, to the fact that I was given a different teaching assignment every two years. I figured, "Different children require different methods, different materials." So I would race off to the library or to the arts-and-crafts store. I'd buy another filing cabinet and join another book club for teachers.

But even when I settled in with the same assignment for a six-year stretch, my frenzy did not abate. My classroom became a veritable curriculum warehouse, stuffed with every innovative whiz-bang gizmo I could buy, borrow, or invent. I spent hundreds of hours reading, constructing, laminating. My husband gave up reminding me that I had promised to put the cut-and-paste factory in our living room out of business, once I figured out what to teach. When I wasn't inventing projects, I was taking courses: cardboard carpentry, architectural awareness, science process, Cuisenaire rods, Chinese art, test construction and evaluation, curriculum development, and so on. I even took two courses in the computer language, BASIC. (I thought maybe I'd missed the point in the first course, so I took another—just to be sure.)

I didn't take those courses on whim, any more than I invented curriculum because I had nothing better to do. I chose my courses deliberately, tying to inform my work as a reading teacher. Although I now look back on much of my frenzied search for methods and media as rather naïve, I don't see it as time wasted. I learned a lot. Mostly I learned to simplify. And then to simplify some more.

But the path to simplicity is littered with complexities. And I suspect that it is hard to figure out how to simplify our lives if we haven't cluttered them in the first place. Sure, we teachers clutter up our classrooms with too much claptrap. The fribble is often alluring at first, and it is hard to recognize that the more gadgets we rely on, the poorer we are—at home as well as at school.

People probably always yearn for gadgets, especially if they haven't had much chance to fool around with them. A university research project makes this point rather nicely. The researcher decided to investigate the effects of computer-assisted instruction in English-as-a-second-language (ESL) classes. He set up a computer-taught group and a control group. Both were instructed in ESL for one year. And guess which group had the more positive attitude about computer-assisted instruction at the end of that year? The youngsters who didn't get to use the computers.

Not surprisingly, we teachers are compulsive pack rats. Fearing the vagaries of future school budgets, we hoard construction paper until it is old and brittle and unusable. We worry that we may need that paper more next year than we need it today. Have you ever known a teacher who could throw away a set of ditto masters? Or half a game of Scrabble? For years I had a gross of tiny, childproof, left-handed scissors. Childproof scissors are a horror in the first place. Those designed for left-handers are beyond description. Why did I keep them? Hey, they were mine, weren't they?

Most of us never use 80% of the materials jammed into our classrooms, but we cling to them "just in case." Because our job is hectic, pressured, stressful, we seldom have a reflective moment to clear our minds, let alone our cupboards. Maybe every teacher should change schools every three years and be allowed to take along only what he or she can carry. However, I must add to this suggestion my own statement of full disclosure: the last time I changed classrooms, after 13 years in the district, it took six strong men and a truck to transfer my belongings. And that was after I had filled two dumpsters.

The good professors must stop yielding to our acquisitive pressures; they must refuse to hand out their 100—or even 10—snazzy new ideas for the well-stocked classroom. They must offer fewer methods, fewer recipes. We teachers need less practicality, not more. We need to have our lives informed by Tolstoy, Jane Addams, Suzanne Langer, Rudolf Arnheim, and their ilk—not by folks who promise the keys to classroom control and creative bulletin boards, along with 100 steps to reading success.

We need a sense of purpose from our professors, not a timetable. Better that they show us a way to find our own ways than that they hand out their own detailed maps of the territory. A map isn't of much use to people who don't know where they're headed. The only way to become familiar with the terrain is to explore a little. I nominate the professors to scout ahead, chart the waters, post the quicksand. I know that I still have to climb my own mountain, but I would welcome scholarly advice about the climbing conditions.

Critics of schools of education insist that prospective teachers would profit more from observing good teachers at work than from taking impractical courses on pedagogy. Maybe so, but what are those novices going to see? Is one observation as good as another? After all, a person can look at "Guernica" and not see it, listen to the "Eroica" and not hear it. E. H. Gombrich says that every observation we make is the result of the questions we ask. And where do novices get the questions? How can they ask intelligent questions without knowing something about the subject? Can anyone really see a classroom without some theoretical, historical, developmental savvy?

No one enters a classroom as a *tabula rasa*, of course. We all know something about schools because we have, for better or for worse, been there. We know how schools are supposed to be. At least we think we do. So we judge schools, as we judge anything, with a notion—or schema—of reality in our heads. Most of us don't just look *at* something; we look *for* something, because we have a hypothesis, a hidden agenda. We observe and evaluate with our minds, our memories, our experiences, our linguistic habits. Obviously, the more we know, the more we see.

But teachers cannot walk into classrooms and simply teach what they know. First, they don't know enough. Second, even this seemingly restrictive world—constrained by bells, desks, and textbooks—contains a rich stock of themes from which teachers must choose their own motifs. They must be flexible and inventive enough to modify the schema they carried into their classrooms.

I was one of those people almost literally picked up off a street corner and allowed to teach in New York City under an emergency credential. I walked into the middle of someone else's lesson plan, and, though it didn't take me 10 minutes to realize that a round-robin reading of "Paul Revere's Ride" was not going to work, it took me quite a while to come up with something much better.

All I could manage at first was to teach as I had been taught. But as I learned more about the students and about ways to get around the assigned curriculum, a more ideal classroom began to emerge in my head. It remains a shadowy image—one I glimpse and even touch occasionally, but one I have long since stopped trying to file neatly in my planbook. That's okay. The bird seen through the window is more provocative than the one in the cage.

Teaching, like art, is born of a schema. That's why we need the professors with their satchels of theory, as well as our own observations and practice. Those who hope to be effective teachers must recognize that teaching is a craft of careful artifice; the profession requires more than a spontaneous overflow of good intentions or the simple cataloguing and distribution of information. It is possible, I suppose, to have an inborn talent for teaching, but I am sure that those teachers who endure and triumph are *made*—rigorously trained—and not born.

Much of the training must be self-initiated. People who have some nagging notion of the ideal classroom tickling their psyches probably look more for patterns that appeal than for practices that are guaranteed to produce higher standardized test scores. Such teachers probably have a capacity for ambiguity; they look for snippets of familiarity but do not insist on sameness. Such teachers have a greater need for aesthetic and psychological satisfaction than for a neat and tidy cupboard. But they also have a willingness to practice the craft, to try out new brushstrokes, to discard dried-out palettes.

Most of us, children and adults alike, have a strong need to make sense of the disparate elements in our lives, to bring them together, to find patterns, to make meaning. This desire for meaning is so strong that some teachers, tired and defeated by the system, rely on ritual to get them through the day, the week, the year. External order and ritual are the only things they have left to give. And these things usually satisfy the casual observer, who believes that teachers who provide clean and orderly classrooms are providing enough.

This is one reason I want the professors in on the act—out of their ivory towers and into our dusty school corridors. Maybe well-informed people, good observers who are not bogged down by school minutiae, could convince us that a tidy desk is far from enough. The professors need to promote the search for a different order, a subtler pattern—one that lies not in behavioral checklists but rather, to use Chia Yi's words, in constant "combining, scattering, waning, waxing."

It was my own search for pattern that led me to try using science as a way to inform, enhance, and give order to my work as a reading teacher. The children and I were far too familiar with the rituals of remedial reading for those routines to fall much short of torture. I've never understood why students who have trouble with a certain system of decoding should be made to rehearse that system over and over again. A few times over the course of a few years, maybe. But surely there comes a time to try a different approach. Reading had already been ruined for my students by the time they came to me. I needed to see how they approached pedagogic puzzlement, and such puzzlement would never occur if I persisted in making them circle blends on worksheets. That's why I learned how to mess around in science.

Tell a poor reader that it's time to read, and watch the impenetrable curtain of defeat and despair descend. So my students and I spent our time on science. All year. We made cottage cheese, explored surface tension, built bridges, figured out optical illusions. And not once did my students associate experiment cards, books on the theory of sound, or my insistence that observations be recorded in writing with the onerous task that they knew reading to be. Children told me that my room was a good place. Too bad, they added, that I wasn't a real teacher.

That reading room, where children were busily measuring, making—and reading—received full parental support and had its moment in the limelight. There were a lot of visitors. The teachers among them invariably asked, "How did you get this job?" Clearly, they intended to apply for one like it.

Get the job? Only in the first year of my teaching career was I ever handed a job. Ever after, I've made my own. No job of any value can be given out, like a box of chalk. We get the jobs we deserve. Maybe that's why so many teachers are disappointed. They believe all those promises that someone else can do the thinking for them.

I held seven different jobs in my school district, and I earned the right to love every one of them. That's not to say that I didn't have plenty of moments of anger, frustration, rage. But I also experienced deep satisfaction.

Because my seven jobs required some pretty dramatic shifts in grade level, people were always asking me, "Where is it better—high school or the primary grades?" It's a question I have never been able to answer, mainly because the more grade levels I taught, the more similarities I saw. Sure, high school dropouts enrolled in an alternative program are harder to tune in to the beauty of a poem than are seventh-graders. Third-graders cry more, talk more; seventh-graders scale more heights and sink into deeper pits. But a common thread runs throughout, and it was that thread I clung to.

Maybe I see this sameness because my teaching is dominated less by skill than by idea—the secret, elusive form. I have a hard time reading other people's prescriptions, let alone writing my own. I always figure that, if you can get the idea right, the specific skill will come. Teaching is too personal, even too metaphysical, to be charted like the daily temperature. Teaching is like a Chinese lyric painting, not a bus schedule.

We need to look very closely at just who is calling for "the upgrading of teacher skills," lest this turn out to be the clarion call of those folks with something to sell. The world does not come to us in neat little packages. Even if we could identify just what a *skill* is, does *more* definitely denote *better*? What profiteth a child whose teacher has gathered up an immense pile of pishposh? We must take care, lest the examiners who claim they can dissect and label the educational process leave us holding a bag of gizzards.

We teachers must recognize that we do not need the behaviorist-competency thugs to chart our course. For us, reality is a feeling state, details of daily routine fade, and what remains is atmosphere, tone, emotion. The ages and the talents of the children become irrelevant. What counts is attitude and endeavor. That's why, even when we try, we often can't pass on a terrific lesson plan to a friend; we probably can't even save it for ourselves to use again next year. It's virtually impossible to teach the same lesson twice.

I'm afraid that all of this sounds rather dim, maybe even dubious. But this is where the professors might step in. There are so many outrageous examples of bad pedagogy that it's easy to overlook the good—easy, but not excusable. The professors need to shape up their own schools of education first—getting rid of Papercutting 306, even if it's the most profitable course in the summer school catalogue. Then they need to get out in the field to work with student teachers, principals, and children.

Is it outrageous to think that the professors might even pop into the classrooms of veteran teachers now and then? Wouldn't it be something if their research occasionally involved real children and real teachers (and if they had to face bells, mandated tests, bake sales, and field trips to mess up their carefully laid plans), instead of four children in a lab staffed by 63 graduate students? That's probably a scary thought for some professors.

I know of one school of education that relegates the observation and direction of student teachers to the local school district. The district, in turn, passes this responsibility on to an administrator who has never taught. In such a situation, pedagogy gets turned upside down and inside out. The outcome is empty platitudes, not effective classroom practice. The student teacher, who is paying for expert training, is being defrauded. The children are being cheated. The system is stupid and immoral. We need teacher trainers who know educational theory and who are savvy about children. Those professors who won't help us should be replaced by ones who will.

But aspiring teachers have a responsibility, too. They must heed the advice of Confucius:

If a man won't try, I will teach him; if a man makes no effort, I will not help him. I show one corner, and if a man cannot find the other three, I am not going to repeat myself.

We teachers must stop asking the education professors for the whole house. I know plenty of teachers who are disappointed, indignant, and eventually destroyed by the fact that nobody has handed them all four corners. But the best we can expect from any program of courses or training is the jagged edge of one corner. Then it is up to us to read the research and to collaborate with the children to find the other three corners. And, because teaching must be a renewable contract, if we don't keep seeking new understanding, we'll find that the corners we thought we knew very well will keep slipping away. There are constant, subtle shifts in the schoolroom. One can never be sure of knowing the floorplan forever and ever.

In trying to renew my faith in myself as a teacher, I find little help in the "how to" books, those nasty little tomes that define learning in 87 steps. I like to think of learning as a wave that washes over the learner, rather than as a series of incremental hurdles to be pre- and posttested. I reject *How to Teach Reading in 100 Lessons,* relying instead on *The Mustard Seed Garden Manual of Painting,* which advises that "neither complexity in itself nor simplicity is enough"—nor dexterity alone nor conscientiousness. "To be without method is worse."

What can we do? What is the solution? In painting, there is an answer: "Study 10,000 volumes and walk 10,000 miles." One more thing is required of teachers. We must also work with 10,000 children.

Susan Ohanian is a freelance writer and former teacher.

11

Psst . . . It Ain't About the Tests

It's Still About Great Teaching

Robert DiGiulio

If you are planning to become a teacher, welcome, and prepare to be overwhelmed. If you are already teaching, you know this already. After a seminar I gave for teachers recently, we were standing by the coffee: "My head is spinning! There's too much to think about: Portfolios, standards-based lessons, differentiated instruction, IEPs, ESTs, continuous assessment, making sure the kids pass those standardized tests, fundraisers, getting the computers to work, inclusion, trying to keep discipline in a classroom where some can't even sit still for a minute!" As I drove home from that seminar, I thought about how right they were. There seemed to be two huge but connected problems here: First, teachers today have been swamped by tasks—often, trivial and unconnected to students—that demand compliance, to the point where it is difficult for teachers to balance or to discern what was really important. Second, teachers have a vague (or all-too-clear) uneasiness, based on a hazy sense of how well they were

---

NOTE: Parts of this essay first appeared in the book *Great Teaching Is Still Great Teaching*, by Robert DiGiulio, copyright 2003. Reprinted with permission from Corwin Press.

doing. There was a lack of useful information that ought to help teachers connect what they were doing to how well students were learning. A common form of data—students' standardized test scores, now all the rage—provide little guidance for teachers, and are among the most useless (and harmful) pieces of data, in terms of helping teachers and future teachers, to say nothing of useless in helping students actually be successful.

Since I began teaching in the inner-city public schools of New York City in 1970, I have been absorbed by the question of good teaching. Along with the New York State and City teacher licensing boards, Al Shanker and the teachers' union defined good teaching in terms of qualifications, years teaching, seniority, number of advanced degrees, and so on. But my first-hand observation of some great teachers contradicted that—I saw no connection between these paper qualifications and how excellent teachers actually were in the classroom. The skills and qualities of great teachers seemed to be increasingly marginalized; crowded out by administrative, compliance paperwork (I call it "ditto worksheets for teachers"), somebody's Great New Idea, and other time killers imposed on teachers. Later, as a school principal, my awareness grew of even darker reasons for the downplaying of good teaching, and I suppose money has a lot to do with it. Simply stated, when one acknowledges someone as being good (or great), there is a corresponding expectation to pay those people well. So while I have heard a lot over thirty years about teacher competency and merit pay, I have yet to hear a sincere effort to acknowledge what is the essence of great teaching. For once that is done, it forces the question of how we should expect it, recognize it, and maybe, pay great teachers well for what they do. I am still waiting for that discussion.

In a sense, I am writing this piece as an historical document. Great teaching has existed since one of the first humans—generously and competently—showed another how to make a fire and how to cook food. Great teaching has been great because it placed the learner's needs and interests first. Today, however, I see a tendency to marginalize great teaching by redefining it as teaching that emphasizes interests other than the needs of students. These other interests include those of special interest groups that often hide their interests behind the cloak of reform and of school improvement. They address alleged defects of teachers and/or public schools, and provide solutions to problems that only they have identified, and narrowly so at that. In these cases, neither the public's best interests nor students' best interests are at the heart of their "solutions." Some groups insist, for example, that standardized testing is essential to accountability. I am not opposed to accountability, and I can agree that under some circumstances standardized tests can provide useful information. But they don't inform teaching; standardized tests are beside the point of great teaching because they are too narrow in scope. While data from well-designed tests can help inform teachers as to their students' mastery of content, those tests cannot provide help for teachers seeking to improve their teaching skills and qualities. No standardized test for students can ever inform us of a teacher's enthusiasm, caring, or belief that students can be successful—three factors that have an enormous effect on student achievement and self-esteem. We simply have to use other means to focus on these important traits.

And focus we must. We see great teachers, and we see the undeniably powerful effect great teachers have on students. Yet, I worry that special-interest agendas are distorting (or submerging) the traditional, common sense notion of what great teaching is. As proof, think about what we know works in schools. After thousands of studies (some better than others), we know a lot about high-quality teaching. We know that there are good and better things that teachers do with and for students, and we know there are not-so-good things that teachers do. Yet despite the research data, and despite our common sense perceptions, how often do we hear about teachers who do the right things? How often do we see what and how they do those good things? I am not simply calling for mere praise for the great, even heroic teacher, although that is long overdue. I am calling for simply naming, noting, identifying what these teachers do, teachers whose students are succeeding—academically and socially—despite unfortunate conditions in their schools and communities. How often do we hear about students who do not bring weapons to school, students who are not violent? Students who don't hurt others; students who have learned how civilized human beings behave, learning much of this, in large part, from a good teacher? I am only asking for "the facts," not for a massive public relations campaign promoting teachers and schools.

When well-organized and well-funded anti-public education voices and special interest group voices have reached a fever pitch so that the acts of great teachers and great teaching are marginalized or disregarded, it is time to speak out. When the elements comprising great teaching are minimized, it is time to speak out. Again, I am concerned not so much that great teachers and their successes are being ignored (which they are), but that the qualities and skills that great teachers bring to great teaching are in danger of vanishing, disappearing from both the public eye and from the cur- riculum of teacher preparation. I speak out not as a cheerleader of great teachers, but as a curator who seeks to keep alive the awareness of the qual- ities and skills that comprise great teaching. These qualities and skills apply to all levels of education, from preschool through graduate school, private school as well as public school. They apply to teaching throughout the world, because they go directly to the heart of how teachers teach so that students learn most effectively.

As we get to the heart of what really matters in fostering student achievement, we realize more and more how important the individual teacher is. We know this; we have known this since the time of the wise Buddha, but we still seem to dance around focusing on the essence of the great teacher. Teacher education college programs are just as guilty as corporate interests: When was the last time you heard an education professor talk about great teaching? Is there anything in any syllabus that refers to great teaching? Yet we know—or *should know*—that this issue should not be summarily ignored. Probably the strongest voice is that of University of Tennessee professor William Sanders (2003), whose research shows how the effective teacher is more important—as a predictor of student success—than any of the other traditional social indicators usually blamed for student failure:

> . . . we've been able to get a very fair measure of the school district, the school, and the individual classroom. And we've been able to demonstrate that ethnicity, poverty, and affluence can no longer be used as justifications for the failure [of students] to make academic progress. The single biggest factor affecting academic growth of any population of youngsters is the effectiveness of the individual classroom teacher. [Furthermore,] [t]he teacher's effect on academic growth dwarfs and nearly renders trivial all these other factors that people have historically worried about.

Fine. But the devil is in the details, and how we define the "effectiveness" of that teacher is the heart of the problem. Shall we use standardized test scores? I think not. What shall we do instead? Richard B. Traina, former President of Clark University, is a research historian who asked, "What makes a good teacher?" (1999, 34). He looked through the biographies and autobiographies of prominent 19th and 20th century Americans, focusing on what they had to say about the traits their best teachers possessed. Traina saw a thread that ran through their stories: The best teachers—the memorable ones—were remembered as being skillful and enthusiastic, having such a solid command of the subject matter that students could "pick up on their excitement" for the subject. Second, these teachers were *caring*—they cared "deeply about each student and about that student's accomplishment and growth." Third, Traina said that these teachers had "distinctive character . . . there was a palpable energy that suffused the competent and caring teacher, some mark-making quality." In short, the memorable teachers were skillful, enthusiastic, caring, and perhaps even idiosyncratic. Dr. Traina's third trait—"distinctive character"—is indeed the most elusive category. Although we can't *teach* teachers to "acquire distinctive character," we certainly can work to not destroy it, by demanding conformity and narrow-definitions of what successful teachers are. Distinctive character is a fragile naturally occurring resource. Like a gemstone, the distinctive character of each teacher is revealed as she or he teaches. Our job is to guard it, and not allow it to be shattered.

Aside from this *je ne sais qua* of distinctive character, what else do great teachers do that helps kids learn? Knowledge and "distinctive character" are part of it, but it is also about efficacy, a teacher's belief that she or he will be successful, because his or her students will be successful. And, to achieve student success, great teachers help move their students via three paths: producing, empowering, and connecting.

Great teachers know that to actually be successful, a student must first do something of value. Simply telling kids they are good won't wash. Student success is fostered by the work students do, by what they produce. This can include participating, performing, creating, practicing, designing, producing, carrying out an experiment, finishing an assignment, or any of hundreds of other activities. Worksheets, on the other hand, are all too often mindless, and require little thinking (input). The quality and value of the output, then, is quite low. Some worksheets may be okay for practicing, or passing time with puzzles, but not for producing. In the final analysis, what the student does will have a greater impact on how successful the student is (and feels he or she is) than what the teacher knows, says, or believes.

Student success is also fostered by empowering students (and students are automatically empowered when they are producing!). Empowering means actively teaching students how to help themselves, how to take responsibility for their work; how to get help: How to ask for help, whom to ask for help, and when to seek help. This is a real-world skill that starts and grows in class and in school. Students must also be weaned from depending on the teachers to provide direction at every step.

The third path to student success lies in helping students make connections. Success is fostered by activities/assignments that draw on—connect with—what students already know, and/or what they do well. Perhaps it is too obvious to state that what I learn best and fastest is that which is closest to what I already know; I learn best what builds on what I already know. What I do not learn well is when I try to make sense of material that is alien to what I presently know. Making connections is a core tenet of constructivism, and classrooms with a constructivist orientation are not only the most productive, but are happier places than classrooms with reward-and-punishment teachers, and far, far better than classrooms with laissez-faire (uninvolved) teachers.

Among its other provisions, the "No Child Left Behind" Act includes a provision that all public schools have a highly qualified teacher in each classroom. Unfortunately, there is nothing promising in that goal, especially when we have created so many alternative routes to licensure that even a measurable pulse may not any longer be a consistent requirement to teach (the poorest school districts in America tend to qualify almost anyone to teach).

Every classroom should have not merely a qualified teacher, but a great teacher. But for this to happen, we must move the definition of "qualified" back from *quantity indicators* (test scores, teachers' college degrees, number of years teaching, and other items easily tallied) and onto *quality,* by teaching teachers about efficacy and caring, about the ways one can empower and engage students, while allowing teachers to retain their "distinctive character." What matters at every turn is the teacher, and all kids deserve great teachers. This need has never before been so pressing.

Robert DiGiulio is professor of Education at Johnson State College in Johnson, Vermont.

12

So What Do You Do Now?

Neil Postman and Charles Weingartner

Y ou are a teacher in an ordinary school, and the ideas in this book make
sense to you . . . What can you do about it, say tomorrow?

1. Your first act of subversion might be conducted in the following way:
write on a scrap of paper these questions:

- What am I going to have my students do today?
- What's it good for?
- How do I know?

Tape the paper to the mirror in your bathroom or some other place
where you are likely to see it every morning. If nothing else, the questions
will begin to make you uneasy about shilling for someone else and might
weaken your interest in "following the syllabus." You may even, after a
while, become nauseous at the prospect of teaching things which have a
specious value or for which there is no evidence that your anticipated
outcomes do, in fact, occur. At their best, the questions will drive you to
reconsider almost everything you are doing, with the result that you will

NOTE: From *Teaching as a Subversive Activity* by Neil Postman and Charles Weingartner,
copyright 1969 by Neil Postman and Charles Weingartner. Used by permission of Dell
Publishing, a division of Random House, Inc.

challenge your principal, your textbooks, the syllabus, the grading system, your own education, and so on. In the end, it all may cost you your job, or lead you to seek another position, or drive you out of teaching altogether. Subversion is a risky business—as risky for its agent as for its target.

2. In class, try to avoid *telling* your students any answers, if only for a few lessons or days. Do not prepare a lesson plan. Instead, confront your students with some sort of problem which might interest them. Then, allow them to work the problem through without your advice or counsel. Your talk should consist of questions directed to particular students, based on remarks made by those students. If a student asks you a question, tell him that you don't know the answer, even if you do. Don't be frightened by the long stretches of silence that might occur. Silence may mean that the students are thinking. Or it may mean that they are growing hostile. The hostility signifies that the students resent the fact that you have shifted the burden of intellectual activity from you to them. Thought is often painful even if you are accustomed to it. If you are not, it can be unbearable.

There are at least two good accounts of what happens when a teacher refrains from telling students answers. One of them appears in Nathaniel Cantor's *The Dynamics of Learning;* the other, in Carl Rogers' *On Becoming a Person.* You may want to read these accounts before trying your experiment. If you have any success at all, you ought to make your experiment a regular feature of your weekly lessons: one hour every day for independent problem solving, or one hour every week. However much you can do will be worth the effort.

3. Try listening to your students for a day or two. We do not mean reacting to what they say. We mean listening. This may require that you do some role playing. Imagine, for example, that you are not their teacher but a psychiatrist (or some such person who is not primarily trying to teach but who is trying to understand). Any questions you ask or remarks you make would, therefore, not be designed to instruct or judge. They would be attempts to clarify what someone has said. If you are like most teachers, your training has probably not included learning how to listen, Therefore, we would recommend that you obtain a copy of *On Becoming a Person* by Carl Rogers. The book is a collection of Rogers' best articles and speeches. Rogers is generally thought of as the leading exponent of non-directive counseling, and he is a rich source of ideas about listening to and understanding other people. You probably will not want to read every article in the book, but do not overlook "Communication: Its Blocking and Facilitation." In this article, Rogers describes a particularly effective

technique for teaching listening: the students engage in a discussion of some issue about which they have strong feelings. But their discussion has an unusual rule applied to it. A student may say anything he wishes but only after he has restated what the previous speaker has said *to that speaker's satisfaction*. Astounding things happen to students when they go through this experience. They find themselves concentrating on what others are saying to the point, sometimes, of forgetting what they themselves were going to say. In some cases, students have a unique experience. They find that they have projected themselves into the frame of mind of another person. You might wish to make this special listening game a permanent part of your weekly lessons. But, of course, you ought to try it yourself first. An additional aid to you in your efforts at listening will be "Do You Know How to Listen?" by Wendell Johnson. The article appeared in *ETC.* in autumn 1949. This publication is edited by S. I. Hayakawa, and we enthusiastically suggest that you become a permanent subscriber.

It is important for us to say that the principal reason for your learning how to listen to students is that you may increase your understanding of what the students perceive as relevant. The only way to know where a kid is "at" is to listen to what he is saying. You can't do this if you are talking.

Invite another teacher to observe your class when you are experimenting with listening. After the lesson, ask your colleague this question: On the basis of what you heard these students say, what would you have them do tomorrow, or next week? Perhaps your colleague will then invite you to observe her class while she experiments with listening. After a while, both of you may find that you are becoming increasingly more effective at designing activities based on what students actually know, feel, and care about.

4. If you feel it is important for your students to learn how to ask questions, try this:

Announce to the class that for the next two days, you will not permit them to make any utterances that are not in the form of questions. Then, present the class with some problem. Tell them that their task is to compile a list of questions, the answers to which might help in solving the problem. If your students require an inducement, tell them you will reward (with A's, gold stars, or whatever sugar cubes you conventionally use) those students who produce the most questions. At this point, you need only be concerned with the quantity of questions, not their quality. Your students probably have had very little experience with question-asking behavior (at least in school), and the primary problem is to get them to begin formulating questions. Later, you can have them examine their questions in an effort to determine if there are certain criteria by which the quality of a question can be evaluated. (For example: Does the question contain unwarranted assumptions? Does it leave important terms undefined? Does it suggest some procedure for obtaining an answer?)

You might use some such problems as the following, depending on the age of your students:

Suppose we wanted to make the school the best possible school we can imagine, what would you need to know in order to proceed?

Read the following speech (for example by the President). What would you need to know in order to evaluate the validity of the speech?

Suppose our job was to make recommendations to improve the traffic problem (or pollution problem or population problem or whatever), what would you need to know in order to suggest a solution?

5. In order to help yourself become more aware of the subjectivity of your judgments, try this experiment:

The next time you grade your students, write down your reasons for whatever grade you assigned to a student. Then, imagine that you are the student. Study the reasons that your teacher gave to explain your grade. Ask yourself if you can accept these reasons and reflect on what you think of a teacher who would offer them. You might discover that your basis for assigning grades is prejudicial to some students, or lacks generosity, or is too vague. You might also discover, as some teachers have, that the conventional grading system is totally inadequate to evaluate the learning process. Some teachers have grown to resent it bitterly and have been driven to invent another system to complement the one they are forced to use.

Another experiment that might be helpful: Each time you give a grade to a student, grade your own perception of that student. The following questions might be useful:

1. To what extent does my own background block me from understanding the behavior of this student?

2. Are my own values greatly different from those of the student?

3. To what extent have I made an effort to understand how things look from this student's point of view?

4. To what extent am I rewarding or penalizing the student for his acceptance or rejection of my interests?

5. To what extent am I rewarding a student for merely saying what I want to hear, whether or not he believes or understands what he is saying?

You may discover that your answers to these questions are deeply disturbing. For example, you may find that you give the lowest grades mostly to those students you least understand, in which case, the problem is yours—isn't it?—not theirs. What we are driving at is this: too many teachers seem to believe that the evaluations they make of their students reflect only the "characteristics," "ability," and "behavior" of the students. The teacher merely records the grade that the student "deserves." This is complete nonsense, of course. A grade is as much a product of the teacher's characteristics, ability, and behavior as of the student's. Any procedure you can imagine that would increase your awareness of the role you play in "making" the student what you think he is will be helpful, even something like the following:

Keep track of the judgments you make about students. Every time you say words such as right, wrong, good, bad, correct, incorrect, smart, stupid, nice, annoying, polite, impertinent, neat, sloppy, etc., keep a record. Do it yourself or have a student do it. You can simply make a check on a sheet of paper that has been divided in two, with one column marked "+" and the other marked "–." Beyond the verbal judgments, you might keep track of the judgments you make that are made visible nonverbally, through facial expression, gesture, or general demeanor. Negative judgments are, not surprisingly, impediments to good learning, particularly if they have the effect of causing the learner to judge himself negatively.

Positive judgments, perhaps surprisingly, can also produce undesirable results. For example, if a learner becomes totally dependent upon the positive judgments of an authority (teacher) for both motivation and reward, what you have is an intellectual paraplegic incapable of any independent activity, intellectual or otherwise.

The point to all of this is to help you become conscious of the degree to which your language and thought is judgmental. You cannot avoid making judgments but you can become more conscious of the way in which you make them. This is critically important because once we judge someone or something we tend to stop thinking about them or it. Which means, among other things, that we behave in response to our judgments rather than to that which is being judged. People and things are processes. Judgments convert them into fixed states. This is one reason that judgments are commonly self-fulfilling. If a boy, for example, is judged as being "dumb" and a "nonreader" early in his school career, that judgment sets into motion a series of teacher behaviors that cause the judgment to become self-fulfilling.

What we need to do then, if we are seriously interested in helping students to become good learners, is to suspend or delay judgments about them. One manifestation of this is the ungraded elementary school. But you can practice suspending judgment yourself tomorrow. It doesn't require any major changes in anything in the school except your own behavior.

For example, the following incident—in this case outside of a classroom— is representative of the difference between a stereotypic and a suspended judgment.

A man and his seventeen-year-old son on Monday evening had a "discussion" about the need for the son to defer his social activities on week nights until he has finished doing all of the home work he has for school the next day.

It is now Wednesday evening, 48 hours later, about 7:30 P.M. Father is watching TV. Son emerges from his room and begins to put on a jacket.

FATHER: Where are you going?

SON: Out.

FATHER: Out where?

SON: Just out.

FATHER: Have you finished your homework?

SON: Not yet.

FATHER: I thought we decided [*that's the way parents talk*] that you wouldn't go out on week nights until you finished your home work.

SON: But I have to go out.

FATHER: What do you mean you "have to?"

SON: I just do.

FATHER: Well, you're not going out. You just have to learn to live up to the terms of the agreements you make.

SON: But. . . .

FATHER: That's all. I want no back talk.

MOTHER: Please. Let him go out. He'll be back soon.

FATHER: I don't want you butting in.

MOTHER: [*to son*] Go ahead. It will be all right
[Son exits.]

FATHER: [*in a rage*] What the hell do you mean by encouraging his impertinence. How do you expect him to learn responsibility if you side with him in an argument with me? How . . .

MOTHER: *[interrupting]* Do you know what tomorrow is?
FATHER: What the hell has that got to do with it? Tomorrow's Thursday.
M0THER: Yes, and it's your birthday.
FATHER: *[silence]*
MOTHER: Your son has been making a birthday gift for you at Jack's house. He wanted it to be a surprise for you tomorrow morning. A nice start for the day. He has just a bit more work to do on it to finish it. He wanted to get it done as early as possible tonight so he could bring it home and wrap it up for tomorrow. And then he'd still have time to do his homework.

Well, you see how easy it is to judge someone as something on the basis of *x* amount of data perceived in one way while simultaneously they are not only not that, but are something quite different.

Judgments are relative to the data upon which they are based and to the emotional state of the judge.

Learning to suspend judgment can be most liberating. Yon might find that it makes you a better learner (meaning maker) too.

6. Along the lines of the above, we would suggest an experiment that requires only imagination, but plenty of it. Suppose you could convince yourself that your students are the smartest children in the school; or, if that seems unrealistic, that they have the greatest potential of any class in the school. (After all, who can say for certain how much potential anyone has?) What do you imagine would happen? What would you do differently if you *acted* as if your students were capable of great achievements? And if you acted differently, what are the chances that many of your students would begin to act as if they *were* great achievers? We believe that the chances are quite good. There is, as we have noted, considerable evidence to indicate that people can become what others think they are. In fact, if you reflect on how anyone becomes anything, you are likely to conclude that becoming is almost always a product of expectations—one's own or someone else's. We are talking here about the concept of the "self-fulfilling prophecy." This refers to the fact that often when we predict that something will happen, the prediction itself contributes to making it happen. Nowhere is this idea more usable than in education, which is, or ought to be, concerned with the processes of becoming.

A *warning*: You will have great difficulty in imagining that your students are smart if you hold on to the belief that the stuff you know about, or would like to know about, constitutes the only ingredients of "smartness."

Once you abandon that idea, you may find that your students do, in fact, know a great deal of stuff, and that it is easier than you supposed to imagine they are the brightest children you ever had.

7. The extent to which you can try the following experiment depends on the degree to which the administration and the school community are rigid. In its most effective form, the experiment involves telling your students that all of them will get A's for the term and, of course, making good on your promise. At first, the students will not believe you, and it has sometimes taken as long as four weeks before all the students accept the situation. Once such acceptance is achieved, the students can begin to concentrate on learning, not their grades. There is no need for them to ask, "When is the midterm?" "Do we have to do a paper?" "How much weight is given to classwork?" and so on. If such questions do arise, you can reply, honestly, by saying that the questions are not necessary since the grades have already been given and each student will receive the highest possible grade the system allows. (We can assure you that such questions will come up because students have been conditioned to think of education as being indistinguishable from grades.) The next step is to help the students discover what kind of knowledge they think is worth knowing and to help them decide what procedures can most profitably be used to find out what they want to know. You will have to remind your students that there is no need for them to make suggestions that they think will please *you*. Neither is there any need for them to accept your suggestions out of fear of reprisal. Once they internalize this idea, they will pursue vigorously whatever course their sense of relevance dictates. Incidentally, they are likely to view your proposals not as threats, but as possibilities. In fact, you may be astonished at how seriously your own suggestions are regarded once the coercive dimension is removed.

If you are thinking that students, given such conditions, will not do any work, you are wrong. Most will. But, of course, not all. There are always a few who will view the situation as an opportunity to "goof off." So what? It is a small price to pay for providing the others with perhaps the only decent intellectual experience they will ever have in school. Beyond that, the number of students who do "goof off" is relatively small when compared with those who, in conventional school environments, tune out.

There is no way of our predicting what "syllabus" your students will evolve. It depends. Especially on them, but also on you and how willing you are to permit students to take control of the direction of their own studies. If you, or your administration and community, could not bear this possibility, perhaps you could try the experiment on a limited basis: for example, for a "unit" or even a specific assignment.

8. Perhaps you have noticed that most examinations and, indeed, syllabi and curricula deal almost exclusively with the past. The future hardly exists in school. Can you remember ever asking or being asked in school a question like "If such and such occurs, what do you think will happen"? A question of this type is usually not regarded as "serious" and would rarely play a central role in any "serious" examination. When a future-oriented question is introduced in school, its purpose is usually to "motivate" or to find out how "creative" the students can be. But the point is that the world we live in is changing so rapidly that a future-orientation is essential for everybody. Its development in schools is our best insurance against a generation of "future shock" sufferers.

You can help by including in all of your class discussions and examinations some questions that deal with the future. For example:

What effects on our society do you think the following technological inventions will have?
   a. the electric car
   b. the television-telephone
   c. the laser beam
   d. the 2,000-mph jet
   e. central data storage
   f. disposable "paper" clothing
   g. interplanetary communication
   h. language-translation machines

Can you identify two or three ideas, beliefs, and practices that human beings will need to give up for their future well-being?

In case you are thinking that such questions as these are usable only in the higher grades, we want to assure you that young children (even third-graders) frequently provide imaginative and pointed answers to future-oriented questions, provided that the questions are suitably adapted to their level of understanding. Perhaps you can make it a practice to include future-oriented questions at least once a week in all your classes. It is especially important that this be done for young children. After all, by the time they have finished school, the future you have asked them to think about will be the present.

9. Anyone interested in helping students deal with the future (not to mention the present) would naturally be concerned, even preoccupied, with media of

communication. We recommend to you, of course, the books of Marshall McLuhan, especially *Understanding Media*. We think that the most productive way to respond to McLuhan's challenge (as he has suggested) is not to examine his statements but to examine the media. In other words don't dwell on the question "Is McLuhan right in saying such and such?" Instead, focus on the question "In what ways are media affecting our society?" Your answers may turn out to be better than McLuhan's. More important, if you allow your students to consider the question, their answers may be better than McLuhan's. And even more important than that, the process of searching for such answers, once learned, will be valuable to your students, throughout their lives.

Therefore, we suggest that media study become an integral part of all your classes. No matter what "subject" you are teaching, media are relevant. For example, if you are a history teacher, you can properly consider questions about the effects of media on political and social developments. If you are a science teacher, the entire realm of technology is open to you and your students, including a consideration of the extent to which technology influences the direction of the evolutionary process. If you are an English teacher, the role of media in creating new literatures, new audiences for literature, and new modes of perceiving literature is entirely within your province. In short, regardless of your subject and the age of your students, we suggest that you include the study of media as a normal part of the curriculum. You might bear in mind that your students are quite likely to be more perceptive and even more knowledgeable about the structure and meaning of newer media than you. For example, there are many teachers who haven't yet noticed that young people are enormously interested in poetry—the poetry that is now on LP records and sung by Joan Baez, Phil Ochs, and Bob Dylan; or that young people are equally interested in essays of social and political criticism as *heard* on records by Lenny Bruce, Bill Cosby, Godfrey Cambridge, Mort Sahl, et al.

10. Before making our final suggestion, we want to say a word of assurance about the revolution we are urging. There is nothing in what we have said that precludes the use, *at one time or another,* of any of the conventional methods and materials of learning. For certain specific purposes, a lecture, a film, a textbook, a packaged unit, even a punishment, may be entirely justified. What we are asking for is a methodological and psychological shift in emphasis in the roles of teacher and student, a fundamental change in the nature of the classroom environment. In fact, one model for such an environment already exists in the schools—oddly, at the extreme ends of the schooling process. A good primary-grade teacher as well as a good graduate-student

adviser operate largely on the subversive assumptions expressed in this book. They share a concern for process as against product. They are learner-and problem-oriented. They share a certain disdain for syllabi. They allow their students to pursue that which is relevant to the learner. But there is a 15-year gap between the second grade and advanced graduate study. The gap can be filled, we believe, by teachers who understand the spirit of our orientation. It is neither required nor desirable that *everything* about one's performance as a teacher be changed. Just the most important things.

11. Our last suggestion is perhaps the most difficult. It requires honest self-examination. Ask yourself how you came to know whatever things you feel are worth knowing. This may sound like a rather abstract inquiry, but when undertaken seriously it frequently results in startling discoveries. For example, some teachers have discovered that there is almost nothing valuable they know that was *told* to them by someone else. Other teachers have discovered that their most valuable knowledge was not learned in a recognizable sequence. Still others begin to question the meaning of the phrase "valuable knowledge" and wonder if anything they learned in school was "valuable." Such self-examination can be most unsettling as you can well imagine. English teachers have discovered that they hate Shakespeare; history teachers, that everything they know about the War of the Roses is useless; science teachers, that they really wanted to be druggists. The process, once begun, leads in many unexpected directions but most often to the question "Why am I a teacher, anyway?" Some honest answers that this question has produced are as follows:

- I can control people.
- I can tyrannize people.
- I have captive audiences.
- I have my summers off.
- I love seventeenth-century nondramatic Elizabethan literature.
- I don't know.
- The pay is good, considering the amount of work I actually do.

Obviously, none of these answers is very promising for the future of our children. But each in its way is a small act of positive subversion because it represents a teacher's honest attempt to know himself. The teacher who *recognizes* that he is interested, say, in exercising tyrannical control over others is taking a first step toward subverting that interest. But the question "Why am I a teacher, anyway?" also produces answers that are encouraging: for example, that one can participate in the making of intelligence and, thereby, in the development of a decent society. As soon as a teacher recognizes that this is, in fact, the reason he became a teacher, then the subversion of our existing educational system strikes him as a necessity. As we have been trying to say: we agree.

Neil Postman is an author and professor at the New School for Social Research.

Charles Weingartner (deceased) was a professor at Queen's College.

PART IV

What Do Good Schools Look Like?

Though a K-8 facility, Thayer is a small school with fewer than four hundred students attending this tasteful stone and brick building situated in a lovely, bucolic setting. As a bedroom community to one of the nation's largest cities, students at Thayer generally hale from homes of considerable affluence. Thayer boasts strong music and art programs, numerous after-school activities, including drama and the usual sports teams, computers with video streaming capabilities in every classroom, and an abundance of actively involved parent volunteers. The teachers at Thayer tend to be happy too. The average class size is under twenty students, and there is so little turnover in the staff that Thayer hasn't advertised a teaching position in years.

This year, like most years before it, students at Thayer Elementary School earned the distinction of having the highest test scores in the state. Tom Rogers, the principal at Thayer for the last six years, takes special pleasure in announcing this fact every year at the June Parent's Night meeting. He states, "Student performance on reading, writing, and math has been consistent enough for the State Department of Education to label the school 'high performing' and 'a model school where exemplary teaching and learning are the norm.'"

The Johnsons were thrilled to move to the Thayer district over the summer. And, when they arrived for their first Parent-Teacher Night in early September, they were brimming with anticipation when their daughter's teacher began her introduction.

"We've purchased a new basal reader for all sixth grade students," the teacher began. "We like this series because each reading is short and the text is accompanied by a teacher's edition that contains plenty of discussion questions, quizzes, and worksheets."

As their daughter's new teacher continued, the Johnsons thumbed through the basal readers. The Johnsons were crestfallen. Between the hard covers of the basal reader were no fewer than 25 great novels, each abridged into 5–10 page versions of the originals. More depressing, their daughter had already read most of the novels in their original form. The teacher continued and encouraged parents to walk around the room and examine student work from the previous year. The Johnsons wondered about the geography worksheets that required, for example, students to identify country names based upon longitude and latitude coordinates, the "A-Z List" which asked students to match Egypt-related vocabulary words with their definitions, and reams of math dittos. By the end of the evening, the Johnsons had serious questions about whether Thayer was the right place for their daughter.

Is Thayer a good school? What are the defining characteristics of a good school?

13

The Paideia Proposal

Rediscovering the Essence of Education

Mortimer Adler

In the first 80 years of this century, we have met the obligation imposed on us by the principle of equal educational opportunity, but only in a quantitative sense. Now as we approach the end of the century, we must achieve equality in qualitative terms. This means a completely on-track system of schooling. It means, at the basic level, giving all the young the same kind of schooling, whether or not they are college bound.

We are aware that children, although equal in their common humanity and fundamental human rights, are unequal as individuals, differing in their capacity to learn. In addition, the homes and environments from which they come to school are unequal—either predisposing the child for schooling or doing the opposite.

Consequently, the Paideia Proposal, faithful to the principle of equal education opportunity, includes the suggestion that inequalities due to environmental factors must be overcome by some form of preschool preparation—at least one year for all and two or even three for some. We know that to make such preschool tutelage compulsory at the public expense would be tantamount to increasing the duration of compulsory schooling from 12 years to

NOTE: From *The Paideia Proposal: An Educational Manifesto* by Mortimer J. Adler. Copyright 1982. Published by Collier Books, Macmillan Publishing Company, (on behalf of the Paideia Group). Reprinted with permission from the Paideia Group.

13, 14, or 15 years. Nevertheless, we think that this preschool adjunct to the 12 years of compulsory basic schooling is so important that some way must be found to make it available for all and to see that all use it to advantage.

The Essentials of Basic Schooling

The objectives of basic schooling should be the same for the whole school population. In our current two-track or multitrack system, the learning objectives are not the same for all. And even when the objectives aimed at those on the upper track are correct, the course of study now provided does not adequately realize these correct objectives. On all tracks in our current system, we fail to cultivate proficiency in the common tasks of learning, and we especially fail to develop sufficiently the indispensable skills of learning.

The uniform objectives of basic schooling should be threefold. They should correspond to three aspects of the common future which all the children are destined:

(1) Our society provides all children ample opportunity for personal development. Given such opportunity, each individual is under a moral obligation to make the most of himself and his life. Basic schooling must facilitate this accomplishment. (2) All the children will become, when of age, full-fledged citizens with responsibilities. Basic schooling must do everything it can to make them good citizens, able to perform the duties of citizenship with all the trained intelligence that each is able to achieve. (3) When they are grown, all (or certainly most) of the children will engage in some form of work to earn a living. Basic schooling must prepare them for earning a living, but not by training them for this or that specific job while they are still in school.

To achieve these three objectives, the character of basic schooling must be general and liberal. It should have a single, required, 12-year course of study for all, with no electives except one—an elective choice with regard to a second language, to be selected from such modern languages as French, German, Italian, Spanish, Russian, and Chinese. The elimination of all electives, with this one exception, excludes what should be excluded—all forms of specialization, including particularized job training.

In its final form, the Paideia Proposal will detail this required course of study, but I will summarize the curriculum here in its bare outline. It consists of three main columns of teaching and learning, running through the 12 years and progressing, of course, from the simple to the more complex, from the less difficult to the more difficult, as the students grow older. Understand: The three columns (see Table 1) represent three distinct modes of teaching and learning. They do not represent a series of courses. A specific course or class may employ more than one mode of teaching and learning, but all three modes are essential to the overall course of study.

The first column is devoted to knowledge in three subject areas: (A) language, literature, and the fine arts; (B) mathematics and natural science; (C) history, geography, and social studies.

The second column is devoted to developing the intellectual skills of learning. These include all the language skills necessary for thought and communication—the skills of reading, writing, speaking, listening and scientific skills; the skills of observing, measuring, estimating, and calculating; and skills in the use of the computer and of other scientific instruments. Together, these skills make it possible to think clearly and critically. They once were called the liberal arts—the intellectual skills indispensable to being competent as a learner.

The third column is devoted to enlarging the understanding of ideas and values. The materials of the third column are books (not textbooks), and other products of human artistry. These materials include books of every variety—historical, scientific, and philosophical as well as poems, stories, and essays—and also individual pieces of music, visual art, dramatic productions, dance productions, film, or television productions. Music and works of visual art can be used in seminars in which ideas are discussed; but as with poetry and fiction, they also are to be experienced aesthetically, to be enjoyed and admired for their excellence.

The three columns do not correspond to separate courses, nor is one kind of teaching and learning necessarily confined to any one class. In this connection, exercises in the composition of poetry, music, and visual works and in the production of dramatic works should be used to develop the appreciation of excellence.

The three columns represent three different kinds of learning on the part of the student and three different kinds of instruction on the part of teachers.

In the first column, the students are engaged in acquiring information and organized knowledge about nature, man, and human society. The method of instruction here, using textbooks and manuals, is didactic. The teacher lectures, invites responses from the students, monitors the acquisition of knowledge, and tests that acquisition in various ways.

In the second column, the students are engaged in developing habits of performance, which is all that is involved in the development of an art or skill. Art, skill, or technique is nothing more than a cultivated, habitual ability to do a certain kind of thing well, whether that is swimming and dancing, or reading and writing. Here, students are acquiring linguistic, mathematical, scientific, and historical *know-how* in contrast to what they acquire in the first column, which is *know-that* with respect to language,

Table 1

	Column One	*Column Two*	*Column Three*
Goals	Acquisition of Organized Knowledge	Development of Intellectual Skills and Skill of Learning	Improved Understanding of Ideas and Values
Means	By Means of Didactic Instruction, Lecturing, and Textbooks	By Means of Coaching, Exercises, Supervised Practices	By Means of Maieutic or Socratic Questioning and Active Participation
Subject Areas, Operations, and Activities	Language, Literature, and Fine Arts; Mathematics and Natural Science; History, Geography, and Social Studies	Reading, Writing, Speaking, Listening, Calculating, Problem Solving, Observing, Measuring, Estimating, Exercising Critical Judgment	Discussion of Books (Not Textbooks) and Other Works of Art; Involvement in Music, Drama, and Visual Arts

literature, and the fine arts, mathematics and science, history geography, and social studies. Here, the method of instruction cannot be didactic or monitorial; it cannot be dependent on textbooks. It must be coaching, the same kind used in the gym to develop bodily skills; only here it is used by a different kind of coach in the classroom to develop intellectual skills.

In the third column, students are engaged in a process of enlightenment, the process whereby they develop their understanding of the basic and controlling ideas in all fields of subject matter and come to appreciate better all the human values embodied in works of art. Here, students move progressively from understanding less to understanding more—understanding better what they already know and appreciating more what they already have experienced. Here, the method of instruction cannot be either didactic or coaching. It must be the Socratic, or maieutic, method of questioning and discussing. It should not occur in an ordinary classroom with the students sitting in rows and the teacher in front of the class, but in a seminar room, with the students sitting around a table and the teacher sitting with them as an equal, even though a little older and wiser.

Of these three main elements in the required curriculum, the third column is completely innovative. Nothing like this is done in our schools, and because it is completely absent from the ordinary curriculum of basic schooling, the students never have the experience of having their minds addressed in a challenging way of being asked to think about the important ideas, to express their thoughts to defend their opinions in a reasonable fashion.

The only thing that is innovative about the second column is the insistence that the method of instruction here must be coaching, carried on either with one student at a time or with very small groups of students. Nothing else can be effective in the development of a skill, be it bodily or intellectual. The absence of such individualized coaching in our schools explains why most of the students cannot read well, write well, speak well, listen well, or perform well any of the other basic intellectual operations.

The three columns are closely interconnected and integrated, but the middle column—the one concerned with linguistic, mathematical, and scientific skills—is central. It both supports and is supported by the other two columns. All the intellectual skills with which it is concerned must be exercised in the study of the three basic subject-matters and in acquiring knowledge about them, and these intellectual skills must be exercised in the seminars devoted to the discussion of books and other things.

In addition to the three main columns in the curriculum, ascending through the 12 years of basic schooling, there are three adjuncts: One is 12 years of physical training, accompanied by instruction in bodily care and hygiene. The second, running through something less than 12 years, is the development of basic manual skills, such as cooking, sewing, carpentry, and the operation of all kinds of machines. The third, reserved for the last year or two, is an introduction to the whole world of work—the range of occupations in which human beings earn their livings. This is not particularized job training. It is the very opposite. It aims at a broad understanding of what is involved in working for a living and of the various ways in which that can be done. If, at the end of 12 years, students wish training for specific jobs, they should get that in two-year community or junior colleges, or on the job itself, or in technical institutes of one sort or another. Everything that has not been specifically mentioned as occupying the time of the school day should be reserved for after-hours and have the status of extra curricular activities.

Please, note: The required course of study just described is as important for what it displaces as for what it introduces.

It displaces a multitude of elective courses, especially those offered in our secondary schools, most of which make little or no contribution to general, liberal education. It eliminates all narrowly I specialized job training, which now abounds in our schools. It throws out of the curriculum and into the category of optional extracurricular activities a variety of things that have little or no educational value.

If it did not call for all these displacements, there would not be enough time in the school day or year to accomplish everything that is essential to the general, liberal learning that must be the content of basic schooling.

The Quintessential Element

So far, I have set forth the bare essentials of the Paideia Proposal with regard to basic schooling. I have not yet mentioned the quintessential element—the sine qua non—without which nothing else can possibly come to fruition, no matter how sound it might be in principle. The heart of the matter is the quality of learning and the quality of teaching that occupies the school day, not to mention the quality of the homework after school.

First, the learning must be active. It must use the whole mind, not just the memory. It must be learning by discovery, in which the student, never the teacher, is the primary agent. Learning by discovery, which is the only genuine learning, may be either unaided or aided. It is unaided only for geniuses. For most students, discovery must be aided.

Here is where teachers come in—as aides in the process of learning by discovery not as knowers who attempt to put the knowledge they have into the minds of their students. The quality of the teaching, in short, depends crucially upon how the teacher conceives his role in the process of learning, and that must be as an aide to the student's process of discovery.

I am prepared for the questions that must be agitating you by now: How and where will we get the teachers who can perform as teachers should? How will we be able to staff the program with teachers so trained that they will be competent to provide the quality of instruction required for the quality of learning desired?

The first part of our answer to these questions is negative: We cannot get the teachers we need for the Paideia program from schools of education as they are now constituted. As teachers are now trained for teaching, they simply will not do. The ideal—an impracticable ideal—would be to ask for teachers who are, themselves, truly educated human beings. But truly educated human beings are too rare. Even if we could draft all who are now alive, there still would be far too few to staff our schools.

Well, then, what can we look for? Look for teachers who are in the process of becoming educated human beings, who are themselves deeply motivated to develop their own minds. Assuming this is not too much to ask for the present, how should teachers be schooled and trained in the future? First, they should have the same kind of basic schooling that is recommended in the Paideia Proposal. Second, they should have additional schooling, at the college and even the university level, in which the same kind of general, liberal learning is carried on at advanced levels—more deeply, broadly, and intensively than it can be done in the first 12 years of schooling. Third, they must be given something analogous to the clinical experience in the training of physicians. They must engage in practice—teaching under supervision, which is another way of saying that they must be coached in the arts of teaching, not just given didactic instruction in educational psychology and in pedagogy. Finally, and most important of all, they must learn how to teach well by being exposed to the performances of those who are masters of the arts involved in teaching.

It is by watching a good teacher at work that they will be able to perceive what is involved in the process of assisting others to learn by discovery. Perceiving it, they must then try to emulate what they observe, and through this process, they slowly will become good teachers themselves.

The Paideia Proposal recognizes the need for three different kinds of institutions at the collegiate level: The two-year community or junior college should offer a wide choice of electives that give students some training in one or another specialized field, mainly those fields of study that have something to do with earning a living. The four-year college also should offer a wide variety of electives, to be chosen by students who aim at the various professional or technical occupations that require advanced study. Those elective majors chosen by students should be accompanied, for all students, by one required minor, in which the kind of general and liberal learning that was begun at the level of basic schooling is continued at a higher level in the four years of college. And we should have still a third type of collegiate institution—a four-year college in which general, liberal learning at a higher level constitutes a required course of study that is to be taken by all students. It is this third type of college, by the way, that should be attended by all who plan to become teachers in our basic schools.

At the university level, there should be a continuation of general, liberal learning at a still higher level to accompany intensive specialization in this or that field of science or scholarship, this or that learned profession. Our insistence on the continuation of general, liberal learning at all the higher levels of schooling stems from our concern with the worst cultural disease that is rampant in our society—that of specialization.

There is no question that our technologically advanced industrial society needs specialists of all sorts. There is no question that the advancement of knowledge in all fields of science and scholarship, and in all the learned specialization. But for the sake of preserving and enhancing our cultural traditions, as well as for the health of science and scholarship, we need specialists who also are generalists—generally cultivated human beings, not just good plumbers. We need truly educated human beings who can perform their special tasks better precisely because they have general cultivation as well as intensely specialized training.

Changes indeed are needed in higher education, but those improvements can not reasonably be expected unless improvement in basic schooling makes that possible.

The Future of Our Free Institutions

I already have declared as emphatically as I know how that the quality of human life in our society depends on the quality of the schooling we give our young people, both basic and advanced. But a marked elevation in the quality of human life is not the only reason improving the quality of schooling is so necessary—not the only reason we must move heaven and earth to stop the deterioration of our schools and turn them in the opposite direction. The other reason is to safeguard the future of our free institutions.

They cannot prosper, they may not even survive, unless we do something to rescue our schools from their current deplorable deterioration. Democracy, in the full sense of that term, came into existence only in this century and only in a few countries on earth, among which the United States is an outstanding example. But democracy came into existence in this century, only in its initial conditions, all of which hold out promises for the future but remain to be fulfilled. And if they are not, our free institutions are doomed to decay and wither away.

We face many insistently urgent problems. Our prosperity and even our survival depend on the solution of those problems—the threat of nuclear war, the exhaustion of essential resources and of supplies of energy, the pollution or spoilage of the environment, the spiraling of inflation accompanied by the spread of unemployment.

To solve these problems, we need resourceful and innovative leadership. For that to arise and be effective, an educated populace is needed. Trained intelligence—not only on the part of leaders, but also on the part of followers—holds the key to the solution of the problems our society faces. Achieving peace, prosperity and plenty could put us on the threshold of an early paradise. But a much better education system than now exists also is needed, for that alone can carry us across the threshold. Without it, a poorly schooled population will not be able to put to good use the opportunities afforded by the achievement of the general welfare. Those who are not schooled to enjoy society can only despoil its institutions and corrupt themselves.

Mortimer Adler (deceased) was a professor at the University of Chicago and founder of the Great Books Movement.

14

When Learning Matters

Using Learning Plans to Educate One Student at a Time

Elliot Washor

One hundred years ago in *Atlantic Monthly*, William James wrote,

> In children we observe a ripening of impulses and interests in a certain deter-
> minate order. Creeping, walking, climbing, imitating, vocal sounds, con-
> structing, drawing, calculating, possess the child in succession. Of course, the
> proper pedagogic moment to work in skill and to clinch the useful habit is
> when the native impulse is most acutely present. Crowd on the athletic
> opportunities, the mental arithmetic, the verse-learning, the drawing, the
> botany, or what not, the moment you have reason to think the hour is ripe.

James' thoughts make me believe that when learning matters, schools are
student-centered. They are places that encourage, generate and sustain the
abilities and talents of every child. Our schools need to be places where

---

NOTE: Previously published in *Personalized Learning*, pp. 1–16, edited by Joseph DiMartino,
John Clarke, and Denise Wolk. Reprinted by permission of Scarecrow Education.

learning matters, but instead most of the time they are places where only what is being taught matters. From early on the content starts to matter more than learning it. This includes at what grade material is taught rather than what students are learning.

Ian Kelly, a first grade student living in Ireland recently presented me with a telling riddle to ponder that went like this:

Question: Who's still talking when everyone has stopped listening?

Answer: The teacher

This riddle lets us in on the secret that every child knows—that in school, teaching matters more than learning.

This chapter will focus on the importance of creating student-centered learning environments using *Personalized Learning Plans* (PLPs) to engage students in their own learning experiences. I discuss my own experience with the difference between the PLPs used at the Met and the *Individualized Education Plans* (IEPs) that are commonly used for students with special needs. The importance of creating a supportive link between the student, family, advisor and mentors in creating a challenging and personalized educational plan for every student is crucial, and examples of how the process works at the Met are presented here. By allowing students the opportunity to learn using hands-on experience they are able to demonstrate proficiency through a variety of non-traditional methods. In the end, we have found that students with PLPs are able to utilize the experience they've gained to determine their future goals for college and beyond.

The Met

The Metropolitan Regional Career and Technical Center (the Met) is a five-year-old Rhode Island public high school with a mission to rethink and revamp the entire delivery of secondary school education. As researcher Adria Steinberg puts it, the Met "turns education on its head" by starting with the student instead of with a preset curriculum and classroom structured learning. The Met is a school that uses real world experiences to build skills and knowledge, one student at a time. By engaging its students in real projects with working adults, the Met prepares them for college, work, and citizenship. It demonstrates how effective a school can be when the entire community is a resource for education.

All Met students have their own Personalized Learning Plan based on their particular interests, which are continually updated by the student and her teacher, parents and mentors. Met students are intrinsically motivated to learn, because they have a say in choosing the work they do.

To carry out their learning plans, Met students establish a unique intern relationship called Learning Through Internship (LTI) with a mentor in the community. The LTI is based on the premise that adolescents need to learn in real world settings and interact effectively with adults. The primary function of the school is to provide the infrastructure that supports that learning. The student works on learning goals and develops a portfolio of work as evidence of achieving those goals. The mentor is a role model, content expert and learning resource.

Over the years, we have enhanced our work around learning plans so they have changed and evolved as we have changed. We have connected them and acculturated them into the Met as we grew from using them with incoming ninth graders to translating learning plans into a driving force for our students' entry into Senior Institute in the eleventh grade and as a resource for our innovative college transcript. The Met's evolution of the learning plan is a statement of what educators can do to make a community accountable for learning and engage families in learning if educators have students and families in mind.

All schools are mandated to use learning plans for children with Special Needs, but does this ensure that learning is personalized? Mandates do not ensure that learning plans are student-centered and that learning really matters. A student-centered environment is key to the success of learning plans that allow for accountability, flexibility and family engagement.

Michael's Story: IEP Versus PLP

The following story is my own account of my son Michael's Individualized Education Plan (IEP) meeting from a school he attended. Here I'm in the role of parent.

In his middle grades my son Michael was diagnosed with a language/reading disability. I will share here what transpired at a learning plan (Individualized Education Plan) meeting at his middle school. These meetings are mandatory for any child who is diagnosed as Special Needs.

As I went into the room you could see some of the testers talking with each other but keeping their distance from me. There were 8–10 people assembled in a circle. The group included the guidance counselor, special education teacher, school psychologist, two school testers, the assistant principal, and two of Michael's teachers. There were eight staff members from the school, and myself as a parent. It was quite intimidating.

The guidance counselor started the meeting. She introduced everyone and then asked the school psychologist to present and analyze the results of the test and observational data. It seems that the data showed Michael was easily distracted, tended to daydream, did a lot of drawing but was not a discipline problem. One tester said he fit into the average range of intelligence showing some deficits and confusion when it came to putting details together. Another said his issues in learning to write are that his fine motor coordination is below par. One by one, each person talked about Michael through the data either from formalized tests or his grades in school. As the meeting went on, one or two more of his teachers came in late and joined us around the circle. Each one pointed out Michael's deficits. It was a very uncomfortable feeling for everyone sitting around the table. I didn't know anyone there.

As they presented their evaluations and remediations, it was also clear that some were uncomfortable talking, some even broke out in hives, and others were displaying their discomfort through their body language.

From my perspective, it was uncomfortable as a parent to hear qualified educational experts talk about my child using test data and a smattering of observations. The intent is to somehow use scientific instruments that give a profile of a child but nothing can be further from the truth. I can't believe the original intent of any law was to mandate testing over really knowing a child well.

All the while I sat there listening, and I must confess I was doodling a bit to deal with my uneasiness. Finally, the guidance counselor said in summation, "So it seems everything is going along well. Michael is receiving some extra support in reading and language development. We are working on his writing. Thanks for coming. Do you have any questions?"

Now, no one in the room knew me, and they only learned that I was a principal because I told them that during our introductions. I said, "I have some things to say. First, all of you talked about Michael through your findings, but do you really know my son? Do any of you know he is a protégé jazz guitarist who practices three hours a night? Do you realize the tremendous intellectual focus, concentration and dexterity it takes to play an instrument at that level? Do you know that athletically he is the fastest student in the school? (So much for his fine or gross motor coordination issues.) And do you know that he is well liked and respected by other students and seems to get along well with all the teachers in the building? People on both sides of his family have been musicians and artists for generations. This may account for his doodling but maybe not. Maybe he is not connected to what he is doing in school. You said, he is easily distracted, and doodles. Do his doodles look anything like this?" I turned the paper I was doodling on around so all could see. I smiled and everyone was a bit relieved. I did this in a way that was not casting blame but opening up a conversation about looking at the strengths and weaknesses. As my friend Bill Ayers from Chicago says, "Our primary responsibility as teachers is to give hope."

After my comments we really started talking about Michael. It was apparent that these folks really do care about children, but there is no way in this system for people to really care. There was no way for these educators to really look at the whole child, strengths and weaknesses, and build learning environments that will use strengths to get at a weakness.

Like most systems, there is a distrust of parents as part of the educational planning where they can be used as a resource. The work of student learning is relegated to what has been mandated either as remedial plans or standards-based reform. These mandates take all the craft, art, and in many cases, even the technical components out of teaching and learning. It is exactly the idea Dewey warned us about when he stated, "All reforms which rest simply upon the enactment of law, or the threatening of certain penalties, or upon changes in mechanical or outward arrangements, are transitory or futile."

Michael graduated from the Met last year, and now attends Wheaton College where he is majoring in music and business. At the Met he had a learning plan where he, his parents, advisors/teachers and mentors were involved in his learning, and we all knew one another well. Everyone was encouraged to sit in on his learning plan meetings. His learning has evolved over the years to a place where things in Michael's life make sense for the person he is, where he wants to go, and what he wants to learn.

The Importance of Family Engagement

My voice is that of a parent and an educator when I agree with Cremin's (1976) statement " . . . the real message of the Coleman and Jencks studies of equal educational opportunities: not that the school is powerless but that the family is powerful." Family Engagement at the Met is very different than most schools and our learning plan meetings are a major part of the difference. The average family comes to the Met to learning plan meetings and exhibitions seven times a year. In the past, these families rarely went into their children's schools. In my own experience, I went to my son's school only for parent night, one or two events, and an IEP meeting. It was not that I didn't want to go to the school; it was that there was nothing for me to go to. As a matter of fact, one time I wanted to see the principal and the secretary told me I would have to wait three weeks for an appointment. The tipping point that gets families engaged at the Met is that families are used as a resource at learning plan meetings and are an important part of the learning process.

Families are not only participants in learning plans but at times are the topic of a project. A Met graduate who is now attending college in Rhode Island did a project on fibromyalgia, a condition with which her mom was diagnosed. This project illustrates the depth of the work that can be accomplished through an LTI, and how Met learning goals are woven into the academic needs of a student and agreed on at a Learning Plan meeting.

When Priscilla Santana came back to school in the fall of 10th grade, she had a new interest. Her mother had had carpal tunnel surgery over the summer and was doing physical therapy as part of her recovery. Priscilla's interest was awakened to physical therapy, and she decided that she wanted to learn more, both for herself and to help her mother. After searching, interviewing and job shadowing, she started an LTI with a mentor in a physical therapy clinic. At a learning plan meeting, Priscilla, her mentor, her parents, and her advisor, Rachel, identified a product that the clinic needed, and it became Priscilla's responsibility and the basis for her project.

The following is an excerpt from Priscilla's learning plan on the project proposal:

Product

An informational pamphlet for patients recently diagnosed with the condition fibromyalgia.

Investigation

First try: Why do there seem to be more cases of fibromyalgia diagnosed in Rhode Island than in Florida, as my mentor thinks from talking to another physical therapist down there? Is it doctor diagnosis and referral to physical therapy? Is it weather-related? Are there more retirees in Florida and therefore it's work-related? What accounts for the difference?

(Continued)

(Continued)

Second try: A thorough understanding of fibromyalgia, its causes, manifestations and various treatment options. Learn the "tender points" used to diagnose patients. Understand the physics of torque for biomechanics and how this translates to lifting objects.

Reflection:

(Synopsis of student's journal writing and student narrative)

The first investigation didn't work because fibromyalgia is a recently developed diagnosis and even the Center for Disease Control had no information. I planned to survey doctors but when I tried to set up an interview with a doctor to look at my survey, he didn't respond. I had no idea that this kind of information might not be available yet and that it would be so hard to get doctors. This was frustrating and made me nervous because I was worried my project wouldn't be good. But then Rachel (my advisor) helped me see that it just meant sometimes projects don't go the way you plan and you have to be on top of it and make a change when you need to. So that's when we changed to the second investigation and I did all the research.

I was so surprised that I could read a lot of the medical journals and get the information I needed. My mentor also helped me by answering my questions to understand what I was reading about. I learned a lot of new terms like pressure points and bone names and what it meant that there might be a disease. I was also surprised to learn about how torque is measured in lifting objects. And when I had to put it all together, I learned how to use PageMaker to put it on a computer layout.

I learned so much in this project, not just about this syndrome, but also about myself and how I learn and how I do a project.

The concept of LTIs goes hand in hand with developing learning plans and portfolios for post high school goals, whether it's college, vocational school, apprenticeships or directly to work. From working on the learning plans, each student will have a portfolio that allows him or her to customize all of their experiences for application to each college or work situation.

Throughout this project Priscilla's parents, her mentor, and her teacher were all in agreement about her learning. Priscilla is now pursuing a college education. Her parents have been part of her education at the Met from her beginning enrollment. They have watched her develop interests in writing, poetry and nursing. They have questioned her on her learning journey as well as gotten to know her teacher Rachel, her mentors and her principals. The learning plan meeting is one of the key places where this forum takes place and everyone can be accountable.

Learning Plans and Accountability

The notion of high stakes accountability has been thrust on schools from the many varied constituencies that want schools to show what children are learning, and to be more precise, to see if what is being taught is being learned, and why it is not. Being accountable is one of those ideas that everyone agrees on, for surely students, schools, teachers, and parents must account for learning. For the most part, accountability has been measured by whether a child achieves a given content or skill standard by passing a test on a certain amount of information.

On the other hand, learning plans offer a way to account for student learning one student at a time, by literally bringing everyone to the table to agree upon what the goals for learning are in a given amount of time, and over an extended period of time. This is what happens at the Met. Our students demonstrate proficiency in what they have learned during student exhibitions that are held at least four times this year. Each student presents work and evidence of learning before a public panel of teachers, parents, mentors, students, and other community members who know him well or bring relevant field expertise. Panelists evaluate the student's work and presentation skills against criteria pre-determined by the teacher and student, and against the standards of their own field. Through these exhibitions, students demonstrate mastery of skills and knowledge. Because a student's work at the Met is not quantified by the use of traditional courses or credits, other methods are needed to document what is accomplished. One of these methods is the creation of a portfolio, a comprehensive collection of artifacts of student work. The contents vary among students, but they typically include final papers and drafts, photos of products, notes, videotape of exhibitions, artwork, narrative reports and other assessments, and a student-authored journal. In the end, Met students prove what they learned through a comprehensive demonstration of skills, not just by fielding questions on a standardized test.

A learning plan meeting is not always easy to facilitate or to participate in. Parents, students, and teachers may disagree but in order to connect everyone to learning, our teachers learn to facilitate and negotiate learning plans starting from student interest, and the skills and knowledge a student has. Then, they develop a way to bring that student toward reaching his/her goals. Learning plans have become part of our culture at the Met. Our accountability to our students, their families and to ourselves is to ensure our students graduate and are prepared to move on to forms of higher education and the workforce. After four years of learning plan meetings and LTIs, the Met's first graduating class had every student accepted to a post secondary institute. Students, their families, their mentors and teachers were involved through learning plan meetings every step of the way where education was planned one student at a time.

How LTIs Help Students Shape Their Own Future

We have students such as John who have amassed experiences in a wide variety of LTI situations. For the Met, John's family and for John, this is fine. John was born in New York City and came to Providence while he was in middle school. When he came to the Met in ninth grade at his first learning plan meeting, he expressed an interest in animation. His first year LTI was at a local graphic design studio, a start-up organization that is contracted by other businesses to do animation and multi-media presentations. He worked along side programmers and business managers alike and developed a flipbook of cartoons and a Claymation video. Simultaneously, he took a short acting class at a local theatre company and discovered he had an interest in theater. His interest led him to a summer job as the sound manager for a local theater group's production of "Fame."

When John returned to school in the fall of his 10th grade year, he found out about internship opportunities with the state judicial system. Just a little over a year before he had been involved with the legislative hearings for the opening of the Met and had testified before the House Finance Committee. This new opportunity interested him. At his 10th grade learning plan meeting, everyone agreed on an LTI at the Supreme and Superior Court of Rhode Island, where he honed in on the juvenile justice system and conducted an opinion survey of people in the court system about why juveniles commit crimes. At the end of 10th grade, John earned a Summer Search scholarship and spent 6 weeks in Colorado in a wilderness-training course and was certified as a lifeguard as well as a CPR instructor. This New York-born teen, in his own words, had trouble getting his feet back on city ground when he returned to Providence.

In 11th grade, John had an LTI with a dance choreographer/educator in the dance department in a local middle school. He worked on the technical aspects of performance and was the stage manager for a production of "Milan." Simultaneously, he, another student and a Met teacher rehearsed for a three person play written by a local playwright entitled "Slow Dance on the Killing Ground," scheduled to go on stage in the spring.

John already had a Summer Search scholarship lined up for the end of his 11th grade year, and had to decide between a performing arts program in London or a language program in Spain to help him develop better literacy in his family's first language, Spanish. The sum of all these experiences was a prelude to his senior year, when he began the process of selecting colleges.

John now attends a college near Worcester, Massachusetts, is majoring in criminal justice, and is still performing in school productions. He was recently on a TV show talking about his first year of college and how an innovative high school prepared him for his college experience.

There have been a few movies made in recent years about learning. One movie, *Billy Elliot,* is the story of a boy with an amazing gift as a dancer. The school he attended never recognized or cared about his interests and passions. In *October Sky,* another student has a passion for rockets and one teacher supported his interests in the face of family and school obstacles. What would it have been like for these children to have had learning plans that allowed them to pursue their interests at their school? I think we all know the answer. It is too scary to think, what if they don't?

Resources

Cotton, K. (1994). *School Size, Climate, and Student Performance.* Portland OR. Northwest Regional Laboratory, U.S. Dept. of Education.

Cremin, L. (1961). The Transformation of the School. *Progressivism in American Education,* 1876–1957. New York: Alfred A. Knopf.

Cremin, L. (1975). *Public Education.* New York: Basic Books, 1975.

Cremin, L. (1988). *American Education: The Metropolitan Experience,* 1876–1980. New York: Harper & Row.

Csikszentmihalyi, M. (1988). Motivation and Creativity: Toward a Synthesis of Structural and Energistic Approaches to Cognition. *New Ideas in Psychology,* 6(2), 159–176.

Csikszentmihalyi, M. (1988). *Optimal Experience.* New York: Cambridge University Press.

Csikszentmihalyi, M. (1990). *Flow*. New York: Harper & Row.

Dewey, J. (1916). *Democracy in Education*, New York: The MacMillan Company.

Dewey, J. (1933). *How We Think*, Second Revised Edition. New York: D.C. Heath & Co.

Hillman, J. (1996). *The Soul's Code*. New York: Random House.

James, W. (1958). *Talks to Teachers on Psychology and to Students on some of Life's Ideals*. New York: W. W. Norton & Co. (originally published 1899).

Klonsky, M & Ford, P. (1994, May). One Urban Solution: Small Schools. *Educational Leadership*, 64–66.

Levine, E. B. (2001) *One Kid at a Time: A Visionary High School Transforms Education*. New York: Teacher's College Press.

Littky, Dennis & Allen, Farrel, Whole-School Personalization, One Student At A Time. *Educational Leadership*, September 1999.

Meier, D. (1995). *The Power of Their Ideas: Lessons For America From a Small School in Harlem*. Boston: Beacon Press.

Montessori, M. (1966). *The Secret of Childhood*. New York: Ballantine Books.

Sarason, S. (1990). *The Predictable Failure of School Reform*. San Francisco: Jossey-Bass.

Schank, R. (2000). *Coloring Outside the Lines: Raising a Smarter Kid by Breaking All the Rules*. New York: Harper Collins.

Steinberg, A. (1996). *Real Learning, Real Work*. New York: Routledge.

Wilson, F. R. (1998). *The Hand: How Its Use Shapes the Brain, Language, and Human Culture*. New York: Pantheon Books.

Elliot Washor is co-director of the Big Picture Company and a former teacher and school principal.

15

What to Look for in a Classroom

Alfie Kohn

When you walk into a "working with" classroom, what aspects of school life are you—or are you not—likely to see?

In describing the climate of a classroom, we are often guided by a certain set of values, a vision of what school *ought* to be like. We might begin with the premise, for example, that an ideal climate is one that promotes deep understanding, excitement about learning, and social as well as intellectual growth.

In such a classroom, students play an active role in decisions, teachers work *with* students rather than doing things *to* them, and the learners' interests and questions drive much of the curriculum. The environment supports children's desire to find out about things, facilitates the process of discovery, and, in general, meets children's needs. A school with this mission has a climate very different from one in which educators are mostly thinking about how they can make students work harder or follow directions.

Put another way, in a "doing to" classroom or school, the adults tend to focus on students' behavior in order to elicit compliance; the preferred

	Good Signs	Possible Reasons to Worry
Furniture	• Chairs around tables to facilitate interaction • Comfortable areas for learning, including multiple "activity centers" • Open space for gathering	• Chairs all facing forward or (even worse) desks in rows
On the Walls	• Covered with students' projects • Evidence of student collaboration • Signs, exhibits, or lists obviously created by students rather than by the teacher • Information about, and personal mementos of, the people who spend time together in this classroom	• Nothing • Commercial posters • Students' assignments displayed, but they are (a) suspiciously flawless, (b) only from "the best" students, or (c) virtually all alike • List of rules created by an adult and/or list of punitive consequences for misbehavior • Sticker (or star) chart— or other evidence that students are rewarded or ranked
Students' Faces	• Eager, engaged	• Blank, bored
Sounds	• Frequent hum of activity and ideas being exchanged	• Frequent periods of silence • The teacher's voice is the loudest or most often heard
Location of Teacher	• Typically working with students so it takes a few seconds to find her	• Typically front and center
Teacher's Voice	• Respectful, genuine, warm	• Controlling and imperious • Condescending and saccharine-sweet

Figure 1   A Visitor's Guide

(Continued)

Figure 1   (Continued)

	Good Signs	Possible Reasons to Worry
Students' Reaction to Visitor	• Welcoming; eager to explain or demonstrate what they're doing or to use visitor as a resource	• Either unresponsive or hoping to be distracted from what they're doing
Class Discussion	• Students often address one another directly • Emphasis on thoughtful exploration of complicated issues • Students ask questions at least as often as the teacher does	• All exchanges involve (or are directed by) the teacher; students wait to be called on • Emphasis on facts and right answers • Students race to be first to answer teacher's "Who can tell me . . . ?" queries
Stuff	• Room overflowing with good books, art supplies, animals and plants, science apparatus; "sense of purposeful clutter"	• Textbooks, worksheets, and other packaged instructional materials predominate; sense of enforced orderliness
Tasks	• Different activities often take place simultaneously • Activities frequently completed by pairs or groups of students	• All students usually doing the same thing • When students aren't listening to the teacher, they're working alone
Around the School	• Appealing atmosphere: a place where people would want to spend time • Students' projects fill the hallways • Library well-stocked and comfortable • Bathrooms in good condition • Faculty lounge warm and inviting • Office staff welcoming toward visitors and students • Students helping in lunchroom, library, and with other school functions	• Stark, institutional feel • Awards, trophies, and prizes displayed, suggesting an emphasis on triumph rather than community

methods are punishments and rewards. In a "working with" environment, the focus is on students' underlying motives in order to help them develop positive values and a love of learning; the preferred methods include the creation of a caring community and a genuinely engaging curriculum.

What Do You See?

When I conduct a workshop, I like to present a conceptual framework that contrasts these two approaches to education. I then invite workshop participants to list familiar practices that exemplify each of them. Participants work in groups, categorizing—and in the process, scrutinizing—various aspects of school life. (For example, if the faculty object to students' clothing, a "working with" response would be to invite students to meet and reflect together on how this problem might be solved. A "doing to" response would be to tell students what they may wear, or simply to force all of them to dress alike.)

These lists tend to grow quickly because there is no limit to the number of examples. And the exercise makes an important point: It is one thing to talk about a learner-centered classroom, and something else again to specify exactly what such a place looks and sounds like. Here, then, in Figure 1, is an abbreviated list—a crib sheet, if you will—that administrators, parents, and others can use to gauge the climate of a classroom and school.

Alfie Kohn is an author, speaker, and social critic.

16

The Idea of Summerhill

A. S. Neill

This is a story of a modern school—Summerhill.

Summerhill was founded in the year 1921. The school is situated within the village of Leiston, in Suffolk, England, and is about one hundred miles from London.

Just a word about Summerhill pupils. Some children come to Summerhill at the age of five years, and others as late as fifteen. The children generally remain at the school until they are sixteen years old. We generally have about twenty-five boys and twenty girls.

The children are divided into three age groups: The youngest range from five to seven, the intermediates from eight to ten, and the oldest from eleven to fifteen.

Generally, we have a fairly large sprinkling of children from foreign countries. At the present time (1960) we have five Scandinavians, one Hollander, one German and one American.

The children are housed by age groups with a house mother for each group. The intermediates sleep in a stone building, the seniors sleep in huts. Only one or two older pupils have rooms for themselves. The boys live two or three or four to a room, and so do the girls. The pupils do not have to stand room inspection and no one picks up after them. They are left free. No one tells them what to wear: they put on any kind of costume they want to at any time.

Newspapers call it a *Go-as-you-please* School and imply that it is a gathering of wild primitives who know no law and have no manners.

It seems necessary, therefore, for me to write the story of Summerhill as honestly as I can. That I write with a bias is natural; yet I shall try to show the demerits of Summerhill as well as its merits. Its merits will be the merits of healthy, free children whose lives are unspoiled by fear and hate.

Obviously, a school that makes active children sit at desks studying mostly useless subjects is a bad school. It is a good school only for those who believe in such a school, for those uncreative citizens who want docile, uncreative children who will fit into a civilization whose standard of success is money.

Summerhill began as an experimental school. It is no longer such; it is now a demonstration school, for it demonstrates that freedom works.

When my first wife and I began the school, we had one main idea: *to make the school fit the child*—instead of making the child fit the school.

I had taught in ordinary schools for many years. I knew the other way well. I knew it was all wrong. It was wrong because it was based on an adult conception of what a child should be and of how a child should learn. The other way dated from the days when psychology was still an unknown science.

Well, we set out to make a school in which we should allow children freedom to be themselves. In order to do this, we had to renounce all discipline, all direction, all suggestion, all moral training, all religious instruction. We have been called brave, but it did not require courage. All it required was what we had—a complete belief in the child as a good, not an evil, being. For almost forty years, this belief in the goodness of the child has never wavered; it rather has become a final faith.

My view is that a child is innately wise and realistic. If left to himself without adult suggestion of any kind, he will develop as far as he is capable of developing. Logically, Summerhill is a place in which people who have the innate ability and wish to be scholars will be scholars; while those who are only fit to sweep the streets will sweep the streets. But we have not produced a street cleaner so far. Nor do I write this snobbishly, for I would rather see a school produce a happy street cleaner than a neurotic scholar.

What is Summerhill like? Well, for one thing, lessons are optional. Children can go to them or stay away from them—for years if they want to. There is a timetable—but only for the teachers.

The children have classes usually according to their age, but sometimes according to their interests. We have no new methods of teaching, because we do not consider that teaching in itself matters very much. Whether a school has or has not a special method for teaching long division is of no significance, for long division is of no importance except to those who want to learn it. And the child who wants to learn long division will learn it no matter how it is taught.

Children who come to Summerhill as kindergartners attend lessons from the beginning of their stay; but pupils from other schools vow that they will never attend any beastly lessons again at any time. They play and cycle and get in people's way, but they fight shy of lessons. This sometimes goes on for months. The recovery time is proportionate to the hatred their last school gave them. Our record case was a girl from a convent. She loafed for three years. The average period of recovery from lesson aversion is three months.

Strangers to this idea of freedom will be wondering what sort of madhouse it is where children play all day if they want to. Many an adult says, "If I had been sent to a school like that, I'd never have done a thing." Others say, "Such children will feel themselves heavily handicapped when they have to compete against children who have been made to learn."

I think of Jack who left us at the age of seventeen to go into an engineering factory. One day, the managing director sent for him.

"You are the lad from Summerhill," he said. "I'm curious to know how such an education appears to you now that you are mixing with lads from the old schools. Suppose you had to choose again, would you go to Eton or Summerhill?"

"Oh, Summerhill, of course," replied Jack.

"But what does it offer that the other schools don't offer?"

Jack scratched his head. "I dunno," he said slowly; "I think it gives you a feeling of complete self-confidence."

"Yes," said the manager dryly, "I noticed it when you came into the room."

"Lord," laughed Jack. "I'm sorry if I gave you that impression."

"I liked it," said the director. "Most men when I call them into the office fidget about and look uncomfortable. You came in as my equal. By the way, what department did you say you would like to transfer to?"

This story shows that learning in itself is not as important as personality and character. Jack failed in his university exams because he hated book learning. But his lack of knowledge about *Lamb's Essays* or the French language did not handicap him in life. He is now a successful engineer.

All the same, there is a lot of learning in Summerhill. Perhaps a group of our twelve-year-olds could not compete with a class of equal age in handwriting or spelling or fractions. But in an examination requiring originality, our lot would beat the others hollow.

We have no class examinations in the school, but sometimes I set an exam for fun. The following questions appeared in one such paper:

Where are the following:—Madrid, Thursday Island, yesterday, love, democracy, hate, my pocket screwdriver (alas, there was no helpful answer to that one).

Give meanings for the following: (the number shows how many are expected for each)—Hand (3) . . . only two got the third right—the standard of measure for a horse. Brass (4). . . . metal, cheek, top army officers, department of an orchestra. Translate Hamlet's To-be-or-not-to-be speech into Summerhillese.

These questions are obviously not intended to be serious, and the children enjoy them thoroughly. Newcomers, on the whole, do not rise to the answering standard of pupils who have become acclimatized to the school. Not that they have less brain power, but rather because they have become so accustomed to work in a serious groove that any light touch puzzles them.

This is the play side of our teaching. In all classes much work is done. If, for some reason, a teacher cannot take his class on the appointed day, there is usually much disappointment for the pupils.

David, aged nine, had to be isolated for whooping cough. He cried bitterly. "I'll miss Roger's lesson in geography," he protested. David had been in the school practically from birth, and he had definite and final ideas about the necessity of having his lessons given to him. David is now a lecturer in mathematics at London University.

A few years ago someone at a General School Meeting (at which all school rules are voted by the entire school, each pupil and each staff member having one vote) proposed that a certain culprit should be punished by being banished from lessons for a week. The other children protested on the ground that the punishment was too severe.

My staff and I have a hearty hatred of all examinations. To us, the university exams are anathema. But we cannot refuse to teach children the required subjects. Obviously, as long as the exams are in existence, they are our master. Hence, the Summerhill staff is always qualified to teach to the set standard.

Not that many children want to take these exams; only those going to the university do so. And such children do not seem to find it especially hard to tackle these exams. They generally begin to work for them seriously at the age of fourteen, and they do the work in about three years. Of course they don't always pass at the first try. The more important fact is that they try again.

Summerhill is possibly the happiest school in the world. We have no truants and seldom a case of homesickness. We very rarely have fights—quarrels, of course, but seldom have I seen a stand-up fight like the ones we used to have as boys. I seldom hear a child cry, because children when free have much less hate to express than children who are downtrodden. Hate breeds hate, and love breeds love. Love means approving of children, and that is essential in any school. You can't be on the side of children if you punish them and storm at them. Summerhill is a school in which the child knows that he is approved of.

Mind you, we are not above and beyond human foibles. I spent weeks planting potatoes one spring, and when I found eight plants pulled up in June, I made a big fuss. Yet there was a difference between my fuss and that of an authoritarian. My fuss was about potatoes, but the fuss an authoritarian would have made would have dragged in the question of morality—right and wrong. I did not say that it was wrong to steal my spuds; I did not make it a matter of good and evil—I made it a matter of my spuds. They were *my spuds* and they should have been left alone. I hope I am making the distinction clear.

Let me put it another way. To the children, I am no authority to be feared. I am their equal, and the row I kick up about my spuds has no more significance to them than the row a boy may kick up about his punctured bicycle tire. It is quite safe to have a row with a child when you are equals.

Now some will say: "That's all bunk. There can't be equality. Neill is the boss; he is bigger and wiser." That is indeed true. I am the boss, and if the house caught fire the children would run to me. They know that I am bigger and more knowledgeable, but that does not matter when I meet them on their own ground, the potato patch, so to speak.

When Billy, aged five, told me to get out of his birthday party because I hadn't been invited, I went at once without hesitation—just as Billy gets out of my room when I don't want his company. It is not easy to describe this relationship between teacher and child, but every visitor to Summerhill knows what I mean when I say that the relationship is ideal. One sees it in the attitude to the staff in general. Rudd, the chemistry man, is Derek. Other members of the staff are known as Harry, and Ulla, and Pam. I am Neill, and the cook is Esther.

In Summerhill, everyone has equal rights. No one is allowed to walk on my grand piano, and I am not allowed to borrow a boy's cycle without his permission. At a General School Meeting, the vote of a child of six counts for as much as my vote does.

But, says the knowing one, in practice of course the voices of the grownups count. Doesn't the child of six wait to see how you vote before he raises his hand? I wish he sometimes would, for too many of my proposals are beaten. Free children are not easily influenced; the absence of fear accounts for this phenomenon. Indeed, the absence of fear is the finest thing that can happen to a child.

Our children do not fear our staff. One of the school rules is that after ten o'clock at night there shall be quietness on the upper corridor. One night, about eleven, a pillow fight was going on, and I left my desk, where I was writing, to protest against the row. As I got upstairs, there was a scurrying of feet and the corridor was empty and quiet. Suddenly I heard a disappointed voice say, "Humph, it's only Neill," and the fun began again at once. When I explained that I was trying to write a book downstairs, they showed concern and at once agreed to chuck the noise. Their scurrying came from the suspicion that their bedtime officer (one of their own age) was on their track.

I emphasize the importance of this absence of fear of adults. A child of nine will come and tell me he has broken a window with a ball. He tells me, because he isn't afraid of arousing wrath or moral indignation. He may have to pay for the window, but he doesn't have to fear being lectured or being punished.

There was a time some years back when the School Government resigned, and no one would stand for election. I seized the opportunity of putting up a notice. "In the absence of a government, I herewith declare myself Dictator. Heil Neill!" Soon there were mutterings. In the afternoon Vivien, aged six, came to me and said, "Neill, I've broken a window in the gym."

I waved him away. "Don't bother me with little things like that," I said, and he went.

A little later he came back and said he had broken two windows. By this time I was curious, and asked him what the great idea was.

"I don't like dictators," he said, and I don't like going without my grub." (I discovered later that the opposition to dictatorship had tried to take itself out on the cook, who promptly shut up the kitchen and went home.)

"Well," I asked, "what are you going to do about it?"

"Break more windows," he said doggedly.

"Carry on," I said, and he carried on.

When he returned, he announced that he had broken seventeen windows. "But mind," he said earnestly, "I'm going to pay for them."

"How?"

"Out of my pocket money. How long will it take me?"

I did a rapid calculation. "About ten years," I said.

He looked glum for a minute; then I saw his face light up. "Gee," he cried, "I don't have to pay for them at all."

"But what about the private property rule?" I asked. "The windows are my private property."

"I know that but there isn't any private property rule now. There isn't any government, and the government makes the rules."

It may have been my expression that made him add, "But all the same I'll pay for them."

But he didn't have to pay for them. Lecturing in London shortly afterward, I told the story; and at the end of my talk, a young man came up and handed me a pound note "to pay for the young devil's windows." Two years later, Vivien was still telling people of his windows and of the man who paid for them. "He must have been a terrible fool, because he never even saw me."

Children make contact with strangers more easily when fear is unknown to them. English reserve is, at bottom, really fear; and that is why the most reserved are those who have the most wealth. The fact that Summerhill children are so exceptionally friendly to visitors and strangers is a source of pride to me and my staff.

We must confess, however, that many of our visitors are people of interest to the children. The kind of visitor most unwelcome to them is the teacher, especially the earnest teacher, who wants to see their drawing and written work. The most welcome visitor is the one who has good tales to tell—of adventure and travel or, best of all, of aviation. A boxer or a good tennis player is surrounded at once, but visitors who spout theory are left severely alone.

The most frequent remark that visitors make is that they cannot tell who is staff and who is pupil. It is true: the feeling of unity is that strong when children are approved of. There is no deference to a teacher as a teacher. Staff and pupils have the same food and have to obey the same community laws. The children would resent any special privileges given to the staff

When I used to give the staff a talk on psychology every week, there was a muttering that it wasn't fair. I changed the plan and made the talks open to everyone over twelve. Every Tuesday night, my room is filled with eager youngsters who not only listen but give their opinions freely. Among the subjects the children have asked me to talk about have been these: The Inferiority Complex, The Psychology of Stealing, The Psychology of the Gangster, The Psychology of Humor, Why Did Man Become a Moralist?, Masturbation, Crowd Psychology. It is obvious that such children will go out into life with a broad clear knowledge of themselves and others.

The most frequent question asked by Summerhill visitors is, "Won't the child turn round and blame the school for not making him learn arithmetic or music?" The answer is that young Freddy Beethoven and young Tommy Einstein will refuse to be kept away from their respective spheres.

The function of the child is to live his own life—not the life that his anxious parents think he should live, nor a life according to the purpose of the educator who thinks he knows what is best. All this interference and guidance on the part of adults only produces a generation of robots.

You cannot make children learn music or anything else without to some degree converting them into will-less adults. You fashion them into accepters of the status quo—a good thing for a society that needs obedient sitters at dreary desks, standers in shops, mechanical catchers of the 8:30 suburban train—a society, in short, that is carried on the shabby shoulders of the scared little man—the scared-to-death conformist.

A. S. Neill (deceased) was the founder of the Summerhill School.

PART V

How Should We
Assess Student Learning?

Mrs. Yan is puzzled. Shayla is one of the hardest working, most motivated students in her 11th grade English class. Shayla participates actively, writes poetry and short fiction, and always offers the most astute insights when class discussion turns to the interpretation of literature.

And yet Shayla struggles on Mrs. Yan's exams and she can't seem to memorize even a simple soliloquy for the oral presentation requirement. In addition, she gets glassy-eyed whenever Mrs. Yan talks about the importance of learning vocabulary as part of SAT preparation.

When reviewing Shayla's performance for the semester, Mrs. Yan noticed that Shayla's poetry and her short fiction, often published in the school's literary magazine, was exemplary, as was her effort and classroom participation. But her performance on exams, research papers, and more formal, oral presentations was, more often than not, deficient.

Struck by these inconsistencies, Mrs. Yan decided that the only fair way to arrive at a final report card grade was to average all Shayla's marks together. However, there was something about this approach that made Mrs. Yan uncomfortable.

For her part, Shayla believes that her grade should reflect her exceptional fiction and poetry, her sophisticated interpretation of literature, and her active class participation. Shayla is not happy with Mrs. Yan's simple solution to the complex problem.

Why assess student learning? What is the purpose of assessment? What does good assessment look like?

17

Grading

The Issue Is
Not How But Why?

Alfie Kohn

Why are we concerned with evaluating how well students are doing? The question of motive, as opposed to method, can lead us to rethink basic tenets of teaching and learning and to evaluate what students have done in a manner more consistent with our ultimate educational objectives. But not all approaches to the topic result in this sort of thoughtful reflection. In fact, approaches to assessment may be classified according to their depth of analysis and willingness to question fundamental assumptions about how and why we grade. Consider three possible levels of inquiry:

Level 1. These are the most superficial concerns, those limited to the practical issue of how to grade students' work. Here we find articles and books offering elaborate formulas for scoring assignments, computing points, and allocating final grades—thereby taking for granted that what students do must receive *some* grades and, by extension, that students ought to be avidly concerned about the ones they will get.

Level 2. Here educators call the above premises into question, asking whether traditional grading is really necessary or useful for assessing students' performance. Alternative assessments, often designated as "authentic," belong in this category. The idea here is to provide a richer, deeper description of students' achievement. (Portfolios of students' work are sometimes commended to us in this context, but when a portfolio is used merely as a means of arriving at a traditional grade, it might more accurately be grouped under Level 1.)

Level 3. Rather than challenging grades alone, discussions at this level challenge the whole enterprise of assessment—and specifically why we are evaluating students as opposed to how we are doing so. No matter how elaborate or carefully designed an assessment strategy may be, the result will not be constructive if our reason for wanting to know how students are doing is itself objectionable.

Grading Rationale I: Sorting

One reason for evaluating students is to be able to label them on the basis of their performance and thus to sort them like so many potatoes. Sorting, in turn, has been criticized at each of the three levels, but for very different reasons. At Level 1, the concern is merely that we are not correctly dumping individuals into the right piles. The major problem with our high schools and colleges, the argument goes, is that they don't keep enough students off the Excellent pile. (These critics don't put it quite this way, of course; they talk about "grade inflation.") Interestingly, most studies suggest that student performance does not improve when instructors grade more stringently and, conversely, that making it relatively easy to get a good grade does not lead students to do inferior work—even when performance is defined as the number of facts retained temporarily as measured by multiple-choice exams (Vasta and Sarmiento 1979, Abrami et al. 1980).

At Level 2, questions are raised about whether grades are reliable enough to allow students to be sorted effectively. Indeed, studies show that any particular teacher may well give different grades to a single piece of work submitted at two different times. Naturally, the variation is even greater when the work is evaluated by more than one teacher (Kirschenbaum et al. 1971). What grades offer is spurious precision, a subjective rating masquerading as an objective assessment.

From the perspective of Level 3, this criticism is far too tame. The trouble is not that we are sorting students badly—a problem that logically should be addressed by trying to do it better. The trouble is that we are sorting them at all. Are we doing so in order to segregate students by ability and teach them separately? The harms of this practice have been well established (Oakes 1985). Are we turning schools into "bargain-basement personnel screening agencies for business" (Campbell 1974, p. 145)? Whatever use we make of sorting, the process itself is very different from—and often incompatible with—the goal of helping students to learn.

Grading Rationale II: Motivation

A second rationale for grading—and indeed, one of the major motives behind assessment in general—is to motivate students to work harder so they will receive a favorable evaluation. Unfortunately, this rationale is just as problematic as sorting. Indeed, given the extent to which A's and F's function as rewards and punishments rather than as useful feedback, grades are counterproductive regardless of whether they are intentionally used for this purpose. The trouble lies with the implicit assumption that there exists a single entity called "motivation" that students have to a greater or lesser degree. In reality, a critical and qualitative difference exists between intrinsic and extrinsic motivation—between an interest in what one is learning for its own sake, and a mindset in which learning is viewed as a means to an end, the end being to escape a punishment or snag a reward. Not only are these two orientations distinct, but they also often pull in opposite directions.

Scores of studies in social psychology and related fields have demonstrated that extrinsic motivators frequently undermine intrinsic motivation. This may not be particularly surprising in the case of sticks, but it is no less true of carrots. People who are promised rewards for doing something tend to lose interest in whatever they had to do to obtain the reward. Studies also show that, contrary to the conventional wisdom in our society, people who have been led to think about what they will receive for engaging in a task (or for doing it well) are apt to do lower quality work than those who are not expecting to get anything at all.

These findings are consistent across a variety of subject populations, rewards, and tasks, with the most destructive effects occurring in activities that require creativity or higher-order thinking. That this effect is produced by the extrinsic motivators known as grades has been documented with students of different ages and from different cultures. Yet the findings are rarely cited by educators.

Studies have shown that the more students are induced to think about what they will get on an assignment, the more their desire to learn evaporates, and, ironically, the less well they do. Consider these findings:

• On tasks requiring varying degrees of creativity, Israeli educational psychologist Ruth Butler has repeatedly found that students perform less well and are less interested in what they are doing when being graded than when they are encouraged to focus on the task itself (Butler and Nissan 1986; Butler 1987, 1988).

• Even in the case of rote learning, students are more apt to forget what they have learned after a week or so—and are less apt to find it interesting— if they are initially advised that they will be graded on their performance (Grolnick and Ryan 1987).

• When Japanese students were told that a history test would count toward their final grade, they were less interested in the subject—and less likely to prefer tackling difficult questions than those who were told the test was just for monitoring their progress (Kage 1991).

• Children told that they would be graded on their solution of anagrams chose easier ones to work on—and seemed to take less pleasure from solving them—than children who were not being graded (Harter 1978).

As an article in the *Journal of Educational Psychology* concluded, "Grades may encourage an emphasis on quantitative aspects of learning, depress creativity, foster fear of failure, and undermine interest" (Butler and Nissan 1986, p. 215). This is a particularly ironic result if the rationale for evaluating students in the first place is to encourage them to perform better.

Grading Rationale III: Feedback

Some educators insist that their purpose in evaluating students is neither to sort them nor to motivate them, but simply to provide feedback so they can learn more effectively tomorrow than they did today. From a Level 2 perspective, this is an entirely legitimate goal—and grades are an entirely inadequate means of reaching it. There is nothing wrong with helping students to internalize and work toward meeting high standards, but that is most likely to happen when they experience success and failure not as reward and punishment, but as information (Bruner 1961, p. 26). Grades make it very difficult to do this. Besides, reducing someone's work to a letter or number simply is not helpful; a B+ on top of a paper tells a student nothing about what was impressive about that paper or how it could be improved.

But from Level 3 comes the following challenge: Why do we want students to improve? This question at first seems as simple and bland as baby food; only after a moment does it reveal a jalapeno kick: it leads us into disconcerting questions about the purpose of education itself.

Demand vs. Support

Eric Schaps (1993), who directs the Developmental Studies Center in Oakland, California, has emphasized "a single powerful distinction: focusing on what students ought to be able to do, that is, what we will demand of them—as contrasted with focusing on what we can do to support students development and help them learn." For lack of better labels, let us call these the "demand" and "support" models.

In the demand model, students are workers who are obligated to do a better job. Blame is leveled by saying students "chose" not to study or "earned" a certain grade—conveniently removing all responsibility from educators and deflecting attention from the curriculum and the context in which it is taught. In their evaluations, teachers report whether students did what they were supposed to do. This mind-set often lurks behind even relatively enlightened programs that emphasize performance assessment and—a common buzzword these days—outcomes. (It also manifests itself in the view of education as an investment, a way of preparing children to become future workers.)

The support model, by contrast, helps children take part in an "adventure in ideas" (Nicholls and Hazzard 1993), guiding and stimulating their natural inclination to explore what is unfamiliar; to construct meaning; to develop a competence with and a passion for playing with words, numbers, and ideas. This approach meshes with what is sometimes called "learner-centered" learning, in which the point is to help students act on their desire to make sense of the world. In this context, student evaluation is, in part, a way of determining how effective we have been as educators. In sum, improvement is not something we require of students so much as something that follows when we provide them with engaging tasks and a supportive environment.

Supportive Assessment

Here are five principles of assessment that follow from this support model:

1. Assessment of any kind should not be overdone. Getting students to become preoccupied with how they are doing can undermine their interest in what they are doing. An excessive concern with performance can erode curiosity—and, paradoxically, reduce the quality of performance. Performance-obsessed students also tend to avoid difficult tasks so they can escape a negative evaluation.

2. The best evidence we have of whether we are succeeding as educators comes from observing children's behavior rather than from test scores or grades. It comes from watching to see whether they continue arguing animatedly about an issue raised in class after the class is over, whether they come home chattering about something they discovered in school, whether they read on their own time. Where interest is sparked, skills are usually acquired. Of course, interest is difficult to quantify, but the solution is not to return to more conventional measuring methods; it is to acknowledge the limits of measurement.

3. We must transform schools into safe, caring communities. This is critical for helping students to become good learners and good people, but it is also relevant to assessment. Only in a safe place, where there is no fear of humiliation and punitive judgment, will students admit to being confused about what they have read and feel free to acknowledge their mistakes. Only by being able to ask for help will they be likely to improve.

Ironically, the climate created by an emphasis on grades, standardized testing, coercive mechanisms such as pop quizzes and compulsory recitation, and pressure on teachers to cover a prescribed curriculum makes it more difficult to know how well students understand—and thus to help them along.

4. Any responsible conversation about assessment must attend to the quality of the curriculum. The easy question is whether a student has learned something; the far more important—and unsettling—question is whether the student has been given something worth learning. (The answer to the latter question is almost certainly no if the need to evaluate students has determined curriculum content.) Research corroborates what thoughtful teachers know from experience: when students have interesting things to do, artificial inducements to boost achievement are unnecessary (Moeller and Reschke 1993).

5. **Students must be invited to participate in determining the criteria by which their work will be judged, and then play a role in weighing their work against those criteria.** Indeed, they should help make decisions about as many elements of their learning as possible (Kohn 1993). This achieves several things: It gives them more control over their education, makes evaluation feel less punitive, and provides an important learning experience in itself. If there is a movement away from grades, teachers should explain the rationale and solicit students' suggestions for what to do instead and how to manage the transitional period. That transition may be bumpy and slow, but the chance to engage in personal and collective reflection about these issues will be important in its own right.

And If You Must Grade . . .

Finally, *while conventional grades persist, teachers and parents ought to do everything in their power to help students forget about them.* Here are some practical suggestions for reducing the salience.

- *Refrain from giving a letter or number grade for individual assignments,* even if you are compelled to give one at the end of the term. The data suggest that substantive comments should replace, not supplement, grades (Butler 1988). Make sure the effect of doing this is not to create suspense about what students are going to get on their report cards, which would defeat the whole purpose. Some older students may experience, especially at first, a sense of existential vertigo: a steady supply of grades has defined them. Offer to discuss privately with any such student the grade he or she would probably receive if report cards were handed out that day. With luck and skill, the requests for ratings will decrease as students come to be involved in what is being taught.

- Never grade students while they are still learning something and, even more important, do not reward them for their performance at that point. Studies suggest that rewards are most destructive when given for skills still being honed (Condry and Chambers 1978). If it is unclear whether students feel ready to demonstrate what they know, there is an easy way to find out: ask them.

- *Never grade on a curve.* The number of good grades should not be artificially limited so that one student's success makes another's less likely. Stipulating that only a few individuals can get top marks regardless of how well everyone does is egregiously unfair on its face. It also undermines collaboration and community. Of course, grades of any kind, even when they are not curved to create artificial scarcity—or deliberately publicized—tend to foster comparison and competition, an emphasis on relative standing. This is not only destructive to students' self-esteem and relationships but also counterproductive with respect to the quality of learning (Kohn 1992). As one book on the subject puts it: "It is not a symbol of rigor to have grades fall into a normal distribution; rather, it is a symbol of failure: failure to teach well, to test well, and to have any influence at all on the intellectual lives of students" (Milton et al. 1986, p. 225).

• *Never give a separate grade for effort.* When students seem to be indifferent to what they are being asked to learn, educators sometimes respond with the very strategy that precipitated the problem in the first place: grading students' efforts to coerce them to try harder. The fatal paradox is that while coercion can sometimes elicit resentful obedience, it can never create desire. A low grade for effort is more likely to be read as "You're a failure even at trying." On the other hand, a high grade for effort combined with a low grade for achievement says, "You're just too dumb to succeed." Most of all, rewarding or punishing children's efforts allows educators to ignore the possibility that the curriculum or learning environment may have something to do with students' lack of enthusiasm.

References

Abrami, P. C., W. J. Dickens, R. P. Perry, and L. Leventhal. (1980). "Do Teacher Standards for Assigning Grades Affect Student Evaluations of Instruction?" *Journal of Educational Psychology* 72: 107–118.

Bruner, J. S. (1961). "The Act of Discovery." *Harvard Educational Review* 31: 21–32.

Butler, R. (1987). "Task-Involving and Ego-Involving Properties of Evaluation." Journal of Educational Psychology 79: 474–482.

Butler, R. (1988) "Enhancing and Undermining Intrinsic Motivation." *British Journal of Educational Psychology* 58 (1988): 1–14.

Butler, R., and M. Nissan. (1986). "Effects of No Feedback, Task-Related Comments, and Grades on Intrinsic Motivation and Performance." *Journal of Educational Psychology* 78: 210–216.

Campbell, D. N. (October 1974) "On Being Number One: Competition in Education." *Phi Delta Kappan*: 143–146.

Condry, J., and J. Chambers. (1978). "Intrinsic Motivation and the Process of Learning." In *The Hidden costs of Rewards: New Perspectives on the Psychology of Human Motivation,* edited by M. R. Lepper and D. Greene. Hillsdale, NJ: Lawrence Erlbaum.

Grolnick, W. S., and R. M. Ryan. (1987). "Autonomy in Children's Learning: An Experimental and Individual Difference Investigation." *Journal of Personality and Social Psychology* 52: 890–898.

Harter, S. (1978). "Pleasure Derived from Challenge and the Effects of Receiving Grades on Children's Difficulty Level Choices." *Child Development* 49: 788–799.

Kage, M. (1991). "The Effects of Evaluation on Intrinsic Motivation." Paper presented at the meeting of the Japan Association of Educational Psychology, Joetsu, Japan.

Kirschenbaum, H., R. W. Napier, and S. B. Simon. (1971). *Wad-Ja-Get?: The Grading Game in American Education.* New York: Hart.

Kohn, A. (1992). *No Contest: The Case Against Competition.* Rev. ed. Boston: Houghton Mifflin.

Kohn, A. (September 1993). "Choices for Children: Why and How to Let Students Decide." *Phi Delta Kappan:* 8–20.

Milton, O., H. R. Pollio, and J. A. Eison. (1986). *Making Sense of College Grades.* San Francisco: Jossey-Bass.

Moeller, A. J., and C. Reschke. (1993). "A Second Look at Grading and Classroom Performance. *Modern Language Journal* 77: 163–169.

Nicholls, J. C., and S. P. Hazzard. (1993). *Education as Adventure: Lessons from the Second Grade.* New York: Teachers College Press.

Oakes, J. (1985). *Keeping Track: How Schools Structure Inequality.* New Haven: Yale University Press.

Schaps, E. (October 1993). Personal communication.

Vasta, R., and R. F. Sarmiento. (1979). "Liberal Grading Improves Evaluations But Not Performance," *Journal of Educational Psychology* 71: 207–211.

Alfie Kohn is an author, speaker, and social critic.

18

The Courage to Be Constructivist

*Martin G. Brooks and
Jacqueline Grennon Brooks*

For years, the term constructivism appeared only in journals read primarily by philosophers, epistemologists, and psychologists. Nowadays, *constructivism* regularly appears in the teachers' manuals of textbook series, state education department curriculum frameworks, education reform literature, and education journals. Constructivism now has a face and a name in education.

A theory of learning that describes the central role that learners' ever-transforming mental schemes play in their cognitive growth, constructivism powerfully informs educational practice. Education, however, has deep roots in other theories of learning. This history constrains our capacity to embrace the central role of the learner in his or her own education. We must rethink the very foundations of schooling if we are to base our practice on our understandings of learners' needs.

One such foundational notion is that students will learn on demand. This bedrock belief is manifested in the traditional scope and sequence of a

NOTE: From *Educational Leadership*, 57(3), pp. 18–24. Association for Supervision and Curriculum Development, Alexandria, VA. Copyright © 1999 ASCD. Reprinted by permission. All rights reserved.

typical course of study and, more recently, in the new educational standards and assessments. This approach to schooling is grounded in the conviction that all students can and will learn the same material at the same time. For some students, this approach does indeed lead to the construction of knowledge. For others, however, it does not.

The people working directly with students are the ones who must adapt and adjust lessons on the basis of evolving needs. Constructivist educational practice cannot be realized without the classroom teacher's autonomous, ongoing, professional judgment. State education departments could and should support good educational practice. But too often they do not.

Their major flaw is their focus on high-stakes accountability systems and the ramifications of that focus on teachers and students. Rather than set standards for professional practice and the development of local capacity to enhance student learning, many state education departments have placed even greater weight on the same managerial equation that has failed repeatedly in the past: State Standards = State Tests; State Test Results = Student Achievement; Student Achievement = Rewards and Punishments.

We are not suggesting that educators should not be held accountable for their students' learning. We believe that they should. Unfortunately, we are not holding our profession accountable for learning, only for achievement on high-stakes tests. As we have learned from years of National Assessment of Educational Progress research, equating lasting student learning with test results is folly.

The Emerging Research from Standards-Driven States

In recent years, many states have initiated comprehensive educational reform efforts. The systemic thinking that frames most standards-based reform efforts is delectably logical: Develop high standards for all students; align curriculum and instruction to these standards; construct assessments to measure whether all students are meeting the standards; equate test results with student learning; and reward schools whose students score well on the assessments and sanction schools whose students don't.

Predictably, this simple and linear approach to educational reform is sinking under the weight of its own flaws. It is too similar to earlier reform approaches, and it misses the point. Educational improvement is not accomplished through administrative or legislative mandate. It is accomplished through attention to the complicated, idiosyncratic, often paradoxical, and difficult to measure nature of learning.

A useful body of research is emerging from the states. With minor variations, the research indicates the following:

• Test scores are generally low on the first assessment relating to new standards. Virginia is an extreme example of this phenomenon: More than 95 percent of schools failed the state's first test. In New York, more than 50 percent of the states' 4th graders were deemed at risk of not graduating in 2007 after taking that state's new English language arts test in 1999.

• Failure, or the fear of failure, breeds success on subsequent tests. After the first administration of most state assessments, schools' scores rise because educators align curriculum closely with the assessments, and they focus classroom instruction directly on test-taking strategies.

• To increase the percentages of students passing the state assessments—and to keep schools off the states' lists of failing schools—local district spending on student remediation, student test-taking skills, and faculty preparation for the new assessments increases.

• Despite rising test scores in subsequent years, there is little or no evidence of increased student learning. A recent study by Kentucky's Office of Educational Accountability (Hambleton et al., 1995) suggests that test-score gains in that state are a function of students' increasing skills as test takers rather than evidence of increased learning.

When Tests Constrict Learning

Learning is a complex process through which learners constantly change their internally constructed understandings of how their worlds function. New information either transforms their current beliefs—or doesn't. The efficacy of the learning environment is a function of many complex factors, including curriculum, instructional methodology, student motivation, and student developmental readiness. Trying to capture this complexity on paper-and-pencil assessments severely limits knowledge and expression.

Inevitably, schools reduce the curriculum to only that which is covered on tests, and this constriction limits student learning. So, too, does the undeviating, one-size-fits-all approach to teaching and assessment in many states that have crowned accountability king. Requiring all students to take the same courses and pass the same tests may hold political capital for legislators and state-level educational policymakers, but it contravenes what years of painstaking research tells us about student learning. In discussing the inordinate amount of time and energy devoted to preparing students to take and pass high-stakes tests, Angaran (1999) writes

> Ironically, all this activity prepares them for hours of passivity. This extended amount of seat time flies in the face of what we know about how children learn. Unfortunately, it does not seem to matter. It is, after all, the Information Age. The quest for more information drives us forward. (P. 72)

We are not saying that student success on state assessments and classroom practices designed to foster understanding are inherently contradictory. Teaching in ways that nurture students' quests to resolve cognitive conflict and conquer academic challenges fosters the creative problem solving that most states seek. However, classroom practices designed to prepare students for tests clearly do not foster deep learning that students apply to new situations. Instead, these practices train students to mimic learning on tests.

Many school districts question the philosophical underpinnings of the dominant test-teach-test model of education and are searching for broader ways for students to demonstrate their knowledge. However, the accountability component of the standards movement has caused many districts to abandon performance-based assessment practices and refocus instead on preparing students for paper-and-pencil tests. The consequences for districts and their students are too great if they don't.

Constructivism in the Classroom

Learners control their learning. This simple truth lies at the heart of the constructivist approach to education.

As educators, we develop classroom practices and negotiate the curriculum to enhance the likelihood of student learning. But controlling what students learn is virtually impossible. The search for meaning takes a different route for each student. Even when educators structure classroom lessons and curriculums to ensure that all students learn the same concepts at the same time, each student still constructs his or her own unique meaning through his or her own cognitive processes. In other words, as educators we have great control over what we teach, but far less control over what students learn.

Shifting our priorities from ensuring that all students learn the same concepts to ensuring that we carefully analyze students' understandings to customize our teaching approaches is an essential step in educational reform that results in increased learning. Again, we must set standards for our own professional practice and free students from the anti-intellectual training that occurs under the banner of test preparation.

The search for understanding motivates students to learn. When students want to know more about an idea, a topic, or an entire discipline, they put more cognitive energy into classroom investigations and discussions and study more on their own. We have identified five central tenets of constructivism (Grennon Brooks & Brooks, 1993).

• First, constructivist teachers seek and value students' points of view. Knowing what students think about concepts helps teachers formulate classroom lessons and differentiate instruction on the basis of students' needs and interests.

• Second, constructivist teachers structure lessons to challenge students' suppositions. All students, whether they are 6 or 16 or 60, come to the classroom with life experiences that shape their views about how their worlds work. When educators permit students to construct knowledge that challenges their current suppositions, learning occurs. Only through asking students what they think they know and why they think they know it are we and they able to confront their suppositions.

• Third, constructivist teachers recognize that students must attach relevance to the curriculum. As students see relevance in their daily activities, their interest in learning grows.

• Fourth, constructivist teachers structure lessons around big ideas, not small bits of information. Exposing students to wholes first helps them determine the relevant parts as they refine their understandings of the wholes.

• Finally, constructivist teachers assess student learning in the context of daily classroom investigations, not as separate events. Students demonstrate their knowledge every day in a variety of ways. Defining understanding as only that which is capable of being measured by paper-and-pencil assessments administered under strict security perpetuates false and counterproductive myths about academia, intelligence, creativity, accountability, and knowledge.

Opportunities for Constructing Meaning

Recently, we visited a classroom in which a teacher asked 7th graders to reflect on a poem. The teacher began the lesson by asking the students to interpret the first two lines. One student volunteered that the lines evoked an image of a dream. "No," he was told, "that's not what the author meant." Another student said that the poem reminded her of a voyage at sea. The teacher reminded the student that she was supposed to be thinking about the first two lines of the poem, not the whole poem, and then told her that the poem was not about the sea. Looking out at the class, the teacher asked, "Anyone else?" No other student raised a hand.

In another classroom, a teacher asked 9th graders to ponder the effect of temperature on muscle movement. Students had ice, buckets of water, gauges for measuring finger-grip strength, and other items to help them consider the relationship. The teacher asked a few framing questions, stated rules for handling materials safely, and then gave the students time to design their experiments. He posed different questions to different groups of students, depending on their activities and the conclusions that they seemed to be drawing. He continually asked students to elaborate or posed contradictions to their responses, even when they were correct.

As the end of the period neared, the students shared initial findings about their investigations and offered working hypotheses about the relationship between muscle movement and temperature. Several students asked to return later that day to continue working on their experiments.

Let's consider these two lessons. In one case, the lesson was not conducive to students' constructing deeper meaning. In the other case, it was. The 7th grade teacher communicated to her students that there is one interpretation of the poem's meaning, that she knew it, and that only that interpretation was an acceptable response. The students' primary quest, then, was to figure out what the teacher thought of the poem.

The teacher spoke to her students in respectful tones, acknowledging each one by name and encouraging their responses. However, she politely and calmly rejected their ideas when they failed to conform to her views. She rejected one student's response as a misinterpretation. She dismissed another student's response because of a procedural error: The response focused on the whole poem, not on just the designated two lines.

After the teacher told these two students that they were wrong, none of the other students volunteered interpretations, even though the teacher encouraged more responses. The teacher then proceeded with the lesson by telling the students what the poet really meant. Because only two students offered comments during the lesson, the teacher told us that a separate test would inform her whether the other students understood the poem.

In the second lesson, the teacher withheld his thoughts intentionally to challenge students to develop their own hypotheses. Even when students' initial responses were correct, the teacher challenged their thinking, causing many students to question the correctness of their initial responses and to investigate the issue more deeply.

Very few students had awakened that morning thinking about the relationship between muscle movement and temperature. But, as the teacher helped students focus their emerging, somewhat disjointed musings into a structured investigation, their engagement grew. The teacher provoked the students to search for relevance in a relationship they hadn't yet considered by framing the investigation around one big concept, providing appropriate materials and general questions, and helping the students think through their own questions. Moreover, the teacher sought and valued his students' points of view and used their comments to assess their learning. No separate testing event was required.

What Constructivism Is and Isn't

As constructivism has gained support as an educational approach, two main criticisms have emerged. One critique of constructivism is that it is overly permissive. This critique suggests that constructivist teachers often abandon their curriculums to pursue the whims of their students. If, for example, most of the students in the aforementioned 9th grade science class wished to discuss the relationship between physical exercise and muscle movement rather than pursue the planned lesson, so be it. In math and science, critics are particularly concerned that teachers jettison basic information to permit students to think in overly broad mathematical and scientific terms.

The other critique of constructivist approaches to education is that they lack rigor. The concern here is that teachers cast aside the information, facts, and basic skills embedded in the curriculum—and necessary to pass high-stakes tests—in the pursuit of more capricious ideas. Critics would be concerned that in the 7th grade English lesson described previously, the importance of having students understand the one true main idea of the poem would fall prey to a discussion of their individual interpretations.

Both of these critiques are silly caricatures of what an evolving body of research tells us about learning. Battista (1999), speaking specifically of mathematics education, writes,

> Many . . . conceive of constructivism as a pedagogical stance that entails a type of nonrigorous, intellectual anarchy that lets students pursue whatever interests them and invent and use any mathematical methods they wish, whether those methods are correct or not. Others take constructivism to be synonymous with

"discovery learning" from the era of "new math," and still others see it as a way of teaching that focuses on using manipulatives or cooperative learning. None of these conceptions is correct. (P. 429)

Organizing a constructivist classroom is difficult work for the teacher and requires the rigorous intellectual commitment and perseverance of students. Constructivist teachers recognize that students bring their prior experiences with them to each school activity and that it is crucial to connect lessons to their students' experiential repertoires. Initial relevance and interest are largely a function of the learner's experiences, not of the teacher's planning. Therefore, it is educationally counterproductive to ignore students' suppositions and points of view. The 7th grade English lesson is largely nonintellectual. The 9th grade science lesson, modeled on how scientists make state-of-the-art science advancements, is much more intellectually rigorous.

Moreover, constructivist teachers keep relevant facts, information, and skills at the forefront of their lesson planning. They usually do this within the context of discussions about bigger ideas. For example, the dates, battles, and names associated with the U.S. Civil War have much more meaning for students when introduced within larger investigations of slavery, territorial expansion, and economics than when presented for memorization without a larger context.

State and local curriculums address what students learn. Constructivism, as an approach to education, addresses *how* students learn. The constructivist teacher, in mediating students' learning, blends the *what* with the *how*. As a 3rd grader in another classroom we visited wrote to his teacher, "You are like the North Star for the class. You don't tell us where to go, but you help us find our way." Constructivist classrooms demand far more from teachers and students than lockstep obeisance to prepackaged lessons.

The Effects of High-Stakes Accountability

As we stated earlier, the standards movement has a grand flaw at the nexus of standards, accountability, and instructional practice. Instructional practices designed to help students construct meaning are being crowded out of the curriculum by practices designed to prepare students to score well on state assessments. The push for accountability is eclipsing the intent of standards and sound educational practice.

Let's look at the effects of high-stakes accountability systems. Originally, many states identified higher-order thinking as a goal of reform and promoted constructivist teaching practices to achieve this goal. In most states, however, policymakers dropped this goal or subsumed it into other goals because it was deemed too difficult to assess and quantify. Rich evidence relating to higher-order thinking is available daily in classrooms, but this evidence is not necessarily translatable to paper-and-pencil assessments. High-stakes accountability systems, therefore, tend to warp the original visions of reform.

Education is a holistic endeavor. Students' learning encompasses emerging understandings about themselves, their relationships, and their relative places in the world. In addition to academic achievement, students develop these understandings through nonacademic aspects of schooling, such as clubs, sports, community service, music, arts, and theater. However, only that which is academic and easily measurable gets assessed, and only that which is assessed is subject to rewards and punishments. Jones and Whitford (1997) point out that Kentucky's original educational renewal initiative included student self-sufficiency and responsible group membership as goals, but these goals were dropped because they were deemed too difficult to assess and not sufficiently academic.

Schools operating in high-stakes accountability systems typically move attention away from principles of learning, student-centered curriculum, and constructivist teaching practices. They focus instead on obtaining higher test scores, despite research showing that higher test scores are not necessarily indicative of increased student learning.

Historically, many educators have considered multiple-choice tests to be the most valid and reliable form of assessment—and also the narrowest form of assessment. Therefore, despite the initial commitment of many states to performance assessment, which was to have been the cornerstone of state assessment efforts aligned with broader curriculum and constructivist instructional practices, multiple-choice questions have instead remained the coin of the realm. As Jones and Whitford (1997) write about Kentucky,

> The logic is clear. The more open and performance based an assessment is, the more variety in the responses; the more variety in the responses, the more judgment is needed in scoring; the more judgment in scoring, the lower the reliability. . . . At this point, multiple choice items have been reintroduced, performance events discontinued. (P. 278)

Ironically, as state departments of education and local newspapers hold schools increasingly accountable for their test results, local school officials press state education departments for greater guidance about material to be included on the states' tests. This phenomenon emboldens state education departments to take an even greater role in curriculum development, as well as in other decisions typically handled at the local level, such as granting high school diplomas, determining professional development requirements for teachers, making special education placements, and intervening academically for at-risk students. According to Jones and Whitford (1997),

> [In Kentucky] there has been a rebound effect. Pressure generated by the state test for high stakes accountability has led school-based educators to pressure the state to be more explicit about content that will be tested. This in turn constrains local school decision making about curriculum. This dialectical process works to increase the state control of local curriculum. (P. 278)

Toward Educational Reform

Serious educational reform targets cognitive changes in students' thinking. Perceived educational reform targets numerical changes in students' test scores. Our obsession with the perception of reform, what Ohanian (1999) calls "the mirage theory of education," is undermining the possibility of serious reform.

History tells us that it is likely that students' scores on state assessments will rise steadily over the next decade and that meaningful indexes of student learning generally will remain flat. It is also likely that teachers, especially those teaching in the grades in which high-stakes assessments are administered, will continue to narrow their curriculum to match what is covered on the assessments and to use instructional practices designed to place testing information directly in their students' heads.

We counsel advocacy for children. And vision. And courage.

Focus on student learning. When we design instructional practices to help students construct knowledge, students learn. This is our calling as educators.

Keep the curriculum conceptual. Narrowing curriculum to match what is covered on state assessments results in an overemphasis on the rote memorization of discrete bits of information and pushes aside big ideas and intellectual curiosity. Keep essential principles and recurring concepts at the center.

Assess student learning within the context of daily instruction. Use students' daily work, points of view, suppositions, projects, and demonstrations to assess what they know and don't know and use these assessments to guide teaching.

Initiate discussions among administrators, teachers, parents, school boards, and students about the relationship among the state's standards, the state's assessments, and your district's mission. Ask questions about what the assessments actually assess, the instructional practices advocated by your district, and the ways to teach a conceptual curriculum while preparing students for the assessments. These are discussions worth having.

Understand the purposes of accountability. Who wants it, and why? Who is being held accountable, and for what? How are data being used or misused? What are the consequences of accountability for all students, especially for specific groups, such as special education students and English language learners?

Students must be permitted the freedom to think, to question, to reflect, and to interact with ideas, objects, and others—in other words, to construct meaning. In school, being wrong has always carried negative consequences for students. Sadly, in this climate of increasing accountability, being wrong carries even more severe consequences. But being wrong is often the first step on the path to greater understanding.

We observed a 5th grade teacher return a test from the previous day. Question 3 was, "There are 7 blue chips and 3 green chips in a bag. If you place your hand in the bag and pull out 1 chip, what is the probability that you will get a green chip?" One student wrote, "You probably won't get one." She was "right"—and also "wrong." She received no credit for the question.

References

Angaran, J. (1999, March). Reflection in an age of assessment. *Educational Leadership, 56*, 71–72.

Grennon Brooks, J., & Brooks, M. G. (1993). *In search of understanding: The case for constructivist classrooms.* Alexandria, VA: ASCD.

Hambleton, R., Jaeger, R. M., Koretz, D., Linn, R. L., Miliman, J., & Phillips, S. E. (1995). *Review of the measurement quality of the Kentucky instructional results information system* 1991–1994. (Report prepared for the Kentucky General Assembly.) Frankfort, KY: Office of Educational Accountability.

Jones, K., & Whitford, B. L. (1997, December). Kentucky's conflicting reform principles: High stakes accountability and student performance assessment. *Phi Delta Kappan, 78*(4), 276–281.

Ohanian, S. (1999). *One size fits few.* Portsmouth, NH: Heinemann.

Martin G. Brooks is the superintendent of Valley Stream Central High School District in Valley Stream, New York.

Jacqueline Grennon Brooks is an associate professor in the Professional Education Program at the State University of New York at Stony Brook.

19

The Standards Fraud

William Ayers

The goals of school reform—to provide every child with an experience that will nourish and challenge development, extend capacity, encourage growth, and offer the tools and dispositions necessary for full participation in the human community—are simple to state but excruciatingly difficult to enact. Hannah Arendt once argued, "Education is the point at which we decide whether we love the world enough to assume responsibility for it and by the same token save it from that ruin which, except for renewal, except for the coming of the new and the young, would be inevitable . . . and where we decide whether we love our children enough not to expel them from our world and leave them to their own devices, nor to strike from their hands their chance of undertaking something new, something unforeseen by us, but to prepare them in advance for the task of renewing a common world." That's a lot, much of it dynamic and ever-changing, much of it intricately interdependent. Yet it is what we must seek, if our ideal is education in a democracy.

Today, there is no more insistent or attractive distraction from that ideal than the "standards movement" that Deborah Meier takes on. This conservative push, dressed up as a concern for standards, is at its heart a fraud. It promotes a shrill and insistent message, simple and believable in its own right, while

NOTE: Reprinted with kind permission of the author.

it subtly shifts responsibility away from the powerful, making scapegoats of the victims of power.

High academic standards (as well as social and community standards) are essential to good schools, and such standards, in part, demonstrate a commitment to high expectations for all students. A watered-down curriculum, vague or meaningless goals, expectations of failure—these are a few of the ingredients of academic ruin, and they have characterized urban schools for too long. Standards exist, whether or not we are explicit about them, and standards of some sort are everywhere. I'm all for clarity of standards, for a more explicit sense of what we expect from students. The questions, however, are: What do we value? What knowledge and experience are of most worth? How can we organize access to that worthwhile knowledge and experience? When we look at this school or classroom, what standards are being upheld? Who decides? These kinds of deep and dynamic questions are never entirely summed up, never finished; they are forever open to the demands of the new. Standards setting, then, should not be the property of an expert class, the bureaucrats, or special interests. Rather, standard setting should be part of the everyday vocation of schools and communities, the heart and soul of education, and it should engage the widest public. Standard setting means systematically examining and then reexamining what we care about, what we hope for, what the known demands of us next. Standard setting, often by other names, is already the work of successful schools and many, many effective classrooms.

The "standards movement" is flailing at shadows. All schools in Illinois, for example, follow the same guidelines: These standards apply to successful schools as well as collapsing ones. These written, stated standards have been in place for decades. And yet Illinois in effect has created two parallel systems—one privileged, adequate, successful, and largely white; the other disadvantaged in countless ways, disabled, starving, failing, and African-American. Some schools succeed brilliantly while others stumble and fall. Clearly something more is at work here.

The American school crisis is neither natural nor uniform, but particular and selective; it is a crisis of the poor, of the cities, of Latino and African-American communities. All the structures of privilege and oppression apparent in the larger society are mirrored in our schools. Chicago public school students, for example are overwhelmingly children of color and children of the poor. More than half of the poorest children in Illinois (and over two thirds of the bilingual children) attend Chicago schools. And yet Chicago schools must struggle to educate children with considerably fewer human and material resources than neighboring districts have. For example,

Chicago has fifty-two licensed physics teachers in the whole city, and a physics lab in only one high school. What standard does that represent?

In the last two years, 50,000 kids attended summer school in Chicago in the name of standards. Tens of thousands were held back a grade. It is impossible to argue that they should have been passed along routinely has been the cynical response for years. But failing that huge group without seriously addressing the ways school has failed them—that is, without changing the structures and cultures of those schools—is to punish those kids for the mistakes and errors of all of us. Further, the vaunted standard turns out to be nothing more than a single standardized test, a relatively simpleminded gate designed so that half of those who take it must not succeed.

The purpose of education in a democracy is to break down barriers, to overcome obstacles, to open doors, minds, and possibilities. Education is empowering and enabling; it points to strength, to critical capacity, to thoughtfulness and expanding capabilities; it leads to an ability to work, to contribute, to participate. It aims at something deeper and richer than simply imbibing and accepting existing codes and conventions, acceding to whatever is before us. The larger goal of education is to assist people in seeing the world through their own eyes, interpreting and analyzing through their own experiences and thinking, feeling themselves capable of representing, manifesting, or even, if they choose, transforming all that is before them. Education, then, is linked to freedom, to the ability to see and also to alter, to understand and also to reinvent, to know and also to change the world as we find it. Can we imagine this at the core of all schools, even poor city schools?

If city schools are to be retooled, streamlined, and made workable, and city schools are to become palaces of learning for all children (and why shouldn't they be?), then we must fight for a comprehensive program of change. Educational resources must be distributed fairly. Justice—the notion that all children deserve a decent life, and that those in the greatest need deserve the greatest support—must be our guide. There is no single solution to the obstacles we face. But a good start is to ask what each of us wants for our own children, What are our standards? I want a teacher in the classroom who is thoughtful and caring, not a mindless clerk or deskilled bureaucrat but a person of substance, depth, and compassion. I want my child to be seen, understood, challenged, and nourished. I want to be able to participate in the community, to have some voice and choice in the questions the school faces.

And so the set of principles outlined by Meier are useful. A small school—as metaphor and practice—is a good starting point. Better yet, one where school people find common cause with students and parents, remaking schools by drawing on strengths and capacities of communities rather than their deficiencies and difficulties. Such a school must focus on shared problems, and find solutions that are collective and manageable. It must talk of solidarity rather than "services," people as self-activated problem solvers and citizens rather than passive "clients" or "consumers." And it must focus on the several deep causes of school failure: the inequitable distribution of educational resources, the capacity of a range of self-interested bureaucracies to work against the common good, and the profound disconnect between schools and the communities they are supposed to serve.

The solutions to the problems we face in a democracy are, as Meier appropriately puts it, more democracy. If the standards guiding schools today are weak or watery—and in many instances they are—the answer is not silence, credulousness, and passivity, but a broader and deeper and more lively engagement with the widest possible public. This is messy and complicated, but true to the ideal of letting the people decide. School is a public space where the American hope for democracy, participation, and transformation collides with the historical reality of privilege and oppression, the hierarchies of race and class. We should all work to raise expectations for our children, to reform and restructure schools, to prepare all students for a hopeful and powerful future, to drive resources to the neediest communities, to demand successful and wondrous learning environments for everyone, to involve teachers, parents, and communities— the public in public schools—in the discussion of what's important for kids to know and experience. At that point the conservative "standards movement," geared to simple, punitive, one-size-fits-all solutions, can be swept aside for something so much better.

William Ayers is a Distinguished Professor of Education and Senior University Scholar at the University of Illinois at Chicago.

20

A Mania for Rubrics

Thomas Newkirk

Near the beginning of the film *Dead Poets Society*, the English teacher played by Robin Williams forces his students to read aloud—from the absurd preface to their anthology. Works of literature, the preface states, can be evaluated by graphing two qualities: importance and execution. Midway through the reading, Mr. Williams' character tells his students to rip out the offending pages. Art can never be so mechanically reduced.

This movie's warning is relevant today because we are now in the middle of a resurgence of mechanical instruction in writing. Driven by state testing, teachers are being pulled toward prompt-and-rubric teaching that bypasses the human act of composing and the human gesture of response.

Proponents of rubrics will claim that they are simply trying to be clear about criteria that are too often tacit and unexplained. By using rubrics, the argument goes, we are giving students more precise and analytic reasons for the evaluations they receive. By placing these criteria in the clear light of day, students will come to see evaluations as less subjective, less what the teacher "likes."

If this were truly the case, who could disagree? The crux of the issue is this: Do rubrics clarify the process of sensitive response? Or do they distort,

---

NOTE: Previously published in *Education Week*, September 2000. Reprinted with permission.

obscure, or mystify that response? And to answer that question, we need to think carefully about what we do when we read student work (when we are at our best)—and what we want from an evaluator.

Personally, I have never been able to use rubrics that establish predetermined weighting systems. I always cheat. I work backwards, determining the impression or sense I had of the writing, a unitary evaluative reaction. Then I jimmy the categories so that they fit my general reaction, hoping to escape detection. In other words, I am not thinking of multiple criteria (organization, detail, mechanics) as I read, parceling out my attention.

As I read, I feel myself in a magnetized field. I am drawn to—or released from—the text I am reading. Initially, this response is more physical than cognitive or analytic; when the text is working I feel more alert, and a good line or image propels me forward. At other times, I feel slack, unmagnetized, as if nothing is drawing me in, drawing me on. This lack of attraction may come from too little detail (or too much), from a lack of direction, absence of personality or voice, from dialogue that doesn't reveal character, but the immediate sensation is physical. The student's text has let me go.

Rather than reveal processes like the one I have described, rubrics conceal or mystify them. They fail to reveal the narrative, moment-by-moment process of evaluation. Their formal and categorical ratings belie—or worse, short-circuit—the work of the reader. Terms like "organization" fail to clarify (or even locate) the disruption in the reader's sense of continuity. Rubrics fail to provide a *demonstration* of the reading process that can later be internalized by the writer.

The very authoritative language and format of rubrics, their pretense to objectivity, hides the human act of reading. The key qualities of good writing (organization, detail, a central problem) are represented as something the writing *has*—rather than something the writing *does*.

All of this, of course, assumes that the purpose of rubrics is to convey response. More often, however, they are used to enforce uniformity of evaluation—as a preparation to test-taking. A striking example appeared in the February 2000 issue of *Educational Leadership*, describing the way kindergartners were prepped for a drawing test. I will quote from the article so that I might not be accused of exaggeration.

After the teacher explained what elements of the drawing were needed to get a score of 4, she said, "Notice that this drawing shows the ground colored green and brown. There are also a tree, the sky, some clouds, and the sun." She then showed a picture earning a 3, in which the tree, clouds, and sun were not as clearly defined. After this explanation, she asked each student to create "artwork that met the requirement of the level-4 drawing" and rate the artwork of a partner. Children spent the rest of class time "improving their drawings until all the student pictures either met the level-4 rubric or went up at least one level."

This is not *preparation*—it is capitulation. This developmentally inappropriate task is presented not as educational malpractice, but as a "success" for standards-based instruction. Which only goes to prove the education writer Alfie Kohn's point: that the standards movement is going to make satire obsolete.

Thomas Newkirk is a professor of English at the University of New Hampshire.

PART VI

How Does One
Develop a Critical Voice?

It's August 26th and, together with my colleagues, I'm gearing up for yet another—in a seemingly endless series—professional development workshop designed to tell me how to "do it right." Every year, usually right before school begins, the district brings in a math consultant, or a behavior specialist, or a literacy coach, or a curriculum expert, or an assessment guru or . . . for goodness sake, who knew there were so many authorities on teaching that don't have their own classrooms, may never have worked with kids?

Dutifully, I attend the scheduled sessions anyway, as I always do. There are no surprises. The other teachers have gotten too used to the routine. The district has brought in a consultant for the day to train us to use newly established reading standards. We take our seats and thumb through our resource packages as the consultant makes a PowerPoint presentation on the importance of the standards, exactly how they will be implemented, and how the state assessment will monitor student reading achievement. We listen attentively. There are a few questions and the consultant does her best to answer concerns. Most concerns are deflected with the statement, "This is the direction that everybody is heading." After lunch, small grade-level focus groups meet. The discussions are collegial, cordial; as teachers we are all compliant. Time well spent. Very professional. Everyone agrees. I guess I better start modifying my plans to align with the new district approach.

How should a teacher respond? If a teacher disagrees, then what words should he or she use? What shall be the tone?

21

Teachers as Transformative Intellectuals

Henry Giroux

The call for educational reform has gained the status of a recurring national event, much like the annual Boston Marathon. There have been more than 30 national reports since the beginning of the 20th century, and more than 300 task forces have been developed by the various states to discover how public schools can improve educational quality in the United States.[1] But unlike many past educational reform movements, the present call for educational change presents both a threat and challenge to public school teachers that appears unprecedented in our nation's history. The threat comes in the form of a series of educational reforms that display little confidence in the ability of public school teachers to provide intellectual and moral leadership for our nation's youth. For instance, many of the recommendations that have emerged in the current debate either ignore the role teachers play in preparing learners to be active and critical citizens, or they suggest reforms that ignore the intelligence, judgment and experience that teachers might offer in such a debate. Where teachers do enter the debate, they are the object of educational reforms that reduce them to the status of high-level technicians carrying out dictates and objectives decided

NOTE: Previously published in *Social Education*, May 1985. Reprinted with permission from the National Council for the Social Studies.

by "experts" far removed from the everyday realities of classroom life.[2] The message appears to be that teachers do not count when it comes to critically examining the nature and process of educational reform.

The political and ideological climate does not look favorable for teachers at the moment. But it does offer them the challenge to join in a public debate with their critics as well as the opportunity to engage in a much-needed self-critique regarding the nature and purpose of teacher preparation, inservice teacher programs and the dominant forms of classroom teaching. Similarly, the debate provides teachers with the opportunity to organize collectively so as to struggle to improve the conditions under which they work and to demonstrate to the public the central role that teachers must play in any viable attempt to reform the public schools.

In order for teachers and others to engage in such a debate, it is necessary that a theoretical perspective be developed that redefines the nature of the educational crisis while simultaneously providing the basis for an alternative view of teacher training and work. In short, recognizing that the current crisis in education largely has to do with the developing trend towards the disempowerment of teachers at all levels of education is a necessary theoretical precondition in order for teachers to organize effectively and establish a collective voice in the current debate. Moreover, such a recognition will have to come to grips not only with a growing loss of power among teachers around the basic conditions of their work, but also with a changing public perception of their role as reflective practitioners.

I want to make a small theoretical contribution to this debate and the challenge it calls forth by examining two major problems that need to be addressed in the interest of improving the quality of teacher work, which includes all the clerical tasks and extra assignments as well as classroom instruction. First, I think it is imperative to examine the ideological and material forces that have contributed to what I want to call the proletarianization of teacher work; that is, the tendency to reduce teachers to the status of specialized technicians within the school bureaucracy, whose function then becomes one of managing and implementing curricula programs rather than developing or critically appropriating curricula to fit specific pedagogical concerns. Second, there is a need to defend schools as institutions essential to maintaining and developing a critical democracy and also to defending teachers as transformative intellectuals who combine scholarly reflection and practice in the service of educating students to be thoughtful, active citizens. In the remainder of this essay, I will develop these points and conclude by examining their implications for providing an alternative view of teacher work.

Toward a Devaluing and Deskilling of Teacher Work

One of the major threats facing prospective and existing teachers with the public schools is the increasing development of instrumental ideologies that emphasize a technocratic approach to both teacher preparation and classroom pedagogy. At the core of the current emphasis on instrumental and pragmatic factors in school life are a number of important pedagogical assumptions. These include: a call for the separation of conception from execution; the standardization of school knowledge in the interest of managing and controlling it; and the devaluation of critical, intellectual work on the part of teachers and students for the primacy of practical considerations.[3]

This type of instrumental rationality finds one of its strongest expressions historically in the training of prospective teachers. That teacher training programs in the United States have long been dominated by a behavioristic orientation and emphasis on mastering subject areas and methods of teaching is well documented.[4] The implications of this approach, made clear by Zeichner, are worth repeating:

> Underlying this orientation to teacher education is a metaphor of "production," a view of teaching as an "applied science" and a view of the teacher as primarily an "executor" of the laws and principles of effective teaching. Prospective teachers may or may not proceed through the curriculum at their own pace and may participate in varied or standardized learning activities, but that which they are to master is limited in scope (e.g., to a body of professional content knowledge and teaching skills) and is fully determined in advance by others often on the basis of research on teacher effectiveness. The prospective teacher is viewed primarily as a passive recipient of this professional knowledge and plays little part in determining the substance and direction of his or her preparation program.[5]

The problems with this approach are evident in John Dewey's argument that teacher training programs that emphasize only technical expertise do a disservice both to the nature of teaching and to their students.[6] Instead of learning to reflect upon the principles that structure classroom life and practice, prospective teachers are taught methodologies that appear to deny the very need for critical thinking. The point is that teacher education programs often lose sight of the need to educate students to examine the underlying nature of school problems. Further, these programs need to substitute for the language of management and efficiency a critical analysis of the less obvious conditions that structure the ideological and material practices of schooling.

Instead of learning to raise questions about the principles underlying different classroom methods, research techniques and theories of education, students are often preoccupied with learning the "how to," with "what works," or with mastering the best way to teach a *given* body of knowledge. For example, the mandatory field-practice seminars often consist of students sharing with each other the techniques they have used in managing and controlling classroom discipline, organizing a day's activities and learning how to work within specific time tables. Examining one such program, Jesse Goodman raises some important questions about the incapacitating silences it embodies. He writes:

> There was no questioning of feelings, assumptions, or definitions in this discussion. For example, the "need" for external rewards and punishments to "make kids learn" was taken for granted; the educational and ethical implications were not addressed. There was no display of concern for stimulating or nurturing a child's intrinsic desire to learn. Definitions of *good kids* as *"quiet kids," workbook work* as "reading," *on task time* as "learning," and *getting through the material on time* as "the goal of teaching"—all went unchallenged. Feelings of pressure and possible guilt about not keeping to time schedules also went unexplored. The real concern in this discussion was that everyone "shared."[7]

Technocratic and instrumental rationalities are also at work within the teaching field itself, and they play an increasing role in reducing teacher autonomy with respect to the development and planning of curricula and the judging and implementation of instruction. This is most evident in the proliferation of what has been called "teacher-proof" curriculum packages.[8] The underlying rationale in many of these packages reserves for teachers the role of simply carrying out predetermined content and instructional procedures. The method and aim of such packages is to legitimate what I call management pedagogies. That is, knowledge is broken down into discrete parts, standardized for easier management and consumption, and measured through predefined forms of assessment. Curricula approaches of this sort are management pedagogies because the central questions regarding learning are reduced to the problem of management, i.e., "how to allocate resources (teachers, students and materials) to produce the maximum number of certified . . . students within a designated time."[9] The underlying theoretical assumption that guides this type of pedagogy is that the behavior of teachers needs to be controlled and made consistent and predictable across different schools and student populations.

What is clear in this approach is that it organizes school life around curricular, instructional and evaluation experts who do the thinking while teachers are reduced to doing the implementing. The effect is not only to deskill teachers, to remove them from the processes of deliberation and reflection, but also to routinize the nature of learning and classroom pedagogy. Needless to say, the principles underlying management pedagogies are at odds with the premise that teachers should be actively involved in producing curricula materials suited to the cultural and social contexts in which they teach. More specifically, the narrowing of curricula choices to a back-to-basics format, and the introduction of lock-step, time-on-task pedagogies operate from the theoretically erroneous assumption that all students can learn from the same materials, classroom instructional techniques and modes of evaluation. The notion that students come from different histories and embody different experiences, linguistic practices, cultures and talents is strategically ignored within the logic and accountability of management pedagogy theory.

Teachers as Transformative Intellectuals

In what follows, I want to argue that one way to rethink and restructure the nature of teacher work is to view teachers as transformative intellectuals. The category of intellectual is helpful in a number of ways. First, it provides a theoretical basis for examining teacher work as a form of intellectual labor, as opposed to defining it in purely instrumental or technical terms. Second, it clarifies the kinds of ideological and practical conditions necessary for teachers to function as intellectuals. Third, it helps to make clear the role teachers play in producing and legitimating various political, economic and social interests through the pedagogies they endorse and utilize.

By viewing teachers as intellectuals, we can illuminate the important idea that all human activity involves some form of thinking. In other words, no activity, regardless of how routinized it might become, can be abstracted from the functioning of the mind in some capacity. This is a crucial issue because by arguing that the use of the mind is a general part of all human activity we dignify the human capacity for integrating thinking and practice, and in doing so highlight the core of what it means to view teachers as reflective practitioners. Within this discourse, teachers can be seen not merely as "performers professionally equipped to realize effectively any goals that may be set for them. Rather [they should] be viewed as free men and women with a special dedication to the values of the intellect and the enhancement of the critical powers of the young."[10]

Viewing teachers as intellectuals also provides a strong theoretical critique of technocratic and instrumental ideologies underlying an educational theory that separates the conceptualization, planning and design of curricula from the processes of implementation and execution. It is important to stress that teachers must take active responsibility for raising various questions about what they teach, how they are to teach, and what the larger goals are for which they are striving. This means that they must take a responsible role in shaping the purposes and conditions of schooling. Such a task is impossible within a division of labor in which teachers have little influence over the ideological and economic conditions of their work. This point has a normative and political dimension that seems especially relevant for teachers. If we believe that the role of teaching cannot he reduced to merely training in the practical skills, but involves, instead, the education of a class of intellectuals vital to the development of a free society, then the category of intellectual becomes a way of linking the purpose of teacher education, public schooling and inservice training to the very principles necessary for developing a democratic order and society.

I have argued that by viewing teachers as intellectuals those persons concerned with education can begin to rethink and reform the traditions and conditions that have prevented schools and teachers from assuming their full potential as active, reflective scholars and practitioners. It is imperative that I qualify this point and extend it further. I believe that it is important not only to view teachers as intellectuals, but also to contextualize in political and normative terms the concrete social functions that teachers perform. In this way, we can be more specific about the different relations that teachers have both to their work and to the dominant society.

A fundamental starting point for interrogating the social function of teachers as intellectuals is to view schools as economic, cultural and social sites that are inextricably tied to the issues of power and control. This means that schools do more than pass on in an objective fashion a common set of values and knowledge. On the contrary, schools are places that represent forms of knowledge, language practices, social relations and values that are representative of a particular selection and exclusion from the wider culture. As such, schools serve to introduce and legitimate *particular* forms of social life. Rather than being objective institutions removed from the dynamics of politics and power, schools actually are contested spheres that embody and express a struggle over what forms of authority, types of knowledge, forms of moral regulation and versions of the past and future should be legitimated and transmitted to students. This struggle is most visible in the demands, for example, of right-wing religious groups currently trying to institute school prayer, remove certain books from the school library, and include certain forms of religious teachings in the science curricula. Of course, different demands are made by feminists, ecologists, minorities and other interest groups who believe that the schools should teach women's studies, courses on the environment, or black history. In short, schools are not neutral sites, and teachers cannot assume the posture of being neutral either.

In the broadest sense, teachers as intellectuals have to be seen in terms of the ideological and political interests that structure the nature of the discourse, classroom social relations and values that they legitimate in their teaching. With this perspective in mind, I want to conclude that teachers should become transformative intellectuals if they are to subscribe to a view of pedagogy that believes in educating students to be active, critical citizens.

Central to the category of transformative intellectual is the necessity of making the pedagogical more political and the political more pedagogical. Making the pedagogical more political means inserting schooling directly into the political sphere by arguing that schooling represents both a struggle to define meaning and a struggle over power relations. Within this perspective, critical reflection and action become part of a fundamental social project to help students develop a deep and abiding faith in the struggle to overcome economic, political and social injustices, and to further humanize themselves as part of this struggle. In this case, knowledge and power are inextricably linked to the presupposition that to choose life, to recognize the necessity of improving its democratic and qualitative character for all people, is to understand the preconditions necessary to struggle for it.

Making the political more pedagogical means utilizing forms of pedagogy that embody political interests that are emancipatory in nature; that is, using forms of pedagogy that treat students as critical agents; make knowledge problematic; utilize critical and affirming dialogue; and make the case for struggling for a qualitatively better world for all people. In part, this suggests that transformative intellectuals take seriously the need to give students an active voice in their learning experiences. It also means developing a critical vernacular that is attentive to problems experienced at the level of everyday life, particularly as they are related to pedagogical experiences connected to classroom practice. As such, the pedagogical starting point for such intellectuals is not the isolated student but individuals and groups in their various cultural, class, racial, historical and gender settings, along with the particularity of their diverse problems, hopes and dreams.

Transformative intellectuals need to develop a discourse that unites the language of critique with the language of possibility, so that social educators recognize that they can make changes. In doing so, they must speak out against economic, political and social injustices both within and outside of schools. At the same time, they must work to create the conditions that give students the opportunity to become citizens who have the knowledge and courage to struggle in order to make despair unconvincing and hope practical. As difficult as this tack may seem to social educators, it is a struggle worth waging. To do otherwise is to deny social educators the opportunity to assume the role of transformative intellectuals.

Notes

1. K. Patricia Cross, "The Rising Tide of School Reform Reports," *Phi Delta Kappan*, 66:3 (November 1984), p. 167.

2. For a more detailed critique of the reforms, see my book with Stanley Aronowitz, *Education Under Siege* (South Hadley, MA: Bergin and Garvey Publishers, 1985); also see the incisive comments on the impositional nature of the various reports in Charles A. Tesconi, Jr., "Additive Reforms and the Retreat from Purpose," *Educational Studies* 15:1 (Apring 1984), pp. 1-11: Terrence E. Deal, "Searching for the Wizard: The quest for Excellence in Education," *Issues in Education* 2:1 (Summer 1984), pp. 56–67; Svi Shapiro, "Choosing Our Educational Legacy: Disempowerment or Emancipation?" *Issues in Education* 2:1 (Summer 1984), pp. 11–22.

3. For an exceptional commentary on the need to educate teachers to be intellectuals, see John Dewey, "The Relation of Theory to Practice," in John Dewey, *The Middle Words, 1899-1924*, edited by Jo Ann Boydston (Carbondale, Southern Illinois University Press, 1977), [originally published in 1904]. See also, Israel Scheffler, "University Scholarship and the Education of Teachers," *Teachers College Record*, 70:1 (1968), pp. 1–12; Henry A. Giroux, *Ideology, Culture, and the Process of Schooling* (Philadelphia: Temple University Press, 1981).

4. See for instance, Herbert Kliebard, "The Question of Teacher Education," in D. McCarty (ed.) *New Perspectives on Teacher Education* (San Francisco: Jossey-Bass, 1973).

5. Kenneth M. Zeichner, "Alternative Paradigms on Teacher Education," *Journal of Teacher Education* 34:3 (May–June 1983), p. 4.

6. Dewey, op. cit.

7. Jesse Goodman, "Reflection and Teacher Education: A Case Study and Theoretical Analysis," *Interchange* 15:3 (1984), p. 15.

8. Michael Apple, *Education and Power* (Boston: Routledge & Kegan Paul, Ltd., 1982).

9. Patrick Shannon, "Mastery Learning in Reading and the Control of Teachers and Students," *Language Arts* 61:5 (September 1984), p. 488.

10. Israel Scheffler, op. cit., p. 11.

Henry Giroux is the Waterbury Chair of Secondary Education at Pennsylvania State University.

22

Resistance and Courage

A Conversation With Deborah Meier

Alan Canestrari: What does teaching require these days?

Deborah Meier: First of all, any kind of teaching requires toughness. You have to have firm convictions about a whole lot of stuff that you are not, in fact, always so sure about. But, if a kid asks can he sharpen his pencil or go to the bathroom, you have to exercise a judgment pretty fast and firmly even if more than one good answer might make sense, or even be the right one. You have to be tough on yourself, so that at the end the day you're left with a bunch of unanswered questions of the "Could I have . . . ?" or "Maybe next time . . . ." or even, "Did I just blow a great moment for . . . ?" And, you need to carve out of an exceedingly unleisurely profession, time to think . . . enough time to think about these sticky matters over time, realizing that all the odd living and reading you do can help you in finding the answers. And then, you need to be tough enough to stick to it.

Bruce Marlowe: Suppose your way of doing your work, exercising judgment—about those little things you mention like going to the bathroom or the big things about what's worth teaching—is very different than your colleagues' ways? Or very different from what the principal, school district, or state is invested in?

Meier: Now that's tougher still. And, these days, that's what many of us are struggling with—the plethora of external regulation about what our work is and how we do it. But of course in fact with rare exceptions, those of us involved all our lives in public education have rarely been in situations where we have had to deal with anything less.

Today, though, we are witnessing something new. And there are some tough choices facing us in the teaching field as a result. After a decade or more of considerable "laissez-faire" between the mid 70s and the early 90s (it varied by locale) we're witnessing a retightening of the screws—with more of the screws coming from higher and more remote places, in a setting in which technology makes it harder to hide. The culture of privacy has been ripped apart—for reasons both good and bad. Thus, the kind of quiet, behind-closed-doors resistance that flourished during my earliest teaching years is more problematic. Today, the standardized curriculums and lesson plans which were always part of the traditional public schools—even when ignored—are being republished and reissued, in even greater detail. The old regime has been reinstalled, plus.

Canestrari: So, what lessons would you offer new teachers?

Meier: Number one is: How to survive. It probably helps to remember that this is not new. The technology to enforce it [teacher compliance] is more brutal, but the intent is old and familiar. And, it has, unfortunately, been accepted by too many men and women of good will as a necessity if all children are to meet "high standards."

When I first arrived in New York City there was a loosely enforced grade-by-grade curriculum, and fairly decent guides for carrying it out step-by-step. We survived in part by figuring out where we had space to deviate and where we didn't. In Headstart I was told teaching the names of numbers, letters, and colors was what we'd be tested on in June; but I figured if we did modestly well at that I could spend 90 percent of my time exploring more important stuff like the properties of real life. I realized I never met a kid of 8 who didn't know his colors—unless he was color blind and then drilling colors at age 4 was worse than useless. And the same would be true of the names of letters unless we persisted in teaching them to read formally too early and insisted that we use the names of the letters as a key way into such early instruction. Survival, in other words, depends on making some decisions about what's important, and living by them—most of the time.

Canestrari: Can teachers be effective in changing their conditions?

Meier: Of course, once they learn to survive. The second strategy is to organize—join with others. It starts with being a good colleague in one's own schools. Not easy work. Another way is through teacher and staff organizations. The power of solidarity among working people is still, or once again, obviously vital. As fewer unions exist nationwide natural allies among other working people have lessened. But teacher unions also provide us with links to other organized working people.

But it's important to remember that it's not just joining with the teachers. For example, you may also be a parent. Don't hesitate to speak out in that role also, without feeling that somehow it's unfair or unwise. Not at all. We listen to what doctors say about the kind of medicine they want for their own kids. So you are doubly powerful in this dual role. But even if you decide to be just a parent in your child's school, be a loud one on behalf of the things you believe are good for all kids and teachers.

And then work, within both roles—as teacher and parent—for the strongest and loudest alliance between these two self-interested and powerful groups. If parents and teachers were truly able to use their strength in even a semi-united way, they'd overcome. But, we've allowed a rift to exist between us that serves others, but neither parents nor teacher. This is a time in history when we have to put the issues that unite us to the fore, and agree to disagree on others.

Then there's using your voice. I don't just mean your teacherly voice, but your broader professional voice. Find every way you can to hone your skills as a writer and speaker—to little audiences and big ones, letters to the editors included. And, not just on contentious reform issues. Speak out and write out as an expert on reading, or science, or classroom management, or children's aspirations. Insist on the idea that you are a theorist and an expert, not only a practitioner; don't make it easy to be seen as hardworking, dedicated, loving but a wee bit weak in the head and too prone to sentimentality, or likely to only see the faces in front of you, to miss the important systemic problems!

Then comes the last course of action. For those who can't find any of the above individual or group strategies feasible, and begin to find it hard to face themselves each morning in the mirror, it may be best to change schools, move to another less draconian locale, or even, dare I say it, quit teaching. There is other important work to be done in the world, including work on behalf of children. And, if and when you leave, don't miss the opportunity; don't go quietly and don't go blaming your former colleagues, families, or kids.

Marlowe: Any final advice for new teachers?

Meier: In each and every way that you work in the field, bring the best of yourself as a parent, citizen, and passionate learner into your work, and put "getting along" in perspective. Getting along helps smooth the way, no mean goal, and it makes for more allies, and it makes your voice more effective. Assuming that your colleagues (like the families whose kids you teach) want similar things, acting out of their best intentions is the place to begin. But, watch out when getting along starts becoming a way of life, and other people's good intentions begin to undermine your own. The "courage" you need is the courage to not excuse yourself too often for failing to do what needs doing, for pretending that bad practice—including your own—is good practice, or for seeing yourself and your colleagues as the enemy—or the victims. Victims don't make good teachers—because above all we want our kids to see themselves as competent actors who have learned how to be competent citizens from teachers who saw themselves as that—citizens of their schools and communities.

Deborah Meier is the principal of the Mission Hill Elementary School in Boston, Massachusetts.

23

Speaking in a Critical Voice

Marilyn Page

Three Vignettes

Stan

Last month, a newly crowned Doctor of Education interviewed for a position in social studies teacher education at a large university in the Northeast. He had taught in the elementary grades for twenty-five years and was now hoping to move to a university professorship. He presented his research involving post-Standards changes to geography education and then fielded questions from the audience. When asked what it meant to him to be a teacher in a democracy, he became flustered and skirted the question with responses that didn't relate at all. Here was a social studies teacher who could not define the role of a teacher in a democracy. When asked how teachers in his school were responding to the new learning Standards and to state-mandated testing, he explained that his state was preparing lessons, and directions for delivering all lessons, for all teachers in the state and that the teachers would do exactly what they were told to because they didn't have a union and therefore wouldn't do anything they weren't supposed to do for fear of losing their jobs.

Mary

As a second semester doctoral student, Mary enrolled in the Research in Social Studies Education class at a large mid-Atlantic university. Mary had taught for five years at the elementary level and had obtained a Master's Degree in Education from a Midwestern university known for its first-class reputation in teacher education. In response to an assignment to write a literature review and to analyze the materials critically, Mary confessed: "I don't know what critical thinking is"; "I have never done it"; "I have never learned about it".

John and Jenni

John had been teaching eighth grade for fifteen years. Jenni was a brilliant preservice teacher completing her first student teacher practicum. She had the ability to develop dynamic learning plans, conduct in-depth and purposeful learning experiences, and assess student understanding and content knowledge in multiple ways. During the first four weeks of her five week practicum, she led eighth grade students in an exploratory adventure through the Civil War. The students became the investigators after several stalling tactics usually couched in the terms: "We can't do that"; "It's too hard"; "We've never done that before." The students not only triumphed in the investigatory process but realized exemplary content proficiency, deep comprehension of cause and effect, ability to analyze using different perspectives, ability to relate current issues in the country, and ability to draw and support conclusions. But John, the classroom teacher, could think only of the upcoming tests. He sent Jenni to the library for a day so he could "teach" the students the necessary information to pass the test—information he was sure they had missed because they had not been involved in the traditional rote/recovery mode of instruction and evaluation.

What Is Critical Voice?

One of the similarities among Stan, Mary, and John is the lack of understanding, development, and/or use of critical voice. In Stan's case, he and his fellow teachers were afraid to speak up to state powers concerning the state mandates and prescribed lesson plans. Mary didn't even know what critical voice/thinking meant, let alone how to use it. John was willing to let Jenni try some active learning approaches but then didn't have the belief in the methods or students' ability to learn from anything other than his traditional approach. None of the three teachers spoke up to administrators, state officials, or school boards. They did what they were told, what they had been taught, or what they themselves had experienced in their schooling.

To develop a critical voice, a teacher has to take the time to analyze directives, mandates, and messages from whatever the source and then use that analysis to speak up about issues willingly and strongly to the power sources. To be able to think critically or analytically does not mean to criticize. It means to look at messages and materials through different lenses and from many perspectives; it means to be able to recognize propaganda regardless of its origin; it means to be able to "detect crap" (Postman & Weingartner, 1969); it means to pull apart materials, sort them, question them, reorganize them mentally, and then synthesize the pieces into a coherent understanding and whole.

Teachers and Their Critical Voices

A teacher has to ask herself if she has a critical voice. If she believes she already has a critical voice, then she needs to think about how she will use it. When? Why? And what will happen if she does? What will happen if she doesn't? What is her responsibility in using this voice? If a teacher does not have a critical voice, or like Mary, has not experienced critical thinking or ever heard of it, then that teacher has work to do.

Assumptions About Teaching and Learning

Every teacher has to have a solid grasp of his assumptions about how people learn (Marlowe & Page, 1998) and how that translates into the kind of environment the teacher will provide. Without a grounded philosophy or theory, a new teacher will end up like John or Stan—doing whatever the administration or the state tells him to do. The teacher will not have a base for figuring out the problems in the classroom and will look to a power figure to handle the issue. If a teacher strongly believes in whatever the latest mandate for teaching and learning is and knows why he believes in it, that is one thing. On the other hand, if he doesn't know what his own beliefs are about teaching and learning, he shouldn't be teaching at all.

Since all mandates are generated by or attached to political agenda, every teacher in a democracy has a responsibility to analyze every new mandate in terms of educational validity and to raise his critical voice if he does not agree with the mandate. Teachers need to be able and willing to separate the politics from the mandates. Without thinking teachers, we do not have thinking schools. Without thinking schools, we do not have thinking students or future citizens who can think. Teachers who timidly follow and obey mandates without considering the pros and cons and political agendas attached to the mandates are dangerous. Thinking and questioning teachers will not only tweak and improve our school systems but will work to improve our democracy and model the responsibilities of all citizens.

Stan and John epitomize teachers who, for whatever reason, either do not know how to think critically or if they do, cannot act on their analyses. They should not be teachers in our democracy. They model what is the most dangerous threat to our society—the inability to speak in critical voice. It is hard to believe that Mary received a master's degree and never came in contact with the concept of critical thinking and speaking. But if a teacher does somehow escape these concepts or any discussion about responsibility of a teacher in a democracy, he needs to begin to look at all messages and mandates in-depth. Here is a diagram that will help.

$$SM \Longleftarrow\!\!\!\Longrightarrow RM$$

In this diagram, the M stands for **MESSAGE**. The S stands for **SENDER** and the R stands for **RECEIVER**. The arrows show the reciprocity of message meaning.

What the diagram shows is that there is no meaning in the message without knowing its origin (the sender) and without knowing its destination (the recipient). For example, if a teacher, Mr. Caron, consistently grades students with either A's or B's and another teacher, Ms. Smith, rarely thinks any work is worthy of an A or B, and Johnny goes home with an A from Ms. Smith and an A from Mr. Caron, how might Johnny and his parents translate what those two A grades mean? Now, add to that the information that Johnny is a student who rarely receives an A or B. How does that change the interpretation of the message?

Responsible citizens and especially teachers, given the power they hold in relation to hundreds of future citizens, must continually consider the source of messages, the medium used to deliver the messages, and the recipients, often themselves. A teacher without the ability to think critically or to translate that thinking into a critical voice does a disservice to teaching, to learning, to students, and to our democracy.

Self-Diagnosis: Do You Have and Use Critical Voice?

1. Will you do whatever your principal tells you to do without discussion or question?

2. Will you do whatever your principal tells you to do, but gripe in the teachers' room?

3. Do you fear having to spend most of your time preparing students for standardized tests?

4. If so, will you speak up?

5. Will you sheepishly adhere to new mandates so that you will not lose your job?

6. Are you worried that your students will not have standardized scores as high as other students?

7. Do you have a solid theory/philosophy about how students learn best?

8. If you do and it contradicts what the administration is demanding that you do, will you write a rationale for developing plans that your theory supports?

9. Have you ever written proposals to recommend changes in action or procedure?

10. Are you prepared to go before a school board and argue your point of view?

"Yes" answers to questions 1–3 and 5–6 and "no" answers to 4 and 7–10 indicate lack of critical voice.

Stan, Mary, and John were not thinking in any way that would represent their responsibility in a democracy; that is, to prepare students to be critically empowered thinkers and to use their (the teachers') own critical voices to further the discussion and understanding of how students learn best and how this relates to whatever is the most recent mandate. It takes a teacher who has a grounding in theory and philosophy and who has developed his own critical voice to produce dynamic learning environments that provide students the opportunities to create their own critical voices. Any teacher who cannot or does not develop and speak in critical voice needs to be in a different profession.

References

Gardner, H. (1991). *The unschooled mind: How children think and how schools should teach.* New York: Basic Books.

Kohn, A. (1993). *Punished by rewards: The trouble with gold stars, incentive plans, A's, praise, and other bribes.* Boston: Houghton Mifflin.

Marlowe, B. & Page, M. (1998). *Creating and sustaining the constructivist classroom.* Thousand Oaks, CA: Corwin Press.

Pestalozzi, J. H. (1801/1898). *How Gertrude teaches her children.* (L. E. Holland & F. C. Turner, Trans.). New York: C. E. Bardeen.

Postman, N. & Weingartner, C. (1969). *Teaching as a subversive activity.* New York: Dell Publishing

Marilyn Page is an assistant professor at Pennsylvania State University.

24

Developing a Critical Voice

A Conversation With Alfie Kohn

Bruce Marlowe: How can new teachers develop a critical voice?

Alfie Kohn: Well, new teachers have to be aware, first of all, that we are in a very dark period of American educational history. They should not be under any misapprehensions about the trade-offs and compromises and sacrifices that await them. The worst situation would be for an idealistic teacher, who hopes to excite children about making sense of the world, to land in a school where that is not on the agenda and be thrown for a loop. Different people will make different compromises, but they should keep their eyes wide open about what needs to be done. Sometimes it is necessary to put a clothespin on your nose and get through what is very distasteful. Sometimes it is necessary in placements, internships with a master teacher, to look upon that as a lesson of what not to do when you have your own classroom.

Sometimes you have to take with a grain of salt what your preceptor or college instructor is telling you, if that person is not emphasizing that your first obligation is to do what's in the best interest of children—not to please the administrators, not to raise test scores, not to keep order, not to carry out ludicrous legislative mandates. To help children become engaged and proficient thinkers and good people may require you to close your door, and it may require you to organize and subvert and rebel.

Alan Canestrari: We'd also like to discover how you developed your own critical voice. How did that happen? Give us a little insight into your own personal experience, your history in developing that critical voice.

Kohn: I had a kind of a contrarian spirit even before I began to be professionally involved in education. I've told this story before, but one day in fifth grade when we were given some typical pointless busy work to do, I neatly headed my paper with my name, the date, and "Busy Work." This did not go over well with the teacher. And here it is thirty-five years later and I'm still trying to call people's attention to assignments that are not worth doing, instead of helping teachers figure out tricks to get kids to do what there is not much reason to do. I don't know how I acquired this sensibility but somehow I did. In sixth grade, I was trying to organize other kids to refuse to sing military songs which was the planned assembly for the elementary school graduation. In ninth grade, I publicly turned down an American Legion Award during the Vietnam War.

In terms of my professional career, my first book, published in 1986, argued that research overwhelmingly demonstrates that competition is always a bad thing, contrary to the assumptions of our culture. In subsequent books, I went on to challenge assumptions about the nature of human nature, about the use of rewards, and about other things. It wasn't until the early 90s that I began to systematically focus on educational issues—well after I had been a teacher myself. When I visit terrific classrooms, I wince in retrospect about what I was doing wrong and how much better I could have been had anyone invited me to think about how learning happens, what kids need, or even how to put what kids need at the center rather than asking how to get them to shut up and sit down and do what they're told.

Marlowe: I think that the single most depressing thing is how easily new teachers are co-opted into what they know is just so silly, but they fall into lock-step within six months of landing their first job. And, I think, how could they be co-opted so quickly?

Canestrari: As recently as yesterday, I had this conversation with a group of students who want to have a critical voice but the pressures on them to comply to certification and licensure mandates . . . they themselves don't know exactly what to do with that circumstance.

Kohn: Well, the most frightening scenario is one where these students rarely, if ever, experienced anything different, having been prepared for tests instead of learning to think for themselves, and then are placed into university settings where it is more of the same, to the point that they think this is the way life has to work. They have no memory of a time when schools might have been about something other than compliance, conformity, and test preparation. The second point I would make is that in some preservice programs, I don't think prospective teachers are being shown what a great classroom looks like. There are university classrooms where the teacher talks a good game about critical theory but it is still about lectures and worksheets and grades. The syllabus is created before the instructor meets the students and the point is to cough up the favorite phrases of the professor to get a good grade. The students might as well never have left seventh grade: they're still being led to ask, "Do we have to know this? Will this be on the test?" They're passively taking notes on lectures, and even the discussions are about guessing what's on the instructor's mind. I don't care how much talk there is about Dewey or critical pedagogy; the hidden curriculum here is: This is what a classroom looks like and it's what yours will eventually look like.

Beyond that, even when there is consistency and good modeling going on, I think preservice instructors have an obligation to help future teachers think about what matters and how to fight. It is important to know how to assess children but it is also important to have what Hemingway called a "good crap detector" and to develop a facility and a disposition to organize fellow teachers, to join with one's colleagues to say, "This cannot pass." And I think these issues have to be talked about explicitly.

Marlowe: But many teachers are saying, "We are not doing this." But they are doing it. They are still giving in. The school year is still structured around state exams. The principal says that at ten-thirty every second grade classroom will be working on "x."

Canestrari: And very often, if teachers say, "We are not doing this," they are looked at as cynics, looked at in a negative sort of way, and they are no longer thought of as team players.

Kohn: So it falls to us to explain the importance of not playing for a bad team, and to rethink the meaning of being cynical. Cynicism can be defined as prepping kids to do well on stupid tests when you know better. Skepticism is what leads to appropriate action that affirms what needs to be affirmed. I was in Florida a couple of weeks ago and I was hearing about teachers in a school who were sitting around complaining about how test prep was interfering with doing good instruction, when in the middle of the discussion, it was announced that their school had improved its rating on the state tests and these same teachers started cheering. If we understand that standardized test results are at best meaningless, and at worst likely to cause us to value the wrong things, that high test scores may actually be a reason to worry, given what has been sacrificed to raise those scores, then we have to be consistent in making the release of those results a nonevent whether we do well or poorly. It is not good news when your school does well on tests. There are many reasons to cheer and take pride in one's school. High scores on a bad test is not one of them.

If we look beyond the field of education, to the sociology of corporations and other entities, it takes a lot of energy and passion and courage to stick it out, to stand up, to speak out against the conventional wisdom, and to develop a reputation as a pain in the ass. But, the stakes are too high not to do so when children are suffering as a result of these dictates and mandates and assumptions.

Marlowe: And to retain a sense of humor about it. That's the other thing that worries me. I see a lot of students leaving our program who say, "This is bleak. There is nothing to look forward to." That is not how we want people to be entering the teaching force.

Kohn: In order to laugh, to keep one's sanity, it helps to have people to laugh with. God knows there is enough to laugh at. But developing a supportive community of people to have a glass of wine after school with, to roll one's eyes with, to exchange glances with during the interminable faculty meeting . . . it is vital for people to keep up their morale and to trade concrete suggestions for how to survive in a totalitarian system. That's critical. Sometimes, it is hard to find even one person in your own school, so you have to network with other people in the district, and of course keep up contacts with people you met in college or you know from other places, just so you are reminded periodically that you're not crazy.

Marlowe: What about the relationship between universities and state departments of education? Our students are about to graduate. Up until today, our students were told to take a test called the "Principles of Learning and Teaching," which of course has virtually nothing to do with either. And now, two weeks before graduation, the state has decided that that's not the test. The one you really need is actually an entirely different test.

Kohn: Schools are under pressure to look good not only on ratings but *rankings* of teacher education programs. These are set up in such a way as to guarantee that some will look bad. What they end up doing is playing games like giving PRAXIS tests before teacher candidates start the program so that, *mirabile dictu,* we have a 100 percent passing rate. Of course, it screws over the prospective teachers and drives a lot of them out.

Most of what I, and others, have had to say about the poor design and the immoral uses of student tests applies to the use of standardized tests for teacher candidates as well. They measure what matters least. They make sure that we have a disproportionate number of middle-class white teachers. They prevent many of the finest people from hanging around. And they change the curriculum for the worse, so that a lot of teacher educators are in the position of having to choose between doing what they know is best and doing what's going to raise scores.

Marlowe: I get upset about our students being so easily co-opted and yet, as university professors, we are just as guilty. Why don't all of the universities, all of us in teacher education, simply say to the state department, "Tough noogies"?

Kohn: That's right. If they all say that, then there is strength and unity among teacher education programs just as there could be among elementary school teachers. For example, what if they gave the test and nobody came? Or we refused to hand it out? A lot of people are really struggling and it is getting worse because some states are following the lead of places like Texas and Florida, which are trying to create a seamless pre-K to graduate school entity, a top-down, one-size-fits-all system. . . . I mean, it's something out of a dystopian novel. And its going to get worse before it gets better unless people do stand up and say we refuse to be part of this—to protect not only our preservice teachers but to protect the children who will be ultimately taught by them. Plus, they need to see models of resistance from the teacher-educators—as opposed to hearing, "This is horrible, now let's get back to doing what we're told."

Canestrari: If you could make a comment about No Child Left Behind—do you think this legislation will fold in on itself or will it be something that is going to be around for a long time? The Elementary and Secondary Education Act was around for a long time and this is the first real big change, unfortunately.

Kohn: Yes, it is. Well, the irony is that people who are silent or inactive, who shrug their shoulders and go along with high stakes testing even though they know better, tend to use one of two mutually exclusive rationales for not taking action. Half of the people say, "This too shall pass. I have seen a lot of fads in education, and standards on steroids is just one more." And the other half of the people say, "This is here to stay whether we like it or not. It is part of life and we had better stop arguing about whether it is a good idea and just conform." Those are opposite positions yet they lead to precisely the same result, which is a failure to rebel.

My own sense is that, first, it's not just part of life. "The Many Children Left Behind Act," as I prefer to call it, is not like the weather. It is a reflection of a political decision and, like all political decisions, it can be challenged and ultimately reversed, just as segregation laws were when caring and courageous people refused to cooperate. On the other hand, it is not going to fall of its own weight any time soon because too many powerful people are heavily invested in this corporate-style control of classrooms. In any case, even if it does eventually fall of its own weight, we may lose half a generation before that happens, which is why I think we have a moral obligation to act. I don't accept a model of historical inevitability. Change happens because we make it happen. And, if we don't, sometimes it doesn't, at least not for a very long time.

The Act itself has many disturbing features to it, including various clauses that the right wing managed to tuck in, such as requiring high schools to report information about their students to the military, and a prohibition on acting against organizations like the Boy Scouts that discriminate on the basis of sexual orientation. But, for me, the most disturbing aspect is the notion of forcing every state to test every kid every year. Even apart from the poor quality and the misleading results of the tests, I think annual testing has three predictable results. First, you remove any pockets of time during which real learning can take place. It used to be that, at least in some states, you could do some exploration of ideas in fifth grade after suffering through relentless test prep in fourth grade, for example. Now the entire school has to become a giant test prep center. Second, annual testing presumes that all kids do or should learn at the same rate, proceed in lockstep fashion so that every eight-year-old has to be at this point, every nine-year-old has to be at that point, and so on—which, of course, flies in the face of everything that we know about the varying rates of child development. It has the practical effect of ensuring that many kids will be unnecessarily defined as failures because they were at a different place or learned in a different way. The third result is that if the federal government requires annual testing but doesn't provide adequate funding, then the states are forced to use the cheapest and, therefore, the worst tests, which take a bad thing and make it even worse.

As we speak, in the spring of '03, there are some states like Nebraska and Maine that are experimenting with ways to minimize the destructive impact by trying to use more authentic forms of assessment since the bill [No Child Left Behind], to my knowledge, does not actually use the phrase "standardized testing" at all. Unfortunately, the bill is being implemented by an administration that insists on demanding the worst sort of testing: an ideological commitment to promulgating regulations that would allow the least amount of wiggle room. Interestingly, though, some conservative Republicans, because of their commitment to local control, have been challenging aspects of No Child Left Behind while relatively liberal Senate Democrats like Edwards of North Carolina or Clinton of New York have been pursuing the worst form of one-size-fits-all testing.

Ted Kennedy, my Senator here in Massachusetts, paraded around with George W. Bush, arm in arm, in a mutual orgy of self-congratulation about squeezing the intellectual life out of schools and causing more low-income kids of color to be driven out. His only concern was with funding. It is as if Bush had said he wanted to hit every kid in America on the head with a hammer and Kennedy bravely took to the Senate floor to say, "Yes, but, ah, who is going to, ah, pay for the hahmahs?"

Alfie Kohn is an author, speaker, and social critic.

Epilogue

"Yes, But . . ."

"Yes, but . . . what if the school district adopts basal readers and requires that we use them to the exclusion of other approaches and instructional activities?"

"Yes, but . . . won't I have to teach to the test if the district demands that scores improve?"

"Yes, but . . . what if the principal requires that all second grade classrooms work on math at 9:15, regardless of my kids' needs or interests on a particular day?"

"Yes, but . . . what if the schoolwide discipline policy requires that kids stay in for recess if they don't finish their homework?"

We hear this "Yes, but . . ." response so frequently after introducing common sense—and research-based—notions about teaching and learning that we decided to close the book using this fundamental tension as a point of departure. And, after struggling over the format of the epilogue, we decided to introduce our students to the overarching themes of this book— our own struggle with the "yes, but" question, and the decisions *we* must make after receiving the same kinds of mandates they will soon face as teachers. Then, we simply asked, "What do you think about all of this?" and taped the discussion that ensued. It was really incredible. Thoughtful, reflective, insightful conversation and occasional debate—between students—about which kinds of teacher decisions rise to the level of moral imperatives, about how we got where we are, about whether teachers should make decisions about curriculum, and about the role teachers can— and should—play in the shaping of educational policy and decision making. Although not always sure of why such a conversation is important, all of the students, as seen in the exchange below, are certain that such conversations are a critical part of teacher education and, perhaps more importantly, should also be part and parcel of the ongoing professional development of inservice teachers. Consider this brief excerpt:

Marlowe: I'm noticing that it's hard to get "air time"—everyone seems to have something urgent to say. Is this the kind of conversation that needs to be a built-in feature of teacher education programs?

Ronald: One thing we definitely need more of is this kind of intellectual exchange. I'd like to see conversations like this be a much larger part of our instruction.

Megan: Isn't this what it's really about, carefully listening to and analyzing each other's views? I mean do real teachers do this? Do they ever really get to reflect on their practice, or do they mindlessly go through the motions?

Ted: I know I'm only beginning my student teaching, but I don't see this happening in my school. Is this what faculty meetings are like?

Ryan: I've been a long-term substitute for a whole semester and I've never been in a faculty meeting where there was a conversation like this. And I don't get it. Shouldn't teachers be engaged in this kind of discussion? Isn't this what should happen in a faculty meeting?

This exchange, and many more like it, underscores the perceived importance—even urgency—of addressing the "Yes, but . . ." question. But the students seemed to lack a metacognitive awareness of what transpired and what was accomplished by the discussion.

Listening to the taped transcripts reveals not only deep student reflection about weighty educational issues but also important insights and the kind of evolution in thinking that underscores the value of engaging teachers in the dialectical process. Imagine how our schools might be different if inservice teachers engaged in regular discussions, like the one between our students below, about whether the mandates they face are consistent with their views of what is in the best interest of their students.

Jane: But what do we do when we are asked to do something we know isn't right, or is contrary to what we've learned in some of our classes here? I just had a class in literacy where we talked about how research indicates that "Round Robin" reading is not best practice. And yet the classroom I'm in now as a student teacher . . . that's all they do. It's the whole reading program.

Maya: As a new person, as a first-year teacher, I wouldn't say anything. I mean, you don't have any credibility. You're the new kid on the block and you have to go along at first.

Marlowe: Will it be the same as a tenth-year teacher? How long do you wait to do what you see as the right thing?

Ted: One thing we can count on is that what's wrong today will be right tomorrow. School reforms come in waves.

Canestrari: So will you allow yourself to be swept in and out with the tide?

Kate: Yeah, but I agree with Maya. You want the job, right? You're not going to say, "See ya later," because, I mean, good luck finding another job. There aren't that many out there so you do have to swim with the tide.

Alex: Should you risk losing your job by raising questions? Don't you have a larger responsibility to your family? I mean what do we really know about teaching anyway? We're new. I agree with Maya, too. We have to go along at first. After a while, maybe then you can say something. But definitely not at first.

Marlowe: Is there a point at which you stop saying to yourself, "I'm just going to hold my tongue, and I'm not going to say a thing?" Okay, Jane mentioned round-robin reading. The stakes seem relatively low here. But what about practices that you view as actually harmful? Is there a point at which you will respond to a principal's directive with "No, I won't do that"?

Ronald: I would. I would absolutely refuse if I thought, morally or educationally, something I was asked to do was wrong.

Kate: You need to be respectful, though. Whether you agree or not, you are the rookie. So you can disagree, I guess, but be tactful. Something like, "I know the test scores are down, and I realize that you want more seat time to help my students prepare for the tests, but I'm thinking about doing it a little differently. I've looked into the research. . . ." Something like that, where you go into the discussion with the principal with a knowledge base, with some preparation. Then maybe he will give a little bit, too.

Sally: Isn't there a happy medium here where you can do something of yours and also what the curriculum might dictate? Just so that it's not completely one way or the other. You get to do some of what you want, what you know is right, what will work with kids, and you do some of what they want, too.

Ronald: So it's okay to do the harmful stuff as long as you do the good stuff, too?

Sally: Yeah, well, I mean . . . to some extent, maybe. No, I guess I wouldn't do the bad stuff. That doesn't make sense. I'm thinking there is stuff that needs to be taught that addresses the standards, but I guess actually, no, I won't do it if it's wrong.

We liken this evolving conversation to "spinning plates." As students formulate their positions and develop their own insights they are forced to consider the ideas of others, thereby positioning another "plate" to be spun, another thought that must be considered. It is this emerging complexity that allows insights to move toward solutions. Notice how the following excerpt, focusing on teaching and testing, evolves with increasing clarity.

Jane: As a student teacher, I'm going to be in a predicament next semester. I'm going into a fourth grade class and I've already been told that we will be making a final push to prepare students for statewide assessments in the spring. Here, in our program, we're all told that we're not supposed to teach to the test, but, I mean, my cooperating teacher couldn't have made it any clearer to me.

Canestrari: Testing has become a yearly event. The results are published in the paper and the schools are ranked from low- to high-performing. Do you have to pay attention to these results, or should you simply teach the way you know is best for your students?

Ryan: Well, again, as a beginning teacher, if I'm told that it's imperative that we do better on the tests, I would highly recommend that you teach more to the test. But obviously you could maintain your teaching and still address the test issue.

Jane: Do I drop social studies? Science? My cooperating teacher didn't say specifically, "We're going to drop science," but there's no doubt in my mind that's what she meant when she said, "We need to prepare the students for the test." What would I do? I mean, under those circumstances, can you teach the way you want to or do you have to follow some districtwide strategy for test preparation?

Ronald: If we teach the right way, won't students be prepared for the test anyway?

Kate: No. If there's a statewide assessment in fifth grade in mathematics, and your job is to prepare students to do well on this test, what do you have to give up to do that? I agree that you can do lots of things the right way that will help them in math, but even if you do everything well to teach them math but drop the rest of the curriculum to prepare for the math test, are you serving your students well?

Our students also came to some important conclusions about how deliberate attempts at creating a chorus of teachers' voices may be the profession's greatest hope for continuous renewal—a discussion that echoes our earlier conversation with Deborah Meier regarding the importance of collaboration.

Canestrari: How do good teachers get heard when they have a different vision than the administration about what a classroom should look like?

Mike: You are teaching a science kit lesson and you decide that it is going really well, so you ask the principal to sit in. Everybody is interactive, it's going great, learning is taking place, or maybe someone else in the school is interested in a demonstration so you invite them into the room.

Ronald: Or you teach together. Let's try something here and approach this unit all from the same standpoint, teaching across content areas.

Ryan: Teaming through integration is powerful. Going through the specialists . . . using integrated units and starting off that way. Building consensus, doing things even across grade levels by showing what really works.

Carissa: I think change requires one person first, and then you talk with someone else, and you have a partner and then it grows. Soon, collectively, you can make a push. At some point, districts will realize that you have pockets of teachers yelling so loudly that you can't cover your ears up anymore, and even legislators, people dictating policy, administrators are going to have to start listening to what we know about good teaching.

As we probed further about how the "yes, but . . ." conversation should be initiated, students expanded the focus of the discussion to larger questions about who should participate in such discussions and where they should occur. It was during this part of the conversation that many students realized for the first time that those above them face pressures, too.

Mike: The class I'm in now, if the kids don't do their math homework they have to stay in for recess and instead of working on their math they have to copy the dictionary, starting with *A!* Why don't we just flog them? How silly and absurd is this? I've only been there two days. Do I say anything? Who do I say it to? What if I wasn't just student teaching, but had a job and saw this in the room across the hall? Then what do I do?

Canestrari: One of the things both Professor Marlowe and I are concerned about is that the scope of issues—in which teachers have real opportunities to put in their two cents—seems to be getting increasingly narrow. The conversation is indeed important. So, let's encourage this conversation about authentic assessment, about who gets to graduate, about which classroom management approaches respect student dignity and encourage thoughtful, respectful behaviors . . . but how will you become part of these conversations in your own districts and buildings? How will you make your voices heard? How can your views become part of the basis for how decisions are ultimately made?

Ashley: I think it needs to happen earlier. We need to broaden the conversation to include the principals, the superintendents, and the policymakers at a very early stage. These people should be here in the room with us right now while we're still teacher education students. I want to know how they would defend some of their policies.

Catherine: Those people who ultimately have the power to hire and fire you must be part of the conversation. They need to hear different perspectives, too. And maybe more importantly they need to look at the research regarding best practice and then explain how the policies they are pursuing square with what we're reading. I mean, virtually none of the policies school districts are so rigidly pursuing seem consistent with what we're reading about.

Matt: The people out there who might be roadblocks need to be part of this dialogue. They need to be part of the exchange so that we can see what is really expected of us, what we need to do, what we're really coming up against.

Jennifer: I want to know in advance what they want from me. That's why we need them here.

Marlowe: But I hear Ashley and Catherine suggesting that the reason to invite administrators is to confront them with research that indicates that they're on the wrong course. Aren't they saying, in effect, that one way to make change is to have a real conversation with the decision makers, the ones in the position, to say "You will do ___" in a context where open dialogue is possible?

Steve: Would they come? I mean, how can a principal or a superintendent look us straight in the eye after being confronted with all the research about the harmful effects of high-stakes testing? Are they going to say, "We still think it's best to pursue a policy of retaining kids who don't pass, even though we know the research says retention is harmful"? They really need to discuss their views of the research with us. Help us understand what is driving their decision making.

Canestrari: Well, what is driving these decisions from above? What do you think about this issue that Steve raises?

Bob: It's about money, not kids. Teachers aren't making these decisions and neither are principals or superintendents.

Mike: You're saying that these decisions are political? You really think it's just from legislators who don't know anything about teaching and learning—is that what you're saying?

Jonah: That's just it. We learn about the ideal situation in a classroom, what the research says, but we're not so naïve to think that is what it's really going to be like without hurdles or else we wouldn't be having this conversation. We need to have the decision makers be part of these exchanges because we don't really know what they are having to deal with either. So, maybe instead of confronting them we should be asking them, "What kind of pressure do *you* face as head of the school district? Where is it coming from? What can we do to resist it?" We don't really understand these pressures that administrators themselves are facing, how they're getting squeezed and how it affects teachers and kids down the chain. We're just a small piece of this and we need to figure out how we fit and what we can do about it, but it's going start with a conversation with them.

It also didn't take long for our students to see the very real ways that the mandates they will soon face as teachers mirror those that we face as professors. This became abundantly clear as we pushed our students to reflect more deeply about exactly why they thought the discussion was so fruitful. Like Kohn, in "Grading: The Issue Is Not How But Why?" students were quick to point out that, even at the postsecondary level, mandatory assessment and grading policies often interfere with learning. For many students, what was most unique and liberating about our discussion was simply the fact that it was ungraded. After reflection, the number of instructional activities in their program that were explicitly evaluated struck many students as inconsistent with what professors were telling them about good teaching and learning for its own sake.

Like our students who will soon be teachers, we too often have little say about whether or not to give grades. Similarly, as university professors in a teacher education program, we must worry about how our students will fare on standardized tests, as the state will make judgments about our program based on our students' performance. As Ayers and Brooks and Brooks note, assessment information based on standardized tests is often misleading and can be used to make dubious claims about how much students are actually learning or about the success of academic programs. It is for these reasons that we, too, perpetually face the "Yes but . . ." question, which became clear to our students as the conversation continued.

Canestrari: What's different about the conversation we're having now compared to discussions in other classes? What accounts for this very high level of engagement?

Steve: Look at the situation. Is this high risk or low risk? Are we getting graded? No, we're just having a conversation with no stakes attached and we're really learning the most in this kind of setting. Everyone wants to get involved. Remember what we read about the affective filter? [laughter in class] To get back to the original question, yeah, there is a place for this—we need this at both the undergraduate and graduate level. Look at how everyone gets involved.

Ronald: In this university setting where everything is graded, everything is assessed, how can you maintain this level of engagement given a threatening environment? I mean, we're still in a classroom where every experience, every paper, every assignment is graded and analyzed and evaluated and then we have pre-evals, in-process evals, post-evals . . . I just realized something! This is why kids hate school. Because the energy, the enthusiasm for learning gets sucked right out of them with all the obsessive focus on assessment.

Carissa: So you're really in the same position as we will soon be in as teachers. You have people above you telling you that you must give grades, as just one example. You don't really have a choice, either.

Canestrari: Let me give you a different kind of example. There will be pressure from the state to insure that you pass the exit exam, the teacher certification test. There is actually a number attached. Our accreditation is determined by whether or not a certain number pass this test. If we fall below that number we could lose our accreditation. This is power politics.

Jane: So, are you going to teach to the test?

Marlowe: Here's what's going to happen, because it's happening in schools of education all over the country. Okay, you're in the master's degree program? Here's what we're going to say: As soon as you get here, you have to take the test. You know why? Because if you pass, good for you, and if you fail, well, then, you're not in our program. See, now we have a 100 percent pass rate at graduation time, because the only people *in* our program are those who already passed the test. Isn't this a terrific program?

Canestrari: I don't know if we'll teach to the test, but you can bet you'll get plenty of opportunities to take it over and over again.

Marlowe: We are in the same position as professors as you will soon be as teachers. Look, this is precisely what is happening in many states around the country. Kids are being discouraged from staying in school under a variety of different kinds of pretense; the more poor test takers who actually drop out, the better the pass rates in the end. In fact, for the first time in many years, the high school dropout rate is increasing in many states. When fewer kids take the test needed to graduate, because many have already dropped out, school districts, or states, can say "Hey, look at how our pass rates are improving. We must be doing a better job educating students." But as you can see from the example of those of you right here in the master's degree program, the student pass rates will have absolutely nothing to do with the quality of our educational programming—because only those who pass will be considered "in the program"—but you can bet that is how it will look when the scores get printed in the newspapers.

The students that we engaged in conversation were junior and senior undergraduates and graduate master's degree students that were very close to their final field placements. Ironically, it is at the end of the program, when they are closest to classrooms of their own, that our students become less secure as they reflect on the incongruity between what they are learning at the university and what they are seeing in public school classrooms. At a time when our students should be feeling more confident, more certain about the skills they have acquired, the dispositions they have adopted, they are instead feeling increasingly adrift; dissonance abounds. The "yes, but . . ." question dominates their thinking and causes them to second guess their education and their good instincts.

Why does the "yes, but . . ." phenomenon persist? Might the reason have to do with the increasingly narrow opportunities for dialogue, critique, and dialectic? Compliance without dissent is the order of the day. From the dictates of No Child Left Behind to the principal at the local elementary school outlining district goals and imperatives, opportunities for open discussion and debate are quashed. What passes for conversation within school districts is, increasingly, simply one-way, top-down, vertical communication. Strict training boundaries are established to insure compliance. Today's teachers have to accept more and more and question less and less in the name of accountability. This phenomenon likely starts at the very beginning when students enter a teacher preparation program.

Have we prepared our future teachers for the challenges that await them? Do our teacher education programs have enough emphasis on scholarship, intellectual capital, and tolerance for differing viewpoints? Have we engaged students in a way that allows them to think critically? Have we given them substantial preparation in articulating what's right in a way that either facilitates or causes others to rethink their classrooms? Have we prepared them in the art of resistance and dissent? Our suspicion is that we have not and our conviction is that these questions must frame teacher education.

Perhaps there is hope for those teachers who are prepared differently—hope for those who have internalized Freire's desire for liberation in the form of "problem-posing education" or Giroux's insistence that teachers think of themselves as "transformative intellectuals" or even Postman and Weingartner's urging that teachers be vigilant "crap" detectors. Ohanian warns us that teachers must be educated rather than trained, that offering recipes leads only to the deskilling of teachers, and that teaching practice be informed by philosophy and art and music rather than by experts "who promise the keys to classroom control and creative bulletin boards, along with 100 steps to reading success."

It was through the back and forth of our conversation, the student-to-student exchange, the horizontal communication between faculty and students where all participants were peers, that we were all reminded of the importance and power of these kinds of discussions to inform teaching and learning.

Index